FROM ROMANCE TO REALISM

*50 Years of Growth
and Change in
Young Adult
Literature*

Michael Cart

FROM ROMANCE TO REALISM

50 Years of Growth and Change in Young Adult Literature

HARPERCOLLINS*PUBLISHERS*

Acknowledgments

Every effort has been made to locate the copyright holders of all copyrighted materials and to secure the necessary permission to reproduce them. In the event of any questions arising as to their use the publisher will be glad to make changes in future printings and editions. Thanks are due to the following for permission to reprint the copyrighted material listed below:

"Language of Violence," written by Michael Franti and Mark Pistel. Copyright © 1992 by PolyGram International Publishing, Inc., Beatnigs Music and Songs of PolyGram International, Inc. Used by permission of PolyGram International Publishing. All Rights Reserved.

Library of Congress Cataloging-in-Publication Data
Cart, Michael.
    From romance to realism : 50 years of growth and change in young adult literature / by Michael Cart.
        p.   cm.
    Includes bibliographical references and index.
    ISBN 0-06-024289-2 ISBN 0-06-446161-0 (pbk.)
    1. Young adult fiction, American—History and criticism. 2. American fiction—20th century—History and criticism. 3. Young adults—United States—Books and reading. 4. Teenagers—United States—Books and reading. 5. Young adults in literature. 6. Romanticism—United States. 7. Teenagers in literature. 8. Realism in literature. I. Title.
PS374.Y6C37   1996   95-31734
813'.54099283—dc20   CIP

Typography by Al Cetta
3   4   5   6   7   8   9   10
❖

For Jack Ledwith
Always the best of friends

CONTENTS

PART ONE

THAT WAS THEN

CHAPTER ONE

FROM *SUE BARTON* TO THE SIXTIES

What's in a Name? and Other Uncertainties

If it was in Victorian England that "a separate state called 'childhood' was envisioned," as Canadian critic Sheila Egoff has argued,[1] others would agree it was neither there nor then but in America, instead, where another separate state, "young adulthood," was to be envisioned.

No one agrees, however, as to *when* this transpired or—for that matter *to whom* this statehood was being granted. These disagreements derive, I suspect, from the very ambiguity of the phrase "young adult" and from the fact that the concept it tries to embrace was an evolutionary one. There was, simply, no single, defining moment when a prototypical young adult was first "discovered." And anyway, who were these creatures being called "young adults"—adolescents? teenagers? adults in training wheels?

Alleen Pace Nilsen and Kenneth L. Donelson, in their standard text *Literature for Today's Young Adults*, seem to think they're all one and the same. At least they use the terms "adolescent," "young adult," and even "teenager" interchangeably to identify that "stretching out of the transition between childhood and adulthood" that first appeared, or so they claim, following the Civil War.

"Before then, people were simply considered either children or adults." [2]

This post-Civil War dating raises the intriguing possibility that the fictional March sisters, Jo, Beth, Meg, and Amy, were America's first "official" young adults, and the chronicle of their lives, Louisa May Alcott's *Little Women* (Roberts, 1868), the first young adult novel.

It was not until 1904, however, that psychology officially sanctioned the existence of this "separate state," with the publication by G. Stanley Hall—the first American Ph.D. in psychology and founder of the American Psychological Association—of his massive, two-volume work *Adolescence: Its Psychology* (Appleton, 1904).

Another psychologist, B. Forisha-Kovach, also claims that "until [the twentieth century] adolescence as a stage of life was not formally recognized. Individuals passed from a short childhood into an early adulthood without the marginal in-between space called adolescence."

However, Forisha-Kovach believes that it was not until the *1920s* that it would become clear that adolescents were "a separate generation." [3]

Still others would claim that the idea of adolescence didn't appear until even later. Betty Carter of Texas Woman's University speaks for this group when she notes that "only when society demanded extended education or training for specialized jobs, *which didn't really happen until the Post World War II years* [emphasis added], did circumstances allow teenagers time for this transition, thus signalling the birth of adolescence." [4]

Novelist Natalie Babbitt supports this rough chronology with her amusing observation, "The category *teenager* itself is a new one, of course. It made its first appearance during the Second World War and was created partly by parents, partly by manufacturers, and partly by Frank Sinatra." [5]

Further support for this chronological notion is the fact that—Hall's anomalously early work aside—important studies of adolescence didn't begin to appear until the late forties. R. J. Havighurst's study of adolescent developmental tasks, for example, was published in 1949; Erik Erikson's theory of identity crisis appeared in 1950; Jean Piaget's work on cognitive development came along in 1958; and Lawrence Kohlberg's studies of moral development followed in the sixties.

Institutional awareness of adolescence began to emerge at roughly the same time—at least librarians started to discuss the need to serve this new group circa World War II. In 1963 Kenneth R. Shaffer, then director of the School of Library Science at Simmons

College, recalled "our excitement of nearly a quarter of a century ago when we made the professional discovery of the adolescent—the 'young adult'—as a special kind of library client whose needs could no longer be adequately served either as a child or as an adult reader." [6]

However, it was not until 1958—nearly two decades later—that this "excitement" became institutionalized in the American Library Association's formation of a Young Adult Services Division (now known as the Young Adult Library Services Association, or YALSA).

Ironically, even the formation of a new ALA division did not ensure agreement among its members as to exactly who was to be served by it. Carter points out that "for years the YASD and YALSA boards of directors wrestled with an age-level definition for young adults." [7]

In fact, it was not until 1991 that the YALSA Board finally adopted the recommendations of the National Center for Education Statistics Task Force and officially defined young adults as "those individuals from twelve to eighteen years old" (Carter, p. 13).

And so—as far as the ALA's definition is concerned, at least—the terms "young adult" and "teenager" *are* synonymous (well, almost). But what about that equally ambiguous term "adolescent"? Surely it still wants definition?

For that we will need something more precise, I think, than novelist Isabelle Holland's rather breathless attempt: "An adolescent," she has said, "is a human being on a journey in that great, amorphous sea called adolescence." [8] (The sea is not the only thing that is amorphous here, I fear.)

And so I prefer what my *American Heritage Dictionary* has to say: An adolescent is "a young person who has undergone puberty but who has not reached full maturity." [9]

But better still—because it is more specific—is what psychologist J. W. Santrock offers: "Adolescence is the period of transition from childhood to early adulthood, entered at approximately 11–13 years of age and ending at 18–21 years of age—the exact time period, however, depending on such diverse factors as the surrounding culture and biological development." [10]

Santrock's phrase "biological development" refers, of course, to the onset of puberty (the beginning of the growth spurt and sexual maturation), which—in terms of age—varies with the individual. As for "culture," Nilsen and Donelson make the compelling point that "puberty is a universal experience but adolescence is not." [11]

The more technologically advanced the culture, it seems, the more likely it is to recognize adolescence as a separate and distinct stage of human development, worthy, thus, of a body of literature that addresses the stage in language, themes, and content accessible to those who populate it.

While adolescence is only a small chronological part of the normal life span (less than a decade in duration), it is enormous in developmental terms and in the breadth of interests, sophistication, emotional capacities, and cognitive abilities which separate its youngest and oldest members.

To create a generic literature that can speak cogently to such a bewilderingly amorphous group of readers is a daunting task. Even to try to *define* the phrase "young adult (or adolescent) literature" can be migraine inducing. One sympathizes with Holland when—after pages of trying—she finally throws up her hands and declares, "I am coming more and more to the conclusion that adolescent literature is whatever any adolescent happens to be reading at any given time." [12]

Mertz and England offered a *slightly* more specific definition in 1983: For them, young adult literature was "that realistic and contemporary American fiction which young adults as well as more mature and critical readers can find aesthetically and thematically satisfying and which is, implicitly or explicitly, written for adolescents." [13]

I'm not quite sure what they intend by those two prefixes "im" and "ex" unless it is to acknowledge that some books published as young adult novels were not written for that audience (authors as diverse as John R. Tunis and Robert Cormier have been surprised to learn from their publishers that they had written young adult novels!) and that some other novels written for adults have quickly been embraced by a young adult readership (Maureen Daly's *Seventeenth Summer*, often hailed as the first young adult novel, was actually published as an adult title, for example).

Historically, this matter of literary definition has been a particularly vexing problem for the American Library Association's various committees that—since 1930—have been taxed with the annual selection of the best books for young adults. At the outset, of course, there was no indigenous body of *young adult* literature, and so the first committees had to choose from among books published either for children or for adults. Titles on the first (1930) list ranged, thus, from Will James's autobiography, *Lone Cowboy*, to Edna Ferber's adult novel *Cimarron*.

This situation obtained until 1948, when librarians, apparently recognizing that this new—but still amorphous—group of adolescents had no compelling interest in children's books, decided to confine their choices to adult titles and changed the name of their list to "Adult Books for Young People."

The annual list would remain confined to adult titles until 1973, when there would finally be a body of literature of sufficient size and literary significance, published specifically for adolescents, to warrant the inclusion of "young adult" books.

This welcome inclusion had been presaged by the change of the name of the list in 1966 to "Best Books for Young Adults," the name that is still in use today.

Then—as now—the committee's name seems to contain a built-in—well, let's call it *waffle* factor. Note, for example, that its name is *not* "Best Young Adult Books" but rather "Best Books *for* Young Adults." The waffle comes with the word "for," which implies inclusion of books published not only for young adults but for other readerships as well. Indeed, the committee's current charge is "to select from the year's publications, significant adult and young adult books" ("Policies and Procedures for the Best Books for Young Adults Committee").

Nilsen and Donelson's definition of the genre is particularly relevant here: "For our purposes," they say, "we define 'young adult literature' as any book freely chosen for reading by someone in this age group [i.e., twelve to twenty], which means we do not make a distinction between books distributed by juvenile divisions and adult divisions of publishing houses." [14]

Neither, any longer, does the YALSA Best Books Committee. In fact, as the years since 1973 have passed, these selectors' nets have been cast wider and wider; and when, in 1991, YALSA began including twelve-year-olds in its definition of "young adults," an unstated invitation was issued to return to the 1930 practice of including children's books on the annual list. The result, Carter notes, is the now widespread complaint that the list is "addressing a younger and younger audience." [15]

Another reason for this "youthening" of the list may be "the growing middle-school movement across our nation" and publishers' acknowledgement of this phenomenon by their offering "more titles for that population [grades six to eight, ages eleven to thirteen] than ever before." [16]

Or it may be the fact, as we will see later, that many publishers have abandoned issuing titles for the senior half of the young adult age range, presuming—perhaps—that these older readers are better served by adult books. And there is similar widespread support in YALSA for promoting this notion by dividing the annual Best Books list into two lists, one of which would consist exclusively of adult titles (and more of them, obviously, than can be accommodated by the current aggregate list).

Whatever happens, the field is in flux; but then, it always has been, and why not? For what is adolescence but a state of continuous change—of becoming, not being. For that reason alone, I believe the best definition of "young adult literature" will be the least specific one. And frankly, since it is such a function of our ever-changing ideas of and attitudes toward adolescence, I'm not even sure we need a formal definition. Most observers will settle for what a Supreme Court Justice once said of pornography: "I can't define it; but I know it when I see it."

At least we have been able to define "young adult," and before going any further, we can also define "literature." For starters, British critic and novelist John Rowe Townsend says it is "all works of imagination which are transmitted primarily by means of the written word or spoken narrative—that is, in the main, novels, stories, and poetry." [17]

Since my focus will be on the novel, perhaps we should define that term, too. And for help we can turn to another British critic and novelist, Anthony

11

Burgess. Says he, "the term 'novel' has, in fact, come to mean any imaginative prose composition long enough to be stitched rather than stapled (a book and not a pamphlet)." [18]

What *about* nonfiction, though? It is prose, after all, and imagination certainly goes into its creation. However, it has already been done ample justice by Betty Carter and Richard F. Abrahamson in their splendid study *Nonfiction for Young Adults: From Delight to Wisdom* (Oryx, 1990). For me to write about it after their comprehensive treatment would be redundant.

As for poetry: It remains the difficult stepchild of young adult literature, often neglected and usually misunderstood. Only one title on the "Top One Hundred Countdown" (YALSA's 1994 list of the best young adult books published between 1967 and 1992) is a work of poetry: *American Sports Poems* edited by R. R. Knudson and May Swenson (Orchard, 1988). Poetry obviously wants more attention, but because it is so intrinsically rich as to warrant a book of its own and because it is evaluated by means other than those used to address fiction, I will leave that important work to others more qualified than I.

Romance or Reality?

Obviously a good deal has happened since the establishment of a Best Books list in 1930, and that "good deal" is, in fact, the history and evolution of a literature published specifically *for* young adults, for adolescents, for teenagers, for all those creatures still "on a journey in that great, amorphous sea called adolescence."

Of course, this is not to deny that, for decades before we discovered young adults, books were being published that found an avid readership among people of that age range.

In this category, surely, are *Little Women, Adventures of Huckleberry Finn*, much of Robert Louis Stevenson and Jules Verne, standard titles by Sir Walter Scott, Victor Hugo, and Charles Dickens, and, indeed, countless books by innumerable others. The important distinction, however, is that it would not be until the 1930s—some would say the forties—that a new *type* of book began to emerge, one published (though not always consciously written) for young adults.

Pioneering librarian Margaret A. Edwards, whose program of young adult service at the Enoch Pratt Free Library in Baltimore served as a national model, was among the first to write about the appearance of such "young adult books" in the United States; the geographical specificity is intended, by the way, since young adult books—like their readership—originated in America and were a unique feature of our publishing culture for years. Townsend acknowledges this when he says, simply, "The teenage novel is an American speciality."[19]

Writing in 1954, Edwards reported publisher Little, Brown's editorial bemusement on receiving a manuscript by Helen Boylston in the mid-1930s: "While it was not a piece of literature, it was an entertaining story which did not fit into any category. It was too mature for children and too uncomplicated for adults. In the end, Little, Brown took a chance and published the story under the title 'Sue Barton, Student Nurse' *and the dawn of the modern teen-age story came up like thunder"* (emphasis added). [20]

The thunder was, presumably, the sound of adolescent applause, since *Sue Barton* (for reasons that seem elusive to modern readers struggling through its turgid pages) is one of the most popular books in the history of young adult literature. In 1947—eleven years after its publication—it was chosen in a survey of librarians in Illinois, Ohio, and New York as "the most consistently popular book" among teenage readers, and it remained in print for years along with its six sequels, which saw young Sue finish her training, serve in a variety of professional capacities (visiting nurse, superintendent of nurses, neighborhood nurse, staff nurse), and finally marry the young doctor she had met in book number one.

The popularity of the series surely derived in large part from its verisimilitude. Boylston was a professional nurse herself, but if there's truth in the details of her settings, there are stereotypes in her characters and clichés in the dramatic situations in which they found themselves embroiled. Told in the omniscient third person, the books betray their author's too-smug, patronizing attitude toward her material and her characters—not only Sue but also, and especially, the "quaint" immigrants who are the chief patients at the big-city hospital where Sue receives her training.

Nevertheless, because of its careful accuracy regarding the quotidian details of the nurse's professional life, *Sue Barton* was the prototype of the career story, an enormously popular subgenre among the earliest young adult books.

Rivaling Sue for the affection of later nurse-story lovers was Helen Wells's own fledgling professional, Cherry Ames, whose debut occurred in 1943 (*Cherry Ames, Student Nurse* [Grosset]) and whose subsequent adventures ultimately filled twenty volumes. But in the years that followed, not only nursing but virtually every other career conceivable found itself reported in drearily didactic detail.

A decade before Boylston's initial publication, another influential author for adolescents debuted; it was 1926 when Howard Pease published his first book, *The Tattooed Man* (Doubleday). A much better writer than Boylston, Pease would rival her for popularity. In fact, a 1939 survey of 1,500 California students found that Pease was their favorite author. [21]

Like Boylston, Pease specialized in a literary subgenre: in his case, the boy's adventure story, set—usually—at sea. And again like Boylston, Pease knew his material from firsthand experience. For him this meant service in the U.S. merchant marine during World War I.

In 1938 still another important early writer, who also specialized in genre fiction based on personal experience, made his debut: John R. Tunis, the "inventor" of the modern sports story, published the first of

his many novels, *The Iron Duke* (Harcourt). Tunis had
played tennis and run track as a student at Harvard
and, following service in World War I, had become a
sportswriter for the *New York Post*. What set his work
apart from that of earlier sportswriters was that he focused less on play-by-play accounts of the big game
than on closely observed considerations of character,
social issues, and challenges—not to his characters'
hand-eye coordination but to their personal integrity
and maturation, instead.

In retrospect, any one of these three writers could
be reasonably identified as the first author for young
adults, but most observers would join the redoubtable
Edwards in declaring (on second thought, in her case)
that "it was in 1942 that the new field of writing for
teen-agers became established." [22]

The occasion was the publication of Maureen
Daly's first (and for forty-four years *only*) novel, *Seventeenth Summer* (Dodd, Mead).

Amazingly, the author was only twenty-one when
her history-making work appeared. (How old she was
when she actually wrote the book is moot. Ms. Daly
herself claims she was a teenager, but *The New York
Times* reported that only fifty pages of the book had
been written before the author turned twenty.) [23]

Daly is also quick to point out that her novel was
not published as a young adult book. "I would like, at
this late date [1994], to explain that *Seventeenth Summer*,
in my intention and at the time of publication, was
considered a full adult novel and published and reviewed as such." [24]

As I have already pointed out, the translation by readers or publishers of an adult title into a book for young adults was hardly unprecedented. Scarcely a decade before Daly's first novel appeared, something similar had happened to Rose Wilder Lane's *Let the Hurricane Roar* (Longmans, Green, 1933). Also published as an adult title, it was soon being touted by its publisher as "the first of their series of 'Junior Books.'" [25] (This phrase—"junior book" or "junior novel"—survived as a rather patronizing descriptor of adolescent fiction for decades; as previously noted, it was not until 1966 that the term "Young Adult" was finally used in connection with the ALA's Best Books list.)

John R. Tunis was similarly—and unpleasantly—surprised to learn from his publisher, Alfred Harcourt, that *The Iron Duke* was a book for young readers. He was still fuming thirty years later when he wrote, "That odious term juvenile is the product of a merchandising age." [26]

In the years to come, the same surprise would be in store for authors like Robert Cormier, Bruce Brooks, and Francesca Lia Block, while such books as *The Catcher in the Rye*, *The Lord of the Flies*, *Mr. and Mrs. Bo Jo Jones*, *A Separate Peace*, *To Kill a Mockingbird*, and *Ordinary People*—all published for adults—would be embraced by adolescent readers and welcomed into the young adult canon. In 1975 Holland reported the results of a "recent" survey that showed that the ten favorite novels of "high school youth" were *The Catcher in the Rye*, *Go Ask Alice*, *The Outsiders*, *To Kill a Mockingbird*, *A Separate Peace*, *Jonathan Livingston Seagull*, *The*

Lord of the Flies, Of Mice and Men, Lisa, Bright and Dark, and *The Exorcist.*

"It is interesting," she then observed, "that of the ten favorites eight were published as adult books." [27]

I suspect that the embrace of Daly's novel by a nonadult readership evidenced two things: 1. There now existed an authentic new generation called "young adults," and 2. Its members were not yet finding "young adult" books that spoke to *their* life experience.

But why *Seventeenth Summer* in particular? Well, its theme—first love—offered a timelessly appealing investigation of a universal, rite-of-passage experience; and its plot, as one reviewer noted, rang "true and sweet and fresh and sound." [28]

The freshness and soundness were due to several factors: For one, the book was clearly autobiographical. ("What I've tried to do, you see," Daly told a contemporary interviewer, "is just write about the things that happened to me and that I knew about—that meant a lot to me." [29])

For another, these "things" were still immediate to the author, since she was herself either still in her teens or barely out of them when she was writing. Most importantly, in terms of the success of the novel and its place in the history of young adult literature, it was written in the first-person voice of its adolescent protagonist, Angie Morrow—a fact that made it possible for readers to identify intimately with her and with her experiences. The use of the first-person voice would, thereafter, become one of the most enduring characteristics of the young adult novel.

For its time the book was also fairly bold—and, thus, reader enticing—in its inclusion of scenes showing teenagers unrepentantly smoking and drinking. And yet . . . to modern readers Angie seems hopelessly naive and much younger than her years. Her language now sounds quaintly old-fashioned, and the pacing of her story is not just magisterially but glacially slow, bogging down in so many lengthy passages describing the fauna of Fond du Lac (the book's setting) that it seems more like a botany textbook than a novel. (Daly admits her propensity to "write microscopically about things that happen right at home."[30])

If Angie's diction is now dated, so—more painfully—are her attitudes. Humiliated, for example, by the bad table manners of her new boyfriend, she thinks, "My whole mind was filled with a growing disdain and loathing. His family probably didn't even own a butter knife! No girl has to stand all that" (p. 147).

More significantly, the modern reader cringes as Angie, who has begun dating the desirable (and always so *clean!*) Jack Duluth, rhapsodizes, "It's funny what a boy can do. One day you're nobody and the next day you're the girl that some fellow goes with. Going with a boy gives you a new identity—especially going with a fellow like Jack Duluth" (p. 57).

Despite all this, *Seventeenth Summer* has remained tremendously popular; it's sold more than 1.5 million copies since its publication, and it is still in print and still being read by teenagers today.

Since innovation breeds imitation, it's no surprise that *Seventeenth Summer* spawned succeeding generations of romance novels—and perhaps even the young women's magazine *Seventeen*, which debuted in 1945—all breathlessly recounting first dates and proms and problems of popularity. These books were set in a *Saturday Evening Post* world of white faces and white picket fences surrounding small-town, middle-class lives where the worst thing that could happen would be a misunderstanding that threatened to leave someone dateless for the junior prom.

One of the most popular of these imitations appeared within three years of *Seventeenth Summers'* publication: Betty Cavanna's *Going on Sixteen* (Westminster, 1946). As its title suggests, the book is an almost-homage to Daly. In fact, Cavanna's protagonist, Julie Ferguson, actually mentions having "just last month read a newspaper account of a book written by a girl of seventeen" (p. 89). This is offered in the context of Julie's longing for a career in publishing—not as an author but as a book illustrator, instead. In this respect, Cavanna borrows both from Daly and from career books like Bolyston's. There are other similarities, as well. *Going on Sixteen* is also about the interrelationship of popularity and dating (remember Angie's rhapsodizing about Jack); the book's dust jacket even claims that it offers "numerous useful tips on how to overcome shyness and how to become 'part of things.' "

Cavanna's Julie must have read the book herself, since she finally does become "part of things," finding true love with a neighbor boy named Dick Webster, who habitually calls her "Peanut" (e.g., p. 9) and "Small

Fry" (e.g., p. 38). One supposes these are intended as endearments, but they sound condescending instead. Consider the following: " 'Hey!' Dick scolded, suddenly masculine. 'We've got to get going.' Dick looked at her Dad in a way that said 'Women!' and grabbed her hand authoritatively. 'Come on' " (p. 220).

As this demonstrates, the book is told in the third person and the author is sometimes as condescending to Julie as Dick is (and as Boylston was to Sue Barton).

Ultimately the author of more than seventy books, Cavanna became one of the most popular authors for adolescents in the forties and fifties (*Going on Sixteen* was the third-most-popular book in a 1959 survey of school and public libraries, close behind *Seventeenth Summer*), yet her plots are predictable and her characters are cardboard copies of types borrowed from popular-magazine fiction.

Another romance author who rivaled Cavanna for popularity was Rosamund du Jardin (who was the only writer to be represented by two titles—*Double Date* and *Wait for Marcy*—on that same 1959 survey).

Du Jardin's first book, *Practically Seventeen* (Lippincott) (do you detect a trend in these titles?), was published in 1949 and is also a pale imitation of Daly.

Like *Seventeenth Summer*, for example, *Practically Seventeen* is told in the first person—in the dumbfoundingly arch voice of du Jardin's protagonist, Tobey Heydon (which sounds too much like "hoyden" to be a coincidence). Like Daly's Angie, du Jardin's Tobey has three sisters—two older and one younger. Like Angie's father, Tobey's is a traveling salesman. He is fond of saying that since he is "completely surrounded by females in his own home," he "would go crazy without a sense of humor and that he has had to develop his in self-defense" (p. 4).

"But none of us mind," Tobey hastens to reassure the reader. "He is really sweet, as fathers go" (p. 4).

Also like *Seventeenth Summer*, du Jardin's book is a story of young love—but much slighter in substance and lighter in tone. Tobey's big dilemma—and the theme that unifies the book's highly episodic plot—is whether her relationship with boyfriend Brose (short for Ambrose) will survive until he can lay hands on the class ring he has asked her to wear.

Given the episodic structure of her first novel, it's no surprise to learn that du Jardin had been a successful writer of magazine fiction, her short stories having appeared in such popular women's magazines as *Cosmopolitan, Redbook, Good Housekeeping,* and *McCall's.* Nevertheless, if her rival Cavanna had borrowed character types from magazine fiction, it seems that du Jardin borrowed not only her characters but her situations from the popular radio comedies of the day. Tobey could be Corliss Archer's sister, and her boyfriend, Brose, is surely Henry Aldrich under an assumed name. To give du Jardin credit, there are a few funny moments in her book (as there were in radio serial comedies), and for at-risk teen readers of the nineties there is something pleasantly nostalgic and comforting in reading about peers whose biggest problems are

a) pesky younger sisters, b) who will take you to the big dance (the "Heart Hop," in this case), and c) how to resolve a rivalry for a boy's affection with a visitor from the South (named "Kentucky Jackson").

The dust-jacket blurb speaks—well, *volumes,* not only about *Practically Seventeen,* but also about the type of book that would prevail in publishing for young adults during the forties and fifties. Here's a sample paragraph: "In recent years, permanent recognition and popularity have been accorded the 'junior novel'—the story that records truthfully the modern girl's dream of life and romance and her ways of adjusting to her school and family experiences. *Practically Seventeen* is such a book—as full of life as the junior prom." And about as relevant to today's readers as *Rebecca of Sunnybrook Farm!*

I suspect, though, that du Jardin and Cavanna were not much more relevant to their contemporary readers. In fact, one reason for their astonishing popularity must have been the escape value their books offered. Both of these writers were being avidly read when I was an adolescent in the early and mid-1950s. Of course, being a boy, I would not have been caught dead reading such—uh, *girls'* books, but I did listen to the radio religiously—not because Henry Aldrich or Corliss Archer or Archie Andrews or Judy (*A Date with Judy*) Foster had anything relevant to say about my young life, but because they offered me an escape from its too-real cares and a chance—like most humor of situation and character—to occasionally feel superior to these relentless innocents. No wonder Daly inspired so many imitators—not only Cavanna and du Jardin but also Janet Lambert, Anne Emery, James L. Summers, Jessica Lyon, and the proverbial host of others—and no wonder their work was so widely read. And no wonder, too, that it is now all out of print (except, interestingly enough, for Cavanna's).

No matter; it has been replaced by a spate of equally interchangable new romances that began appearing in the eighties—books that are less known, this time, for their authors' names than for the names of the series in which they appear—the Sweet Valley books, for example, and their seemingly endless spin-offs— "Sweet Valley High," "Sweet Valley University," "Sweet Valley Twins," "The Unicorn Club," and—for the youngest readers—"Sweet Valley Kids."

The resurgence in the popularity of the romance came after a decade of hard-hitting, realistic, and (more often than not) single-problem novels. No wonder young readers were ready for the irresistible lure of escapist romance. Publishers of these new love stories turned the clock back to the days of the forties and fifties, when, as one editor put it, "[the female protagonists] are not worried about how far to go on a date; they're worried about getting a date." [31]

Ladders or Literature?

Not all the young adult or "junior" novels published in the thirties, forties, and early fifties were romances, of course. Enough attempts at more serious fiction had been published to support the first tentative attempts at literary criticism that began to emerge in the 1950s.

For example, Richard S. Alm noted in 1955 that "the last twenty years" had seen "the coming of age of the novel for the adolescent," perhaps because writers, "noting the heightened attention given to adolescents and their problems by psychologists, educators, and librarians, have turned to the personal concerns of the teen-ager as the focus of their problems." [32]

Perhaps, but the writers of "the novel for the adolescent" whom Alm singled out for particular praise were *adult* novelists like Maureen Daly, James Street, Dan Wickenden, William Maxwell, and Marjorie Kinnan Rawlings.

This was consistent, though, with the approach Dwight L. Burton had taken in his earlier essay, "The Novel for the Adolescent," which is typically cited as the first "criticism" of young adult literature. In it Burton devoted the lion's share of his attention to an analysis of work by four *adult* authors whose novels either showed "a keen perception of the adolescent experience" or "have a peculiar appeal to certain elements of the adolescent reading public." [33] (For the record, the four writers were Dan Wickenden, Ruth Moore, C. S. Forester, and Thomas Wolfe.)

The point we infer from both of these early pieces of criticism is that while, by the fifties, there may have been a separate, identifiable body of books that could be called "young adult literature," too many of its constituent titles were what Alm himself had glumly described as "slick, patterned, rather inconsequential stories written to capitalize on a rapidly expanding market." [34]

A year later (1956) another early critic, Frank G. Jennings, was even blunter, writing "the stuff of adolescent literature, for the most part, is mealy-mouthed, gutless, and pointless." [35]

This smacks of dramatic overstatement, but it is true, I think, that "much of the literature written for young adults from 1940 through 1966 goes largely and legitimately ignored today." [36]

Now, About Those Ladders . . .

Adolescence has always been viewed as a period of transition, and so it is not surprising that its literature, in the early years at least, should have been viewed as a ladder—or, more precisely, a *rung* on a ladder between children's and adult literature. This idea of reading "ladders" may have been the inspiration of Dora V. Smith, who, at the University of Minnesota in the 1930s, taught the first college-level course in adolescent literature. At least one of her most celebrated students, G. Robert Carlsen, thinks so, recalling "in her classes we constructed ladders placing titles on the rungs according to our judgment of quality. . . . Through reading guidance a teacher was to move readers from one level to a higher one." [37]

Consistent with this concept is the corollary notion of stages of reading development; i.e., it is possible to identify certain specific types—or categories—of fiction that will appeal to young readers at certain specific ages or class levels in school. In his influential 1967 book, *Books and the Teen-Age Reader* (Harper), Carlsen identified three such stages: 1. Early Adolescence: ages eleven to fourteen, grades five to eight; 2. Middle Adolescence: fifteen to sixteen, grades nine and ten; and 3. Late Adolescence: seventeen to eighteen, grades eleven and twelve.

He then developed four to nine different book categories of unique appeal to students in each stage; e.g., early adolescents would like animal, adventure, and mystery stories; the middle years would welcome war stories and historical novels; and late adolescents would dote on searches for personal values and books of social significance.

To me this smacks of the dogmatic, and accordingly, I prefer another take on this subject—a 1960 journal article by Margaret J. Early, then an associate professor of education at Syracuse University. At least I like the disclaimer with which she begins her study: "If literature, which imitates life, resists classification, how much more resistant is humanity itself!" [38]

Early did not tie her study to chronological age but rather to the progressively increasing intellectual, emotional, and experiential abilities of readers. Thus, her stages were: "Unconscious Enjoyment," "Self-conscious Appreciation," and "Conscious Delight."

"At the highest stage of literary appreciation," Early asserts, "the reader responds with delight, knows why, chooses discriminatingly, and relies on his own judgment."

This type of reading, she concludes, "is an extension of the creative process which produced the literature," [39] a thought that echoes a similar notion, of reading as an act of creative collaboration, offered by Mortimer Adler in his best-selling *How to Read a Book* (Simon & Schuster).

Whether one prefers Carlsen or Early, the same basic idea drives their respective concepts of stages: that as young people develop, their reading tastes will also mature.

Another influential concept of development that influenced adolescent literature and its interpretation in the fifties and sixties was that of "developmental tasks."

This theory was ... *developed* by Robert G. Havighurst, who appeared to view adolescence as a job of work; if teenagers were to be promoted up the career ladder to adulthood, he seemed to be saying, they must first complete seven distinct tasks: 1. achieve new and more mature relations with age-mates of both sexes; 2. achieve masculine or feminine social roles; 3. accept their physiques and use their bodies effectively; 4. achieve emotional independence of parents and other adults; 5. prepare for marriage and family life; 6. prepare for economic careers; 7. acquire a set of values and an ethical system as a guide to behavior—develop an ideology that leads to socially responsible behavior.

"To accomplish them," he claimed, "will lead to happiness and to success with later tasks, while failure leads to unhappiness in the individual, disapproval by society, and difficulty with later tasks."[40]

By the 1990s "task" had evolved into "need," and the Center for Early Adolescence at the University of North Carolina at Chapel Hill was offering "Seven Developmental Needs of Young Adolescents": 1. physical activity; 2. competence and achievement; 3. self-definition; 4. creative expression; 5. positive social interactions with peers and adults; 6. structure and clear limits; 7. meaningful participation.

One example of the influence of Havighurst's theory may be inferred from Alm's 1955 article, cited above. In it, the critic described what he perceived as the prevailing focus of young adult writers' attention: "In the main, these authors deal with an adolescent's relationships with others his own age, with his parents and other adults, and with such worries as deciding upon and preparing for a job, 'going steady,' marrying and facing the responsibilities of adulthood."[41]

Though Alm doesn't acknowledge it, what he has done is simply to parrot Havighurst's list. Carlsen—an influential teacher as well as critic—was more candid, recalling of his teaching methods: "I applied Robert Havighurst's concept of developmental tasks to adolescent books. It seemed to me that the most popular and successful titles, like Daly's *Seventeenth Summer*, were books in which characters were dealing with one or more of the developmental tasks. So we looked not only at the story content, but also at the conflicts and turmoils besetting the characters."[42]

If writers of the time *were* dealing with these issues, most of them weren't doing it in any particularly substantial way, the books they produced remaining undemanding, ephemeral, formula driven, innocent, and naive. By today's standards most of what they wrote could be described as "genre literature." And so it is probably no wonder that their product so readily lent itself to being forced into categories—whether or not these were also tied to reading stages.

Consider, for example, that if Caesar divided Gaul into three parts, G. Robert Carlsen divided young adult literature into ten! (Some years later, *his* students, Nilsen and Donelson, would boil the divisions down to a slightly more manageable six.)

I think that this persistent attempt to transform literature into utilitarian ladders too often turned the early critics' attention from the literature to the reader. I also think that frog-marching literature into ready-made category pens labeled for reading stage suitability smacks of the didactic and dogmatic and *also* threatens to turn literature from art into tool. Nevertheless I do welcome Carlsen's tenfold list of categories, since it provides a convenient framework on which to hang a necessarily brief overview of the best of the novels that were published for young adults in the two and a half decades between *Seventeenth Summer* and the dawn of realistic fiction in the late 1960s. Attention must be paid, and so, to begin, here are the categories à la Carlsen: 1. sports stories; 2. animal stories; 3. stories of olden times; 4. science fiction; 5. stories of foreign cultures; 6. boys and cars; 7. adventure stories; 8. mystery stories; 9. vocational stories; and, 10. stories of moral or ethical dilemmas. (Nilsen and Donelson call the last category "personal problems and initiation"; they also drop numbers 2, 3, 4, and 5 from their later list and add a new one: "society's problems." See their fourth edition, p. 570.)

With the wisdom of thirty to fifty years of hindsight, what do I think are some of the more enduring titles to be published in those early decades?

Well, in the sports category we've already mentioned John R. Tunis and, under the adventure-stories rubric, the work of Howard Pease. Paul Annixter's *Swiftwater* (Wyn, 1950) should also be mentioned here, and if we expand adventure to survival, we can add Robb White (his *Deathwatch* [Doubleday, 1972] remains one of the most popular young adult novels ever written).

As for careers, we've already mentioned the two Helens, Boylston and Wells; Stephen W. Meader, though best remembered for his historical novels, also wrote career books for boys (e.g., his *Snow on Blueberry Mountain* [Harcourt, 1961], is a novel about the business of skiing).

As for car books, Henry Gregor Felsen was their uncrowned king; three of his most popular works—*Hot Rod* (Dutton, 1953), *Street Rod* (Random House, 1953), and *Crash Club* (Random House, 1958)—are, amazingly, still in print, though admittedly in expensive reprint editions that are more likely to appeal to collectors of nostalgia than to contemporary readers.

As for animal stories, Fred Gipson's *Old Yeller* and

Savage Sam (Harper, 1956 and 1962, respectively) are still deservedly read, and, of course, no one has forgotten Walter Farley's thirteen or more Black Stallion books (all published by Random House, beginning in 1941) or—for the youngest adolescents—Marguerite Henry's *King of the Wind* (Rand McNally, 1948) and *Misty of Chincoteague* (Rand McNally, 1947).

Romance, amazingly, is not on Carlsen's list of categories, although he does append a lengthy list of what he calls "girls' stories." Nilsen and Donelson, however, do include love and romance in their groupings and—improbably, considering the period under discussion—add "passion and sex." That there was virtually none of either in the adolescent novels of the time is evidenced by the examples they offer: *adult* titles like Kathleen Winsor's *Forever Amber* (Macmillan, 1944) and Elizabeth Goudge's *Green Dolphin Street* (Coward McCann, 1944).

Aside from *Seventeenth Summer*, almost all the work in the romance category was ephemeral and eminently forgettable, with one important exception: the writings of Mary Stolz, which belong in the first rank along with Daly's, even though Stolz began writing a generation later, her first book, *To Tell Your Love* (Harper), appearing in 1950. Of all the authors we have mentioned, Stolz is the only one still writing today, forty-four years later, and in fact, her newest novel, *Cezanne Pinto* (Knopf), has just been named one of the best books of 1994 by *Publishers Weekly*! (See its November 7, 1994 issue, p. 44.)

Although Stolz's first books did address considerations of young love, it seems a disservice to label them "romance," since even these early titles were set apart from the plethora of undistinguished others by their powers of characterization, style, and insight. And her third book, *The Sea Gulls Woke Me* (Harper, 1951), is often mentioned as one of the most successful novels (in literary cum critical terms) of the first two decades of young adult literature. Stolz's skills as a novelist presaged the birth of that serious literature for young adults that would begin appearing in the late 1960s.

As for Carlsen's rather quaintly labeled "Stories of Olden Times," the obvious choice is Esther Forbes's *Johnny Tremaine* (Houghton Mifflin, 1944), though today it would be considered a children's book and, in fact, it copped the 1944 Newbery Medal as best children's book of that year.

In the category of science fiction Carlsen offers Robert A. Heinlein's *Farmer in the Sky* (Scribner, 1950), which he calls "typical of the best in this category" (p. 52). Today's young adults would undoubtedly prefer Heinlein's adult title and cult classic, *Stranger in a Strange Land* (Putnam, 1961).

Another of Heinlein's contemporaries who should be added to the science fiction list is the amazingly prolific Andre Norton, who began writing for young readers in 1934 and authored more than seventy-five novels for this age group. It's interesting to compare science fiction with another of Carlsen's genre categories: the mystery. While Heinlein and Norton—and others like Ray Bradbury, Arthur C. Clarke, and Lester Del Rey—are still read today, almost none of the

mystery writers' names—and work—have survived:
Who today has heard of or read Lockhart Amerman or
Ruth Park or Marcella Thum or Budd Westreich?

"Stories of foreign cultures" had been a mainstay
of juvenile fiction since the 1920s—though most of the
titles, written by white Americans, were of the "little
children of foreign lands" (most of whom seemed to
be twins) variety. There were exceptions, of course.
Elizabeth Foreman Lewis had written knowledgeably
and insightfully about the lives of young people in
China, having lived and taught there herself. Her first
book, *Young Fu of the Upper Yangtze* (John C. Winston,
1932) won the 1933 Newbery Medal, in fact. However, the best of this type of book seems not to have
appeared until after World War II, "an era," editor/
publisher Margaret K. McElderry writes, "in which
American children's book editors actively sought out
the best in writing and illustration from abroad, an era
that enriched the children's book scene and American
children's reading immensely." [43]

In fact this new era was inaugurated when Ms.
McElderry herself published Margot Benary-Isbert's
The Ark (Harcourt, 1953), the first German book for
young readers to be published in America following
World War II. This area of publishing is one that
particularly demonstrates the blurring of the line that
divided the more serious children's and young adult
(or "junior") novels in the thirties, forties, and fifties.
Consider, for example, that other names Carlsen
cites—names like Clare Huchet Bishop and Ann Nolan

Clark—are today regarded as writers for children. It wasn't until the sixties that books clearly designed for older readers began to appear: Maia Wojciechowska's novel of Spain, *Shadow of a Bull* (Atheneum, 1964); Jack Bennett's novels of South Africa: *Jamie* (Little, Brown, 1963), *Mister Fisherman* (Little, Brown, 1965), and *The Hawk Alone* (Little, Brown, 1965). And in Australia, Patricia Wrightson began regular publication in the early sixties, while her countryman, Ivan Southall, began his career at the end of the decade.

Nevertheless there was about this whole area of "stories of foreign cultures" a kind of well-intentioned innocence that survived into the eighties, when new patterns of immigration and heightened cultural awareness finally created a new kind of multicultural literature distinguished by authentic stories told by people who actually hailed from the cultures they were writing about. The civil-rights movement of the sixties further contributed to the heightening of cultural awareness and tended to cause a blurring of the lines between Carlsen's "foreign cultures" category and that which Nilsen and Donelson call "society's problems," the latter focusing on problems encountered by minorities—principally blacks. But once again most of the titles discussed are by writers for adults—Ralph Ellison, Claude Brown, Richard Wright, Eldridge Cleaver, etc. Nat Hentoff's first young adult novel, *Jazz Country* (Harper, 1965), which deals with black-white relations, is mentioned, but the authors cautiously acknowledge that "perhaps neither blacks nor whites are comfortable with the themes or the characters" (4th ed., p. 572).

The same might be said of Frank Bonham's *Durango Street* (Dutton, 1965), which is told from the point of view of an African-American teenager, although Bonham, like Hentoff, is white. The reason for the caution, of course, is the matter of "political correctness" ("P.C."), which would emerge in the eighties and nineties as a major issue complicating discussions of multicultural books or books that address "society's problems."

P.C. will be dealt with later, but for now it might be cited as a reason that books like those by the once-important writer Florence Cranell Means—who specialized in novels that explored the social problems encountered by minority populations—could probably not be published today simply because she wrote from outside the cultures she was examining.

Means is a special case, whom Nilsen and Donelson identify, in their second edition, as one of "nine outstanding writers for young adults" (p. 584).

Born in 1891 in Baldwinsville, New York, she was the daughter of a Baptist clergyman, and perhaps it was a kind of missionary zeal that inspired her to write, as she put it, "little stories about children of other kinds and colors."

She got her material, initially, from "visiting and retired missionaries" and from "the blessed public library." As her writing career developed along with her interest in other cultures, she began enriching her earlier research with visits to communities of the cultures she was writing about. In retrospect it seems there was hardly a minority group that escaped her benign attention during a career that spanned six decades. Her books include characters who are African Americans (*Shuttered Windows* and *Great Day in the Morning,* Houghton Mifflin, 1938 and 1946); Japanese Americans (*The Moved-Outers,* Houghton Mifflin, 1945), Mexican Americans (*Rafael and Consuelo,* Friendship Press, 1929), and Native Americans (*Our Cup Is Broken,* Houghton Mifflin, 1969).

She herself states that "my emphasis became increasingly on the beauty and needs of our ethnic minorities" (all quotes are from *20th Century Children's Writers, 3rd edition,* edited by Tracy Chevalier. Detroit: St. James Press, 1989, p. 672), and it certainly seems that her intentions were not only good but exemplary. One supposes, from what one reads of her, that she would be the first to applaud the fact that the peoples she wrote about so carefully and, indeed, lovingly have now found their own voices in the books that are being published in the nineties.

From "society's problems" we move, finally, to the category Nilsen and Donelson call "personal problems" and which Carlsen calls "stories of moral or ethical dilemmas."

Writing in 1967, Carlsen chose as his exemplary writer in this category Anne Emery, author of *Sorority Girl* (Westminster, 1952), a title that—in light of the issues we have been discussing—sounds vapid, at best. And yet Emery does deal with some enduring personal

problems—peer pressure, popularity, and group values—
that are still at home in the work of more contemporary—
and critically praised—writers such as Richard Peck.

In due course both the societal- and personal-problem
categories spawned the spate of "problem" novels that
would become such a fixture of the late sixties and the
decade of the seventies.

Adolescents seem to be inherently divided. On the
one hand they are outer directed and passionately concerned about society's problems, especially when they
involve real or perceived injustice. In 1994, for example,
tens of thousands of Southern California young adults
marched to protest a ballot initiative called Proposition
187, which would remove social services from anyone—
including children—found to be an illegal alien. At the
same time, adolescents are the perfect solipsists in their
inner-directed conviction that they are the center of the
universe; hence the popularity of the personal-problem
novel. And from that point it is an easy transition to the
novel of personal initiation, or what Carlsen, in another
source, calls "The Transition." He explains that "perhaps
the single theme most sought by the young adult is the
book that details the movement of a character from adolescence into early adult life." [44]

This transition is a perilous passage, and few adolescents want to undergo it alone. Recognizing this
fact, the celebrated contemporary young adult author
Richard Peck has written that "the great American
theme in the final third of the 20th century has been
the tribalizing of the young." [45]

I don't disagree with this assertion, but I would qualify it by adding three other great themes: alienation, sex, and violence.

Until all these themes found their way into young adult literature, it would remain securely locked in a cell of smugness like the rest of complacent American culture and society in the 1940s and '50s. The 1960s unlocked that cell, liberating young adult literature and opening the doors to what has come to be called the "New Realism." In fact, since there was no "old" realism, I think it is sufficient to say that the real birth of young adult literature came with its embrace of the novel of realism, beginning, as we will see in the next chapter, in the late 1960s.

NOTES

1. Egoff, Sheila, "Beyond the Garden Wall" in *The Arbuthnot Lectures 1970–1979*, compiled by Zena Sutherland. Chicago: American Library Association, 1980, p. 190.

2. Nilsen, Alleen Pace, and Kenneth L. Donelson, *Literature for Today's Young Adults*. Fourth Edition. New York: Harper, 1993, p. 5.

3. Forisha-Kovach, B., "Adolescent Development" in Raymond J. Corsini, ed., *Encyclopedia of Psychology*, 1:22. New York: Wiley, 1984.

4. Carter, Betty, *Best Books for Young Adults: The History, the Selections, the Romance*. Chicago: American Library Association, 1994, p. 9.

5. Babbitt, Natalie, "Between Innocence and Maturity" in Jana Varlejs, ed., *Young Adult Literature in the Seventies*. Metuchen, NJ: Scarecrow, 1978, p. 140.

6. Shaffer, Kenneth R., "What Makes Sammy Read?" *Top of the News*, XIX:9 (March 1963).

7. Carter, *Best Books*, p. 13.

8. Holland, Isabelle, "What Is Adolescent Literature?" in Patricia E. Feehan and Pamela Petrick Barron, ed., *Writers on Writing for Young*

Adults. Detroit: Omnigraphics, 1991, p. 61.

9. *The American Heritage Dictionary of the English Language.* Third Edition. Boston: Houghton Mifflin, 1992, p. 23.

10. Santrock, J.W., "Adolescence," in Corsini, 1:21.

11. Nilsen, 4th ed., p. 5.

12. Holland, "What Is," p. 61.

13. Mertz, Maia Pank, and David A. England, "The Legitimacy of American Adolescent Fiction," *School Library Journal,* 30:119 (October 1983).

14. Nilsen, 4th ed., p. 2.

15. Carter, *Best Books,* p. 13.

16. Ibid., p. 16.

17. Townsend, John Rowe, "Standards of Criticism for Children's Literature" in *The Arbuthnot Lectures, 1970–1979,* compiled by Zena Sutherland. Chicago: American Library Association, 1980, p. 26.

18. Burgess, Anthony, *The Novel Now.* New York: Norton, 1967, p. 16.

19. Townsend, John Rowe, *Written for Children.* Third revised edition. New York: Lippincott, 1987, p. 279.

20. Edwards, Margaret A., "The Rise of Teen-Age Reading," *The Saturday Review,* XXXVII:88 (November 13, 1954).

21. Hutchinson, Margaret, "Fifty Years of Young Adult Reading 1921–1971," *Top of the News,* 30:27 (November 1973).

22. Edwards, "Rise," p. 88.

23. Van Gelder, Robert, "An Interview with Miss Maureen Daly," *The New York Times Book Review,* July 12, 1942, p. 20.

24. Berger, Laura Standley, ed. *Twentieth Century Young Adult Writers.* Detroit: St. James, 1994, p. 170.

25. Nilsen, Alleen Pace, and Kenneth Donelson, *Literature for Today's Young Adults.* Second edition. Glenview, IL: Scott, Foresman, 1985, p. 551.

26. Tunis, John R., "What Is a Juvenile Book?" in Paul Heins, ed., *Cross-currents of Criticism.* Boston: Horn Book, 1977, p. 25.

27. Holland, "What Is," p. 65.

28. Walton, Edith H. "'Seventeenth Summer' and Other Works of Fiction." *The New York Times Book Review,* May 3, 1942, p. 7.

29. Van Gelder, "Interview," p. 2.

30. Daly, Maureen. "Maureen Daly." In Muriel Fuller, ed., *More Junior Authors.* New York: H. W. Wilson, 1963, p. 59.

31. Pollack, Pamela D., "The Business of Popularity: The Surge of Teenage Paperbacks." *School Library Journal,* 28:26 (November 1981).

32. Alm, Richard S., "The Glitter and the Gold" in Richard A. Meade and Robert C. Small, Jr., eds., *Literature for Adolescents: Selection and Use.* Columbus, OH: Charles E. Merrill, 1973, p. 185.

33. Burton, Dwight L., "The Novel for the Adolescent" in Meade and Small, pp. 86–87,

34. Alm, "Glitter," p. 185.

35. Jennings, Frank G., "Literature for Adolescents—Pap or Protein?" *English Journal,* 45:226 (December 1956).

36. Nilsen, 4th ed., p. 574.

37. Carlsen, G. Robert, "Teaching Literature for the Adolescent: A Historical Perspective," *English Journal,* 73:29 (November 1984).

38. Early, Margaret J., "Stages and Growth in Literary Appreciation," *English Journal,* 49:161 (March 1960).

39. Ibid., p. 166.

40. Havighurst, Robert G., *Developmental Tasks and Education.* Quoted in David A. Russell, "The Common Experience of Adolescence," *Journal of Youth Services in Libraries,* 2:61 (Fall 1988).

41. Alm, "Glitter," p. 185.

42. Carlsen, "Teaching," p. 29.

43. McElderry, Margaret K., "Across the Years, Across the Seas: Notes from an Errant Editor," *Journal of Youth Services in Libraries,* 7:373 (Summer 1994).

44. Carlsen, G. Robert, "For Everything There Is a Season" in Meade, p. 119.

45. Peck, Richard, *Love and Death at the Mall.* New York: Delacorte, 1994, p. 47.

CHAPTER TWO

THE SIXTIES
AND THE RISE OF REALISM
But What's It Really Like?

"Teenagers today want to read about teenagers today."
—S. E. Hinton, "Teen-agers Are for Real"

It was the sixties, and something significant was happening in America. Singer-songwriter Bob Dylan, whose music helped define the new decade, underscored this when he wrote the enduring lyric "The times they are a-changin'."

"Never trust anybody over thirty," kids cautioned one another as they set about a wholesale rejection of the status quo and more—a rejection of the whole world adults had made.

Psychologist B. Forisha-Kovach, with dry understatement, calls the stormy sixties a decade "when youth activities were prominent," and says it is one of two eras of particular significance in the evolution of modern ideas of adolescent development. The other era, as we have already pointed out, was the 1920s, the first time when "it became clear that the young were a separate generation."

It would be the sixties, however, "when the 'under 30' generation became a subject of popular concern" that "research on adolescence came into its own."[1]

It would also be the decade when literature for adolescents could be said to come into *its* own, as well. As had been the case in the forties with Maureen Daly and her *Seventeenth Summer*, a sea change would once again be heralded by the appearance of a single young writer—again, a teenage girl—and the publication of her first book: This time the novel was *The Outsiders* (Viking, 1967) and the teenager was S. E. Hinton of Tulsa, Oklahoma.

And so we have two young women and two books, each having far-reaching impacts on young adult literature and each receiving enormous popular attention because of the novelty of their authors' being themselves teenagers when their respective first books were written.

But there the similarities end and the differences begin. For starters, Hinton was writing about boys, not girls (one reason her publisher suggested she use initials rather than her given names, Susan Elizabeth). And she wasn't writing about tree-shaded streets in small-town America. Instead, she was writing about mean urban streets where teenagers didn't have time to agonize over first love and dates for the prom; they were too busy agonizing over whether they would survive the next battle in their ongoing war with a rival gang.

For, in fact, it *was* warfare that Hinton was writing about—class warfare as symbolized by the two gangs that appear in *The Outsiders:* the Greasers and the "Socs."

"Soc" was short for "Socials, the jet set, the West-side rich kids" who "wreck houses and throw beer blasts for kicks" (pp. 10–11). The 1990s reader might also think of "Soc" as a shorthand designation for "sociopath," the kind of amoral, middle class, house-trashing adolescents who populate Robert Cormier's 1991 novel, *We All Fall Down* (Delacorte Press), and who would surely recognize Hinton's rich kids as distant, older cousins.

The members of the other gang, the economically disadvantaged Greasers, are "almost like hoods" and are given to their own antisocial behavior—they "steal things and drive old souped-up cars and hold up gas stations" (p. 11).

Hinton's story is told in the first-person voice of one of the Greasers: fourteen-year-old Ponyboy Curtis, who lives with his older brothers Sodapop and Darry, the latter of whom acts *in loco parentis,* since the brothers' real parents have been killed in a car wreck before the story begins.

Because, as Ponyboy reports, "the three of us get to stay together only as long as we behave" (p. 11), they try to avoid the more law-breaking Greaser activities outlined above, contenting themselves with wearing their "tuff" hair long, dressing in blue jeans and T-shirts, and lifting a fist in the inevitable rumble. (Hinton's situation involving a family of orphans struggling to stay together as a family unit continues to be a staple of literature and film. In fact, not one but two network television shows that debuted in the 1994 season—*Party of Five* [Fox] and *On Our Own* [ABC]—deal with this situation.)

Hinton's was not the first novel to deal with gangs; Frank Bonham's story of Los Angeles gangs, *Durango Street*, had been published in 1965 (and Leonard Bernstein's now-classic musical *West Side Story* had been produced on Broadway in 1958), but there was something about *The Outsiders* that captured the imagination of its readers and spawned a new kind of literature, "books," as Richard Peck has put it, "about young people parents thought their children didn't know" [2] (or, more probably, *wished* they didn't know!). Hinton knew them, though; she went to school with them every day in Tulsa. She knew from personal observation what their lives were like, but she didn't find that kind of first-person reality being depicted in the pages of young adult literature.

"The world is changing," she wrote in an impassioned *New York Times* article, "yet the authors of books for teen-agers are still 15 years behind the times. In the fiction they write, romance is still the most popular theme, with a horse-and-the-girl-who-loved-it coming in a close second." (The horse-girl relationship was still a staple twenty years later; Sib Spooner, the sixteen-year-old protagonist of Bruce Brooks's 1986 novel, *Midnight Hour Encores* [Harper], offers an amusing meditation on this phenomenon, wondering about her peers' equine fascination: "I knew that someday we were all supposed to get into boys. But horses? Nobody I knew had grown up to marry a horse" [p. 3].)

Hinton continues, "Nowhere is the drive-in social jungle mentioned. . . . In short, where is the reality?"[3]

Hinton was not the only one who was wondering.

George Woods, then children's book editor of *The New York Times Book Review*, wrote in 1965, "One looks for modernity, for boldness, for realism. The teen-age novel, especially, should grapple with the delights and the dilemmas of today's teen-agers. Delicacy and restraint are necessarily called for, yet all too often this difficult problem is resolved through avoidance. A critic in touch with the world and aware of the needs of the young expects to see more handling of neglected subjects: narcotics, addiction, illegitimacy, alcoholism, pregnancy, discrimination, retardation. There are few, if any, definitive works in these areas."[4]

Not quite four months before Hinton's piece appeared, Nat Hentoff contributed a similarly scathing indictment of young adult literature to *The Times*. Writing of his own first novel, he asserted, "*Jazz Country* failed, as have most books directed at teen-agers. . . . My point is that the reality of being young—the tensions, the sensual yearnings and sometime satisfactions, the resentment against the educational lock step that makes children fit the schools, the confusing recognition of their parents' hypocrisies and failures—all this is absent from most books for young readers."[5]

A year later, Newbery Medal–winning author

Maia Wojciechowska joined the chorus, criticizing authors of books for the young who "keep going back to their own turn-of-the-century childhoods, or write tepid little stories of high school proms, broken and mended friendships, phony-sounding conflicts between parents and children, and boring accounts of what they consider 'problems.'

"The gulf between the real child of today and his fictional counterpart must be bridged," she concluded.[6]

Hinton's great success was in managing to bridge that gap and, by giving fictional counterparts to the real teenagers she knew, to introduce to young adult fiction new kinds of "real" characters—whether they were the alienated, socioeconomically disadvantaged Greasers or the equally alienated but socioeconomically *advantaged* Socials.

Her novel was innovative, too, in its introduction of thematic relevance. Hinton had been quite right when she pointed out, in her *New York Times* piece, that "violence, too, is a part of teenagers' lives" (p. 29). Before her, though, authors had tended to ignore this basic fact of adolescent life. But Hinton used it to define the daily lives of her characters, as individuals and as gang members, and this use *was* groundbreaking and consistent with the demands of the realistic novel.

As we have seen, Hinton rejected the literature that had been written for her generation, calling it "the inane junk lining the teen-age shelf of the library" (p. 29). And her rejection of the established literature for young adults is consistent with the universal rejection

47

of the status quo that was such a hallmark of the icon-
oclastic sixties, a decade that belonged to the young (a
prosaic but telling bit of evidence being the American
Library Association's establishment, in 1966, of its
Young Adult Services Division).

Because of her own youth, Hinton came to symbolize that rejection and its replacement by a new kind
of literature. Richard Peck, writing of the young adult
authors, like himself, whose work would follow hers,
has said she "may be the mother of us all." [7]

The Young Adult Library Services Association and
the magazine *School Library Journal* confirmed that
opinion in 1988 when they awarded Hinton the first
Margaret A. Edwards Award, a jointly sponsored prize
that recognizes lifetime achievement in writing young
adult books.

Hinton's place in the evolution of young adult literature is secure, but I was struck when I recently re-read
The Outsiders by the realization that it is an odd hybrid:
part realistic novel and part romantic fantasy that, at its
self-indulgent worst, exemplifies what critic Terrence
Rafferty has called "morbid adolescent romanticism." [8]

The Outsiders is redolent of such romanticism. Ironically, it manifests itself in a treatment of violence that
too often seems to sentimentalize it. Consider that the
chief act of violence in the book, the murder—in self-
defense—of a Soc is perpetrated by Johnny, who is
himself an impossibly romanticized character, delicate,
fearful, the "pet" of the other boys, a sixteen-year-
old who seems even younger than fourteen-year-old

Ponyboy. Johnny is then essentially sacrificed on the altar of sentiment when he dies of injuries that he later sustains in rescuing some small children from a burning church.

Johnny is not only himself a romantically idealized character, he is enchanted by other romantic figures—the Southern cavaliers of Margaret Mitchell's *Gone with the Wind*. And this romantic fascination infects Ponyboy himself. Consider what he writes in his journal: "I'd never get past the part where the Southern gentlemen go riding into sure death because they are gallant. Southern gentlemen with big black eyes in blue jeans and T-shirts, Southern gentlemen crumpling under street lights" (p. 166).

Hinton obviously wants the reader to make an equation between Margaret Mitchell's Southern cavaliers and her own gallant Greasers. But the effort seems mawkish and oddly old-fashioned. For her book also espouses the romantic notion of orphaned boys banding together, in the absence of parents, to create a family in the form of a gang. At one point Pony tells Johnny, who is unhappy because his parents ignore him, "Shoot, you got the whole gang. Dally didn't slug you tonight 'cause you're the pet. I mean, golly, Johnny, you got the whole gang."

In real life, of course, gangs are less family than tribe. True to her adolescent fantasy, there are almost no adults in Hinton's world of teenage "tough puppies," as critic Michael Malone calls them. And those that do exist are either ciphers or one-note caricatures of

49

unfeeling evil in their archetypal lack of caring feelings for their sons. Hinton seems almost to invoke the spirit of Peter Pan and his "gang" of lost boys when she introduces the corollary theme of youthful innocence and its loss in the passage from childhood to adulthood. This finds expression in her use of the Robert Frost poem "Nothing Gold Can Stay," which fascinates Pony, although its meaning eludes him. Of course, it is Johnny who, in a melodramatic deathbed note to Pony, will explicate it: "He meant you're gold when you're a kid, like green. When you're a kid everything's new, dawn . . . like the way you dig sunsets, Pony. That's gold."

Johnny goes on to implore Pony to "keep it that way, it's a good way to be" (p. 187). In other words, à la Peter Pan, refuse to grow up.

The book's realism is further compromised by Hinton's style. I think Canadian critic Michele Landsberg may be a bit harsh in her description of it as "fan-magazine prose," [9] but that phrase does accurately capture the tone of Ponyboy's gushing descriptions of the other boys: "a handsome, dark boy with a reckless grin and a hot temper" (p. 155), and: "Soda is handsomer than anyone else I know. Not like Darry—Soda's movie-star kind of handsome, the kind that people stop on the street to watch go by. . . . His eyes are dark brown—lively, dancing, recklessly laughing eyes . . ." (this effusion continues for fully half of page 10). Not only is this a case of outrageous overwriting, but its voice is too obviously not that of a Ponyboy at all; it is a Ponygirl speaking, instead: Hinton herself, who obviously had an adolescent crush on most of the boys she created, boys who are no more credible than the narrator's voice, as they constantly burst into tears, stroke each other's hair, or put their arms around each other or their heads in each other's laps and go to sleep (p. 90). Accordingly I disagree with Richard Peck, who praised Hinton for her aesthetic distance. Not only can we not believe that a boy has written this, we can't believe that *any* streetwise, economically disadvantaged, hard-edged kid would write like this. (Michael Malone says "Hinton's prose can be as fervid, mawkish, and ornate as any nineteenth century romance," and Ponyboy flings "adjectives and archaic phrases around like [English romance writer] Barbara Cartland." [10])

Nor can we believe that kids like the Greasers would limit their oaths to expressions like "Glory!" "Aw, lay off," "Shoot," "Oh, Lordy!" etc.

But then all these boys are even further softened by their names—almost all of them diminutives. Pony's older brother's given name may be Darrell, but everyone calls him "Darry"; the toughest Greaser in the gang is Dallas, but everyone calls him "Dally." Of course, we also have Johnny, and since the name "Pony" can't be further diminished, Hinton adds "boy" to a name matched in silliness only by his older brother's: "Sodapop." The more cynical reader might breathe a prayer of thanksgiving that the Curtis parents died before they could have a fourth son, since

51

they would probably have named him "Linoleum" or "Bisquik"!

The loss of innocence was also the theme of J. D. Salinger's *The Catcher in the Rye* (Little, Brown, 1951), a more distinguished work of fiction that, though published for adults, is also a more viable model for the modern young adult novel than Hinton's. *Catcher*'s most powerful contribution is the idiosyncratic, first-person voice of its narrator, Holden Caulfield. But the book is also quintessentially adolescent in its tone, attitudes, and choice of narrative incidents, many of which are ritually rite-of-passage, including the obligatory (and obligatorily embarrassing) encounter with a prostitute.

Wry, cynical, funny, and intensely self-conscious, Holden's voice is one of the most original in American fiction, and the story he tells, in *The Catcher in the Rye*, is a marvel of sustained style and tone. Even more than *Seventeenth Summer*, it helped establish a tradition of first-person narrative voice for young adult novels. Yet when used without Salinger's artful ability to sustain interest and credibility, a little bit of it goes a very long way. Such a first-person voice can become relentlessly self-indulgent and solipsistic in telling readers far more than they need or care to know about the narrator's angst and agonies. As one later observer put it, "Holden Caulfield has much to answer for in contemporary teenage literature. The combination of first-person stream-of-consciousness with an attempt at up-to-date slang, lots of brand names for food and drink, and the odd dash of faux-naif literary criticism can be lethal." [11]

I don't know that Salinger's use of the first person influenced Hinton's own choice (although Holden's dream of saving small children by catching them as they run through the rye toward a cliff certainly seems to be reflected in Johnny's running into the burning church to save equally at-risk small children). But Holden's tone of voice *is* clearly echoed in Paul Zindel's, whose own first young adult novel, *The Pigman* (Harper), was published in 1968, a year after *The Outsiders*. Zindel's debt to Holden is the more obvious since his characters, like Salinger's, hail from the urban East—New York City, to be precise.

Because he was an accomplished playwright and a demonstrated master of dialogue before entering the young adult field, it is not surprising that Zindel chose to tell his story in not one but two first-person voices: those of teenage friends John and Lorraine, whose brash, colloquial tone invites further comparison with Holden's. There are other similarities: John, like Holden, is "extremely handsome" and a prodigiously gifted liar. He also hates school and has a horror of being a "phony in the crowd" (p. 71).

Further: Holden's favorite word is "madman," and after having some kind of indeterminate breakdown, he tells his story "about this madman stuff" from a sanitarium where he has been sent "to take it easy" (p. 1).

There are also numerous references to mental illness in *The Pigman*. Lorraine tells the reader "how really disturbed" two of her classmates are and believes herself to be paranoid. For his part, John announces he is a lunatic. Neither of these two *is* insane, of course, only terminally smart-alecky—even Lorraine, when she first meets him, thinks of John as "a first-class smart aleck" (p. 15).

This is manifested in their favorite pastime, what they call "telephone marathons," which evolved from a typical adolescent phone prank. (For example, calling up a drugstore and asking if it has Prince Albert in a can. If the respondent answers yes, the caller's rejoinder is "Then let him out.")

The object of John and Lorraine's telephone marathon is to see who can keep a perfect stranger on the line for the longest amount of time. This, of course, invites dissembling—well, lying, actually—and the implied payoff is that the caller gets to feel smugly superior to those he has duped.

It is through such a telephone marathon that John and Lorraine first meet a lonely old man named Mr. Pignati. Improbably, they befriend him (dubbing him the Pigman because of his name and his collection of pig figurines) and in the process begin to learn some degree of self-confidence and self-approval.

The character of Mr. Pignati is the most successful element of the book. He is an original: warmhearted, generous-spirited, intensely likable—even Lorraine and the cynical John fall for him—and the kind of sweetly eccentric older character who would become a fixture in a number of later young adult novels (e.g., the bag lady Amelia in John Donovan's *Remove Protective Coating a Little at a Time* [Harper, 1973] and Polly Prior in Richard Peck's *Remembering the Good Times* [Delacorte, 1985]).

Zindel writes about the real-life inspiration for Mr. Pignati and other characters and incidents from *The Pigman* in his engaging 1992 memoir, *The Pigman & Me* (Harper).

Though at first John and Lorraine's friendship with the Pigman appears to be the perfect antidote to their adolescent anomie and misanthropic malaise, they will ultimately betray him; while he is in the hospital recovering from a heart attack, they decide to host a party at his house. The revelers get out of hand; the pig collection and a dress that had belonged to the Pigman's late and much-loved wife are destroyed. Improbably (a word one uses a lot in describing this book), Mr. Pignati is released early from the hospital and returns home just in time to witness this scene of destruction. As a result he has a heart attack soon thereafter and dies, in the process teaching John and Lorraine a bitter lesson about the need to accept responsibility for one's actions.

Zindel's biographer Jack Forman summarizes critical opinion when he writes, "*The Pigman* was a groundbreaking event because—along with S. E. Hinton's *The Outsiders*—it transformed what had been called the teen 'junior novel' from a predictable, stereotyped story about high school sports and dances to one about complex teenage protagonists dealing with real concerns."[12]

"Complex"? "Real"? Perhaps, but actually John and Lorraine seem more types of disaffected modern youth than real characters (and, frankly, their narrative voices are so similar as to be sometimes indistinguishable). Compared with their parents, however, they are positively

Tolstoyan in their complexities. John's father and mother, whom he contemptuously refers to as "Bore" and "Hyper," are, at best, one-dimensional sitcom exaggerations, at worst, cartoon types. " 'Be yourself! Be individualistic!' he [John's father] called after me. 'But for God's sake get your hair cut. You look like an oddball' " (p. 73).

Some of this is inarguably funny (one difference between Hinton and Zindel is that he has a sense of humor), but its over-the-top exaggerations ultimately compromise its efforts at realism. How is the reader supposed to believe that John is alienated and disaffected because of his failed relationship with his parents when the adults aren't even believable human beings? Lorraine's mother is, equally, a one-dimensional exaggeration of monstrousness—a sour-tempered nurse/harridan who steals from her patients, mistrusts Lorraine, and suspects the Pigman of taking sexual advantage of her daughter. No wonder John thinks, "I would rather be dead than to turn into the kind of grown-up people I knew" (p. 178).

Who wouldn't?

Five years before *The Pigman* was published, Emily Cheney Neville had written humorously about a similarly uneasy relationship between an urban adolescent and his parents in her Newbery Medal–winning book *It's Like This, Cat* (Harper, 1963). But her treatment is the more realistic. Zindel, one suspects, is playing to the house (and overacting in the process), capitalizing on his sixties readership's innate distrust of "anybody over thirty." Even his minor adult characters are grotesque: Mr. Pignati's nurse is simply described as "the fat, huge nurse" (p. 127). Another nurse is "this Transylvanian-looking nun-nurse" (p. 126). Two policemen are "so dumb it was pathetic" (p. 124). A saleslady has "too much makeup and a beehive hairdo" (p. 91). Etc.

A related problem with *The Pigman*—and one that also compromises its effectiveness as a realistic novel—is how contrived many of its situations and effects seem.

Why in the world do John and Lorraine decide to have a party at the Pigman's house—*and* on the night before he is due home from the hospital? And why does he come home early? And why, having received this crushing blow, should he soon thereafter discover that Bobo, his favorite baboon at the zoo, has died?

The obvious answer is that the author is manipulating situation and character, just as he manipulates the reader's emotions in scenes like the one in which the Pigman finally admits to John and Lorraine that his wife is dead or when he later discovers that Bobo is dead: "He went to grab hold of the railing, but let out a tiny cry *almost like a puppy that had been stepped on by mistake. I can still remember the sound of it . . .*" (emphasis added) (p. 173).

This is not realistically expressed emotion. It is sentimental pathos, instead—the same kind of pathos that cheapens Johnny's death in *The Outsiders.*

I have often puzzled over the fact that Hinton and Zindel have traditionally been accorded the lion's share of the credit for ushering in a new age of modern young adult fiction—at the expense, it seems to me, of a third writer whose own first novel was published the same year as Hinton's and a year before Zindel's. I refer to Robert Lipsyte, whose splendid first novel, *The Contender* (Harper), was published in 1967 and is an authentically realistic novel in its theme, its characters, its style, setting, and resolution.

Its theme—becoming and transforming the self—speaks to the quintessential adolescent experience. In *The Contender* it finds its expression in the character of Alfred Brooks, a black teenager who lives with his widowed aunt Pearl in a tiny Harlem apartment. Like the Curtis boys, Alfred is an orphan; his mother is dead and his father has abandoned him. For Alfred the future is nothing but dead ends. A high-school dropout, he is working as a stockboy in a white-owned neighborhood grocery when the reader first meets him. The members of the local street gang jeeringly refer to him as "Good Old Uncle Alfred"—a reference, perhaps, to Uncle Tom, or perhaps simply a reference to the fact that, at seventeen, Alfred is already an old man, without ambition, without purpose, without hope. Until he discovers Donatelli's gym and the unexpected chance to become, through boxing, a contender—not only in the ring, but in life as well.

Lipsyte, like Zindel, was an established writer before he turned to young adult fiction. At the age of twenty-seven he was already one of two internationally syndicated sports columnists for *The New York*

Times. It was a fortuitous conversation with Cus D'Amato, former heavyweight champion Floyd Patterson's trainer, that gave him the inspiration for his novel.

His experience as a journalist, trained to search for the telling detail and for reporting the unflinching, though often unpleasant, truth, guaranteed a book that is a marvel of verisimilitude in the details of its settings: the boxing world and its gritty, New York–streets backdrop. The characters—even the minor ones—are real people, not conventional types, with believable motivations and authentic reactions to each other and to the situations in which they find themselves. They have their own will, not one imposed on them by the author.

And there is no dishonestly happy, Sylvester Stallone *Rocky* kind of resolution. Instead, Alfred ultimately realizes he doesn't have what it takes—the killer instinct—to make it in the ring, but on the road to that recognition he has discovered that he *does* have what it takes to make it in life; that he has developed the necessary strength of character, "the willingness," as his trainer Mr. Donatelli has put it, "to sweat and bleed to get up as high as his legs and his brains and his heart will take him," to help not only himself but his drug-addicted friend, James, as well.

"Why you wanna do all this?" a puzzled James asks his friend.

Alfred's answer is still moving, thirty-seven years later: "Because I know I can, James. And you're my partner (p. 166)."

It is a cautiously—and therefore realistically—optimistic ending that is consistent with the realistic development of theme and plot that preceded it.

The Contender is a model for the kind of novel that George Woods, S. E. Hinton, and Nat Hentoff had called for in the articles quoted earlier in this chapter.

And so it seems ironic to me that Lipsyte's first novel appears never to have achieved the popularity with readers or the stature in the history of young adult literature that Hinton's and Zindel's have. The latter aspect may be changing, however; *The Contender* was one of the hundred young adult books published between 1967 and 1992 to be chosen recently for YALSA's silver anniversary list of the Best of the Best Books for Young Adults ("Top One Hundred Countdown").

As for popularity, it should be acknowledged that the novel has sold more than a million and a half copies since its publication, but I suspect that may be more a measure of its popularity with teachers and librarians than with teenagers themselves.

I base this on the fact that *The Contender* is not only the most realistic of the three titles I have discussed, it is the most successful in literary terms, as well. Alfred's struggle is painfully real, and it *is* painful for the reader to identify with. The world Alfred inhabits *is* ugly—there are no lyrical interludes of escape like Ponyboy and Johnny's excursion to the country. The book is not told in the first person, and so there is none of the zany, wisecracking, adolescent humor of Zindel's narrators. Lipsyte also has more control of his material; as a result there is none of the self-indulgently romantic, Thomas Wolfeian "O lost" qualities that suffuse *The Outsiders*.

Lipsyte's adult characters are real, complex, and—well, *admirable* in a way that Zindel's and Hinton's are not. And all of Lipsyte's characters—and his readers, by extension—have to *work*. They have to take life one painful step at a time. There is no grand romantic catharsis as ending; no self-indulgent masochism either; but instead, a real-life promise of more work and more struggle accompanied by a realistic level of hope and attainable success.

Unfortunately, kids do overstate their emotional life; for them the possibility of tragedy exists in everything. That's surely a reason why their suicide rate is so high and why they might find a kind of self-indulgent catharsis in the death of a character like Mr. Pignati, not to mention a certain masochistic delight in empathetically sharing John and Lorraine's feeling of responsibility for that demise. But in real life, Mr. P. wouldn't necessarily have died. In real life he might have lived on—but incapacitated—and John and Lorraine would then have had to decide, after their ill-fated party, if his friendship was sufficiently important to them to face the burden of assuming responsibility for his ongoing, day-in-and-day-out care. That is the spirit in which *The Contender* was written. And so there is no death or madness or melodrama in it and no chance for self-pity either. Another observer of *The Outsiders*, Michael Malone, has said, sardonically but—I think—accurately in this regard, that "there is no sweeter sorrow than the self-pity of our teens, no pain more rhapsodized than our adolescent anguish; adults simply lose the will to sustain such *Sturm und Drang*." [13]

The Books, They Are A-Changin'

Considerations of Sturm und Drang aside, it is inarguable that *something* was happening to young adult literature in the late sixties; if it was not a full-blown eruption of realism, it was, at least, a transition from a literature that had traditionally offered a head-in-the-sand approach to one that offered a more clear-eyed and less flinching look at the often unpleasant realities of the lives of adolescent Americans.

It would be an uphill battle, though; for not only are young adults inherent romantics, they are inherent reality deniers, too. Author Richard Peck has put it well: "In depicting reality our books are often on a collision course with our readers' most deeply felt beliefs: that they cannot die, or be infected with sexually transmitted diseases, or get pregnant unless they want to, or become addicted to anything. Our books regularly challenge their conviction that the rules don't apply to them. There are limits to the amount of reality the novel form can encompass. Young adult novels test the boundaries." [14]

Lipsyte and, yes, Hinton and Zindel were among the first to test those boundaries and, in the process, to set aside certain shibboleths that had contributed to the rosy unreality of previous young adult novels. The taboos that had hobbled young adult literature in terms of subject and style had flourished in the complicity of silence that authors had maintained in the forties and fifties. But now, in the late sixties and early seventies, a new and bolder generation of authors began to break the taboos with the candor of their voices.

Nilsen and Donelson have written that "these books shared a new candor. Unlike those in most earlier YA novels, protagonists came from lower-class families, and unlike those in earlier YA novels with their idyllic suburban homes, these new characters led difficult and often harsh lives. This was reflected not only in the problems they faced but also in the language they used. Authors wrote the way people really talked—often ungrammatically, sometimes profanely." [15]

Zindel had written the way *two* people talked; in 1973 Alice Childress would go him ten better and write in twelve different voices while also addressing the hard-edged issue of heroin abuse in her novel *A Hero Ain't Nothin' But a Sandwich* (Coward McCann).

S. E. Hinton would also write about drug abuse (*That Was Then, This Is Now* [Viking, 1971]); and as for other taboo-breaking topics, Zindel would write about abortion (*My Darling, My Hamburger* [Harper, 1969]); Norma Klein about a happily unwed parent (*Mom, the Wolfman and Me* [Pantheon, 1972]); John Donovan would break one of the strictest taboos of all when he introduced the subject of homosexuality (*I'll Get There: It Better Be Worth the Trip* [Harper, 1969]); and, in the era of the Vietnam War, Nat Hentoff explored the ethics of the military draft and the hotly topical issue of avoiding it (*I'm Really Dragged But Nothing Gets Me Down* [Simon & Schuster, 1968]).

The Problem with the Problem Novel

In retrospect the period from 1967 to 1975 is remarkable for the boldness with which writers began to break new ground in terms of the subject matter they chose to address. Unfortunately, innovation is too often followed by less talented imitation, and the subject matter too often became the tail that wagged the dog of the novel—the result being the appearance and swift ascendancy of what has come to be called the "problem novel."

Sheila Egoff has described its characteristic deficiencies as well as any other observer: "It was very strongly subject-oriented with the interest primarily residing in the topic rather than in the telling. The topics—all adult oriented—sound like chapter titles from a textbook on social pathology: divorce, drugs, disappearing parents, desertion, and death." [16]

Or think of it this way and you'll understand the problem with the problem novel: It is to young adult literature what the soap opera is to legitimate drama.

Why the new novel of realism so often degenerated into the single-issue problem novel may be an unanswerable question. But it surely has something to do with the rapid pace of change overtaking the lives of young people in the late sixties and early seventies and the perhaps belated recognition by writers and publishers that the novel, if it is to have any hope of offering not only relevance but revelation to its readers, must keep pace with the ever-changing reality of their daily, real-world lives.

Looking back at the decade of the seventies, Egoff pointed out that "adolescents had been steadily assuming more and more of the attributes, perquisites, and problems of their elders. Like adults, teenagers now had money, cars, jobs and also drugs, liquor, sex, and the assorted difficulties arising therefrom."[17]

The powerful newness of these difficulties and the intoxicatingly sudden freedom to write about them caused some writers to forget the totality of the realistic novel's mission: that it must portray not only real-life circumstances—call them problems, if you wish—but also real people living in real settings. Hence this thought from Roger Sutton: "Instead of a character being the focus of the novel, a condition (or social concern) became the subject of examination."[18]

Natalie Babbitt offers another interpretation from the point of view of both author and parent: "When our children come into their teens, we have a kind of last-chance-for-gas-before-the-thruway feeling that now is the moment to drum away, because obviously their personalities are not formed and they are desperately in need of moral instruction."[19]

The didactic possibilities the novel offers for moral and other instruction have tempted many otherwise good writers to confuse realistic fiction with problem-novel-tract or nonfiction-with-a-conscience. A typical example is Robert Lipsyte and his novel *Jock and Jill* (Harper, 1982).

A deeply humane man, Lipsyte had been, for some time, concerned about the dangers that win-at-any-cost coaches and team doctors were visiting on young athletes by forcing them to play injured or to use untested and potentially dangerous drugs. The author imposed his concerns about these problems on the plot of his novel and buried his characters under their too-didactic weight.

Though offered in another connection, what Sheila Egoff has written about the principal difference between the realistic novel and the problem novel not only echoes Babbitt's observation but neatly describes Lipsyte's chief failure in the case of *Jock and Jill*: The realistic novel, Egoff argues, "grows out of the personal vision of the writer," while the problem novel "stems from the writer's social conscience." [20]

Lipsyte made this mistake only once in an otherwise exemplary career. Other, less talented such as Jeannette Eyerly—made a career of the mistake and so their readers found themselves de facto members not of the Book-of-the-Month Club, but of the problem-of-the-month club.

The clearest evidence of this is that when thinking of titles by a writer like Eyerly, one doesn't remember them by the richness of their settings or the complexity of their characters but by the problems these interchangable entities are forced to deal with; thus, *Drop-Out* (1963) is not about people but about the perils of dropping out of school; *A Girl Like Me* (1966) is about teenage pregnancy; abortion is all we remember of *Bonnie Jo, Go Home* (1972); the only memorable aspect of *The World of Ellen March* (1964) is her parents' divorce; and there are also suicide (*The Girl Inside*, 1968), drugs (*Escape from Nowhere*, 1969), politics (*Radigan Cares*, 1970), runaways (*See Dave Run*, 1978 [all Lippincott]), and— well, you get the idea.

It's ironic that while such books were receiving scorn and disapproval from adult reviewers, they were gaining enormous popularity with young adult readers themselves. Deny though they might the relevance of the problems to their own lives, they seemed to dote on reading about how they plagued *other* people!

"Teens," Roger Sutton wryly observed, "don't even read these books so much as they gobble them like peanuts, picking them up by the handful, one right after the other." [21]

Sheila Egoff has offered her own handful of reasons teenagers were so fond of these novels. One is their therapeutic value: "Many children suffer from the very difficulties depicted in these novels and presumably it is good for them to know they are not alone in their suffering." A second is the appeal of the exotic: This is the opposite of the first reason and applies to young readers to whom the problems are foreign. Third, there is the matter of flattery: "Children want to feel grown-up and problem novels offer to youngsters—in simple language that they can perfectly well follow— the implication that they are ready to deal with issues and themes that are indisputably adult." And last are prurience and peer pressure. Young readers get a "delicious frisson" from reading about the formerly unspeakable; as for the latter: "not to have read Judy Blume seems as socially unacceptable as not being familiar with the latest 'in' television show." [22]

Realism and Revisionism

If the problem novel received a well-deserved drubbing from reviewers, the early realistic novel became the target of revisonist thinking too, with regard to its maturity, integrity, and viability as literature.

By November 1969 (revisionism arrived early) Diane Gersoni Stavn was noting that "an unusual number of juvenile novels aimed at an audience of young teens and attempting realism" had been published in 1968 and '69, and charging that "these stories are often written according to the language, structure, and content specifications of children's books." [23]

One of her examples is Zindel's second novel, *My Darling, My Hamburger*, which she criticizes for its having "punished" its protagonists for their sexual experimentation (pregnant Liz has an abortion and doesn't graduate from high school, while her boyfriend Sean will bear a lifetime burden of guilt).

"This moralizing," Stavn asserts, "is that of a children's story undisguised by its allusions to ongoing teen concerns." [24]

Stavn also criticizes Nat Hentoff's 1968 novel *I'm*

Really Dragged But Nothing Gets Me Down on more purely literary grounds, claiming that its characters are "platforms for thoughts not fleshed-out protagonists."[25]

If, by this, we may presume that Stavn is criticizing the author for making too-didactic use of his characters and their circumstances, it's ironic to reflect that Hentoff himself, only a year earlier, had criticized Robert Lipsyte's *The Contender* on the same grounds. (See Hentoff's review in *The New York Times Book Review* for November 5, 1967.) It seems that in young adult literature, as in life, what goes around comes around.

The next broadside came in 1976, with Jane Abramson's "Still Playing It Safe: Restricted Realism in Teen Novels," in which the author argued that "the restrictions on teen fiction result in books that succeed only in mirroring a slick surface realism that too often acts as a cover-up. . . . Books that set out to tackle painful experiences turn into weak testimonies to life's essential goodness"[26] (and reaffirm conventional morality).

This same criticism is still being leveled in the 1990s: Chris Lynch, himself a young adult author, recently wrote, "my plea is authenticity," and explained that "when writers hear the term Young Adult, they get the feeling that 'the gloves are on.'"[27]

The celebration of conventional morality and an insistence on happy resolution—more than any delicacy in the selection of subject matter—can be cited as valid examples of young adult writers keeping the gloves on in the seventies. George Nicholson, then editor in chief of Delacorte Press, told an interviewer in 1982, "We want to have an uplifting, affirmative quality to books written for children."[28]

There is nothing wrong with affirmation, of course, unless it compromises aesthetic inevitability by forcing an unrealistically happy ending on an otherwise realistically downbeat story; e.g., it turns out that the woman Oedipus slept with wasn't his mother after all, and at story's end, a gifted eye surgeon is found whose uncanny abilities enable him to restore the self-blinded king's sight. Rex redux!

This kind of manipulation transforms realism into romance and demonstrates the kind of "cockeyed optimism" and "false notes of uplift" that Abramson also criticized in what she called "teen novels."[29]

I think she was quite correct in her criticism. On the other hand, it should be remembered that the kind of realistic novel that was being written in the 1960s and early 1970s was firmly rooted in the traditions of nineteenth-century American realism and its essentially optimistic view that goodness would prevail and that man had the power of free will to make it so. It was not until Robert Cormier's *The Chocolate War* arrived in 1974 (Pantheon) that there was the first hint of determinism and the notion that evil might conceivably carry the day. But at that, it could be argued that Cormier does not operate in the tradition of realism but, rather, in that of naturalism, which views human beings as victims of social and natural forces.

One can also argue all day about a related issue: considerations of mode. For example, critic Roger Sutton disputes Nilsen and Donelson's calling the newly realistic novels "ironic" and, occasionally, "tragic," arguing that they are (*pace* Northrop Frye) "low mimetic comedy" instead. [30]

Most readers will be happy simply to acknowledge that whatever they were, they were at least *different* from the fiction of the forties and fifties, and the best of them were good enough, as we shall see in the next chapter, for some now to call the seventies a "golden age" of young adult literature.

Others—who use the phrase "problem novel" as a pejorative—are less sanguine. Though technically the problem novel and the realistic novel are synonymous ("What's a novel without a problem?" Marilyn Kriney, publisher of HarperCollins Children's Books, cogently asks), practically speaking, there are differences— which we have already discussed—separating them, and as the seventies drew to a close, the separation would become positively cavernous.

Despite its occasional lapses, the novel of realism was gradually evolving into a richer and more rewarding kind of fiction (a process that is ongoing); the problem novel, on the other hand, was rapidly devolving into something—well, *ridiculous*. As competition for readers' attention became ever more brisk, the problems being addressed had to become ever more sensational, until the problem novel reached an arguable nadir in books like Scott Bunn's *Just Hold On* (Delacorte, 1982), the plot of which has been helpfully summarized by J. D. Reed: "Heroine Charlotte Maag, 16, is raped by her father, an Albany pediatrician. She befriends fellow loner

Stephen Herndon, who is hiding the shame and rejection of his own physician-father's alcoholism. By mid-story Charlotte is on the sauce, Stephen is involved in a homosexual affair with a football star named Rolf, and both tumble into bed with another couple after a bourbon and pot party. At novel's end, Stephen is near catatonia and Charlotte is institutionalized." [31]

This kind of wretched excess suggested that the genre was not only overripe but also overdue for satire. Daniel M. Pinkwater took the cue and presented readers with his own *Young Adult Novel* (Crowell), a hilarious takeoff on a genre—the problem novel—that had always taken itself far too seriously. A nice coincidence is that Pinkwater's send-up was published the same year as Bunn's book, which, in retrospect, seems almost a send-up of itself while simultaneously sounding the death knell for the subgenre it represented. Bunn's book—and others like it—almost sounded the same toll for the realistic novel, too, as readers—finally exhausted by shrill sensationalism—turned for relief to a resurgence of the romance novel in the 1980s.

But first, about that golden age . . .

NOTES

1. Forisha-Kovach, "Adolescent Development," p. 22.
2. Peck, *Love and Death at the Mall*, p. 154.
3. Hinton, S. E., "Teen-agers Are for Real," *The New York Times Book Review*, (August 27, 1967), p. 26.
4. Woods, George, "Screening Books for Review," *Wilson Library Bulletin*, 41:169 (October 1966).

5. Hentoff, Nat, "Tell It As It Is," *The New York Times Book Review,* May 7, 1967, p. 3.
6. Wojciechowska, Maia, "An End to Nostalgia," *School Library Journal,* 15:13 (December 1968).
7. Peck, Richard, "The Silver Anniversary of Young Adult Books," *Journal of Youth Services in Libraries,* 6:19 (Fall 1993).
8. Rafferty, Terrence, "Superhero," *The New Yorker,* LXX:93 (May 23, 1994).
9. Landsberg, Michele, *Reading for the Love of It.* New York: Prentice Hall, 1987, p. 215.
10. Malone, Michael, "Tough Puppies," *The Nation,* 242:277 (March 8, 1986).
11. Hoffman, Mary, "Growing Up: A Survey," *Children's Literature in Education,* 15:178 (1984).
12. Forman, Jack, "Paul Zindel," in Laura Standley Berger, ed., *Twentieth-Century Young Adult Writers.* Detroit: St. James Press, 1994, p. 733.
13. Malone, "Tough Puppies," p. 278.
14. Peck, *Mall,* p. 159.
15. Nilsen, Alleen Pace, and Kenneth L. Donelson, "The New Realism Comes of Age," *Journal of Youth Services in Libraries,* 1:275 (Spring 1988).
16. Egoff, "Beyond the Garden Wall," p. 196.
17. *Ibid.,* p. 194.
18. Sutton, Roger, "The Critical Myth: Realistic YA Novels," *School Library Journal,* 29:33 (November 1982).
19. Babbitt, "Between Innocence and Maturity," p. 140.
20. Egoff, Sheila, *Thursday's Child.* Chicago: American Library Association, 1981, p. 67.
21. Sutton, "Critical," p. 33.
22. Egoff, "Beyond," p. 196.
23. Stavn, Diane Gersoni, "Watching Fiction for Today's Teens: Notes of a Critical Voyeur," *School Library Journal,* 16:139 (November 1969).
24. *Ibid.,* p. 140.
25. *Ibid.,* p. 139.
26. Abramson, Jane, "Still Playing It Safe: Restricted Realism in Teen Novels," *School Library Journal,* 22:38 (May 1976).
27. Lynch, Chris, "Today's YA Writers: Pulling No Punches," *School Library Journal,* "Up for Discussion," 40:37–38 (January 1994).

28. Reed, J. D., "Packaging the Facts of Life," *Time*, 120:65 (August 23, 1982).

29. Abramson, "Still Playing," p. 39.

30. Sutton, "Critical," p. 33.

31. Reed, "Packaging," p. 66.

CHAPTER THREE

THE SEVENTIES— A GOLDEN AGE?
All That Glitters . . .

In June 1994 a hundred librarians, educators, editors, and authors gathered in Miami Beach, Florida, for a two-day conference preceding the annual American Library Association convention. Assembled under the auspices of the Young Adult Library Services Association, the conferees had a mandate: to choose a silver-anniversary selection of the one hundred "best of the best" young adult books published between 1967 and 1992.

There was ample precedent for this exercise: Similar gatherings had been held in 1975, 1983, and 1988 and had produced lists dubbed, respectively, "Still Alive in '75" (1960–1974 titles), "The Best of the Best Books" (1970–1983), and "Nothin' But the Best" (1966–1986).

Of the four, the Miami list was the most ambitious in terms of the number of titles selected (100) and the time span under consideration (25 years). Since the occasion was also, in effect, a silver anniversary of the modern young adult novel, participants were encouraged to look beyond earlier annual best book inclusions to insure reconsideration of worthy titles that either had been overlooked or had been ineligible—the case with titles published before 1973 when only adult books had been considered for the lists (a reason why a scant twenty percent of the titles on that first 1960–74 best of the best list were young adult books; a secondary reason may have been YASD's collection development guideline then in force, which recommended that young adult collections in libraries contain a ratio of twenty percent young adult titles to eighty percent adult titles).

Like its three predecessors, the 1994 list offers insights into the evolution of young adult literature and the importance, in that process, of the decade of the 1970s. One example: The only five books that could claim the distinction of having appeared on all three earlier lists were, once again, chosen for the 1994 list and all five were published—you guessed it—in the seventies. This seems to support the claim of some earlier observers that "if any classics of the young adult novel have been produced, they are likely to have been published during the seventies."[1] For the record the fab five are:

Angelou, Maya, *I Know Why the Caged Bird Sings* (Random House, 1970)
Guy, Rosa, *The Friends* (Holt, 1973)
Plath, Sylvia, *The Bell Jar* (Harper, 1971)
Swarthout, Glendon, *Bless the Beasts and Children* (Doubleday, 1970)
White, Robb, *Deathwatch* (Doubleday, 1972)

Further evidence of the importance of the seventies comes from the fact that fully twelve of the thirteen titles that have now appeared on three of the four "Best of the Best" lists were also published in that decade. They are:

Anonymous, *Go Ask Alice* (Prentice-Hall, 1971)
Baldwin, James, *If Beale Street Could Talk* (Dial, 1974)
*Childress, Alice, *A Hero Ain't Nothin' But a Sandwich* (Coward McCann, 1973)
*Cormier, Robert, *The Chocolate War* (Pantheon, 1974)
Duncan, Lois, *Killing Mr. Griffin* (Little, Brown, 1978)
Guest, Judith, *Ordinary People* (Viking, 1976)
Holman, Felice, *Slake's Limbo* (Scribner, 1974)
McKinley, Robin, *Beauty* (Harper, 1978)
Peck, Richard, *Are You in the House Alone?* (Viking, 1976)
Scoppettone, Sandra, *Trying Hard to Hear You* (Harper, 1974)

*Sleator, William, *House of Stairs* (Dutton, 1974)
Wersba, Barbara, *Run Softly, Go Fast* (Atheneum, 1970)

(If you're wondering, the one title not published in the seventies is Nancy Garden's lesbian love story, *Annie on My Mind* [Farrar, Straus], which was published in 1982.)

The three titles marked with an asterisk (*) do not appear on the 1994 list; however, this does not mean that their authors' work has gone out of favor, only that newer titles from the respective bodies of their work were selected for inclusion this time around.

Aside from the importance of the seventies, a number of other lessons can be drawn from these lists; one is that a certain inertia is endemic to them. Once a title makes a best of the best list, it tends to remain on successive lists, and the more times the book appears, the more likely it is that it will remain; that is one of the main reasons, I suspect, that Robb White's *Deathwatch*, the exciting story of a teenage guide who becomes a sadistic hunter's target, is a fixture. It is hardly great literature, but—like Richard Connell's classic short story "The Most Dangerous Game" (which may have inspired White)—it addresses a timeless theme, survival, which is a staple of "boys' books." And, though I may presume too much here, I suspect that its perpetual inclusion is a librarian's effort to hook those male readers. That may also be the reason that White's logical successor, Gary Paulsen, has had more titles (thirteen) on the annual best books lists than any other writer.

Another "lesson" of the lists is the crossover appeal that certain adult books demonstrate by finding and holding an adolescent audience. Note that three of the five books that have now appeared on all four of the superlists were first published as adult books. Two of these three are novels—*Bless the Beasts and Children* and *The Bell Jar*—and each not only attracted an enthusiastic young adult readership but garnered immediate professional support, too, being named to the annual best book list the year of its respective publication.

Beasts is a reliable old warhorse that appeals to the ever-green idealism of adolescents by suggesting, dramatically, that it is possible for young people to recognize the wrong and to right it without adult assistance. Even more appealing than self-sufficiency is the satisfaction readers—who themselves are alienated—find in seeing outsiders and underdogs triumph.

The Bell Jar is the more sophisticated and "literary" of the two and continues, accordingly, to command a strong adult readership as well—thanks to Plath's stature as a poet and to the tragic circumstances of her life and death (which have recently been rehearsed yet again in Janet Malcolm's new biography of her and her husband, British poet Ted Hughes: *The Silent Woman* [Knopf, 1994]).

The Bell Jar also offers its adolescent readers the seductive subjects of mental illness and suicide (currently the third-leading cause of adolescent death).

Though a more successful novel in terms of its literary strengths, *The Bell Jar* has enjoyed enduring popularity among adolescents for much the same reason, I suspect, that John Neufeld's young adult novel *Lisa, Bright and Dark* (Phillips, 1969) more briefly did; i.e., their titillating (to teens) treatment of a descent into mental illness. *Lisa* was one of the ten most popular books with high school students in the 1970s, according to a contemporary survey, but it failed to capture the adult support enjoyed by *The Bell Jar.* Accordingly it has never appeared on a best books list, nor did it register on a 1972 survey of high school English teachers. However, a third seventies title that deals with insanity *has* been enthusiastically embraced by both teenage and adult readers: Judith Guest's *Ordinary People.* The suicide-prone protagonist this time is not a girl but a boy, seventeen-year-old Conrad, who is consumed by guilt over his brother's death.

Presuming a protagonist remains unsuccessful at suicide, he or she will inevitably come of age, and that arrival, along with the obligatory rites of passage along the way, provides another great theme of young adult literature. It's no surprise, accordingly, that autobiographies should be fixtures of the best books lists or that one of the greatest autobiographies of the twentieth century, Maya Angelou's *I Know Why the Caged Bird Sings,* should be one of the four-time honorees. The now-famous poet's story is an even more powerful celebration of the triumph of the human spirit than Swarthout's *Bless the Beasts.* The book continues to find new generations of readers not only on its own merits but because of its author's public stature and her personal celebrity, both of which were cemented by her participation in the 1992 inaugural ceremonies for President Bill Clinton.

The fifth title to appear on all four of the retrospective best of the best lists is a young adult novel, Rosa Guy's *The Friends*. The first book in a trilogy (*Ruby*, 1976, and *Edith Jackson*, 1978 [all Viking], are the other two), Guy's novel tells the story of the Cathys, a family of black West Indian immigrants trying to make a new life in New York's Harlem. The Cathy daughters, Phyllisia and Ruby, are bullied and rejected by their classmates because of their Islands speech, exotic in its rhythms, diction, and inflections, and because of the significant cultural differences that isolate them from their peers. Bullied and beaten, the younger sister, Phyllisia, turns in desperation to another girl in her class for support, a black American, Edith Jackson. Careless about her personal cleanliness, wearing old clothes full of holes, indifferent to education and contemptuous of her teacher's authority, Edith is also an outsider. With the death of her mother and the later disappearance of her father, Edith assumes the role of teenage family head that another outsider, Darry Curtis, had played in Hinton's *The Outsiders*. We learn more about her ceaseless struggles to keep her family together in the third book in Guy's trilogy, *Edith Jackson*.

As a seventies novel, *The Friends* is historically

important because it is one of the first books written for young adults to deal realistically (though occasionally histrionically) with immigrants as outsiders, with their attendant difficulties of acculturation, and also with the complex interrelationship of class, racism, and economic privation. Herself a West Indian immigrant and founding president of the Harlem Writers' Guild, Guy wrote from firsthand experience (African-American poet June Jordan had also written from firsthand experience of life in the ghetto in her own 1971 novel, *His Own Where* [Crowell].)

Guy's second novel, *Ruby*, is also historically important as the first young adult novel to deal with the issue of lesbianism. We will discuss it in more detail when we examine the treatment of homosexuality in adolescent books; also to be discussed then will be another seventies novel, Sandra Scoppettone's *Trying Hard to Hear You*, which deals with male homosexuality and is another of the titles on our list of three-time honorees.

The 1994 best of the best list ("The Top One Hundred Countdown") includes a number of other titles that, in terms of their topical and thematic content, are historically important: *Go Ask Alice* and *A Hero Ain't Nothin' But a Sandwich* deal with drug abuse, for example. Rape is the subject of Richard Peck's *Are You in the House Alone?* Like Zindel's *The Pigman*, Lois Duncan's *Killing Mr. Griffin* explores the issue of adolescent acceptance of responsibility when, in this case, a gang of teens is responsible for the death of their eponymous teacher (Duncan had explored the same theme in her earlier *I Know What You Did Last Summer* [Little, Brown, 1973]).

Slake's Limbo by Felice Holman introduces several other important themes that began enriching young adult novels in the seventies: Aremis Slake, like Ponyboy Curtis and Edith Jackson, is an orphan, but the story that Felice Holman has told about him is not presented as a realistic novel like Hinton's and Guy's but as an allegory, instead. Though occasionally too self-consciously "artistic" in its use of language and too-obvious symbolism, it is powerfully successful, nevertheless, in engendering emotional responses to society's cruelties and man's inhumanity to other "men" who are smaller and weaker. In recounting Slake's 121-day odyssey in New York's subways, where he has fled to escape the brutal streets of New York, Holman has also written a classic story of survival. (Slake's sanctuary, a cave he discovers in a subway tunnel, recalls another cave—though above-ground in Central Park—that provided similar refuge to Alfred Brooks and his friend James in Robert Lipsyte's *The Contender.*)

Barbara Wersba's *Run Softly, Go Fast* explores another timeless theme: the uneasy relationship of fathers and sons, a theme that also informs other novels of the seventies, such as Robert Newton Peck's *A Day No Pigs Would Die* (Knopf, 1973) and Richard Peck's *Father Figure* (Viking, 1978).

The list also contains the first important work of two quite different but equally important practitioners of speculative fiction: Robin McKinley (*Beauty*) and William Sleator (*House of Stairs*).

The most important of the titles to appear in the seventies, and arguably the single most important title in the history of young adult literature to date, is *The Chocolate War*, by Robert Cormier. Its publication marked not only the debut of a singular talent on the stage of young adult literature but also turned it in a dramatic new direction, by, as Annie Gottlieb has put it, "setting free the subject of despair." [2] Cormier had the courage to write a novel of thematic weight and substance that actually suggested that there might be no happy endings in young adult lives; that conventional morality (see chapter two) might not prevail; that evil might be real and even institutionalized; and that there are powerful, faceless forces that will destroy us if we disturb them. This may not be a revolutionary concept in the history of deterministic philosophy, but in the 1970s it *was* revolutionary as a view of the world upon which to construct a young adult novel. And it opened enormous areas of thematic possibility for writers who would come after Cormier. Of course, it is possible that the area had earlier been opened for him by William Golding, who had already examined the operation of evil in the lives of the young in his adult novel *The Lord of the Flies* (Coward, McCann, 1962). (In turn, Golding is indebted to Richard Hughes and his great 1928 novel *A High Wind in Jamaica* [Harper].) However, I suspect that it was Graham Greene, not Golding, who was the more powerful influence on the evolution of Cormier's anguished, guilt-ridden view of the world, a possibility to be explored in more detail in the context of our later discussion of Cormier's 1991 novel, *We All Fall Down.* (For a definitive look at the body of Cormier's work, readers are referred to Patty Campbell's excellent biocritical study *Presenting Robert Cormier* [Twayne, 1991]).

The same year that *The Chocolate War* was published, James Baldwin's *If Beale Street Could Talk* also appeared. This inner-city love story was, like Guy's *The Friends* and Jordan's *His Own Where*, one of the first novels to deal realistically with the African-American experience. Though published for adults, it spoke powerfully to adolescents and was widely read by them. In fact, Nilsen and Donelson report that their mentor, G. Robert Carlsen, has said that if he were giving prizes for the best book published each year for young adults, he would have given the 1974 prize to Baldwin instead of Cormier, "even though *The Chocolate War* is really the better book."[3]

For Carlsen, what tipped the balance to *Beale Street* was its greater popularity with readers. The part that such popularity should play in evaluating the merits of a book for young adults has occasioned much lively debate over the years, particularly among members of the best books committees, as I discovered when I served in 1989. The committee guidelines then—as now—in force were silent on this particular point, though the committee members were certainly not! For my part, I think that if popularity is to be a major consideration, then we might as well declare R. L. Stine and Francine Pascal to be the greatest young adult authors of the century and have done with it.

Nevertheless, as in the case of *Beale Street*, popularity and merit do sometimes meet, and Baldwin's novel was not only named to the 1974 best books list but was subsequently chosen for three of the four retrospective best of the best lists (including that of 1994).

If the seventies were the years of the problem novel, it is now clear that they were also years that saw the emergence of a body of extraordinarily significant serious fiction and, in the novels of another major talent, John Donovan, one of the great themes of young adult literature: alienation. Whether set on a remote mountain in New Hampshire or in the steel-and-glass canyons of Manhattan, each of the four YA books by this poet laureate of loneliness (*I'll Get There: It Better Be Worth the Trip* [1969], *Wild in the World* [1971], *Remove Protective Coating a Little at a Time* [1973], and *Family* [1976; all Harper]) features characters who are painfully isolated and estranged through social circumstance or by families' failures of communication.

In developing this important theme, Donovan earned a reputation, as John Rowe Townsend put it, for being a "taboo buster."[4] He cheerfully employed expletives that had previously been declared off-limits in books for this age range and dealt frankly with such subjects as adolescent sexual experimentation, parental alcoholism, death, and, in his first book, *I'll Get There*, an (arguably) homosexual encounter between the thirteen-year-old protagonist, Davy, and his best friend, Altschuler.

Since his parents' divorce, Davy tells us, he has been living with his grandmother in a small Massachusetts town. When she dies, he is sent to live with his mother, a borderline alcoholic, in her Manhattan apartment. He is also reunited, in the form of weekend visits, with his father, who has remarried. Davy's cynical assessment of his parents' lack of enthusiasm for him is expressed in what he says of his much-loved dog, Fred: "When you make a dog like Fred part of your family, he is a full-time member, not just someone who will be around when you want him to" (p. 45).

Unfortunately Fred is killed by a hit-and-run driver soon after Davy and Altschuler give physical expression to their friendship (they kiss each other and, subsequently spending the night together, do what is only described as "it"). Davy is emotionally devastated and consumed by guilt: "Nothing would have happened if I hadn't been fooling around with Altschuler," he thinks bitterly (p. 172).

Eventually, in part through his father's support and in part through finally sharing his feelings with Altschuler, Davy comes to terms with his guilt and the boys resume their friendship.

Though this is the most cautiously optimistic of Donovan's books, most readers will realize that when Altschuler sighs, "Life should be beautiful," he is articulating a goal whose attainment—for these two emotionally vulnerable kids from fractured families—will represent a very difficult trip, indeed.

The family of John Gridley, the protagonist of Donovan's second novel, *Wild in the World*, is beyond fractured: Its twelve other members are dead! Indeed, the first six pages of the book (to the horror of some contemporary critics) are the omniscient narrator's laconic report of the deaths—by suicide, fire, fever, and accident—of John's parents and ten siblings. The youngest, John, is left alone to manage the family farm on a remote mountain in New Hampshire. Emotionally he is as burnt out as any character from Grahame Greene, going through the motions of living but, in fact, simply waiting for his turn to die.

This changes when a stray dog (or is it a wolf?) appears on the farm and John adopts it as a pet and calls it "Son." The name is symbolic of the emotions that the creature reawakens in John, emotions that reach ripeness when the man nurses the dog back to health after it is bitten by a rattlesnake. Reflecting on his newfound capacity for expressing emotion, John thinks, "Son taught me a lot. Human critters hold back."

Ultimately it is not Son but John who dies—of pneumonia. His untimely death, though it has tragic elements, is at least partially redeemed by his earlier discovery of a life-affirming love for Son. That the wolf/dog lives on gives tangible expression to the survival of that love. *Wild in the World*'s powerful themes are expressed in an understated, almost laconic style that lends the story the timeless power of folklore or parable.

Donovan returns to the breezy, wry—and J. D. Salinger–influenced—first-person voice and urban setting of *I'll Get There* in his third novel, *Remove Protective Coating a Little at a Time*. Unlike Davy Ross, fourteen-year-old Harry Knight is not the product of a broken home, but his parents, Bud and Toots, are more like self-absorbed older siblings than father and mother. Though rich in material matters, Harry is obviously impoverished in terms of family love, support, and attention. He finds these, almost by accident, in the seventy-two-year-old person of Amelia Myers, a self-sufficent, eccentric street person whom he meets in Central Park.

Learning to care for Amelia and to feel responsible for her enable Harry to remove the protective coating of emotional isolation and alienation in which he has encased himself.

Donovan's consistent thematic concerns reach their arguable apogee in his fourth and final novel for young adults, *Family*, the story of the escape from a college lab of four apes who were to have been part of a scientific experiment. Three of the apes—Sasha, the narrator; Dilys, a mature female; and Lollipop, an infant—have been born in captivity. The fourth—the largest and the most powerful, a male named Moses who, like his Biblical namesake, leads the others out of captivity and into the wilderness—is a "natural," born in the wild. From him the other three acquire not only the more sophisticated language of the wild apes but also a learned past consisting of stories, legends, and traditions. Donovan, of course, is offering ironic commentary on human society here; note that it is the wild creature—

not the apparently "civilized" ones—that has the more advanced culture. At any rate, Moses's lessons and leadership help them establish a very nontraditional family unit and, in it, a context of connectedness that few of Donovan's earlier human characters experienced.

Telling the apes' story in Sasha's first-person voice gives Donovan the ironic distance he needs to comment on the failings of human society, especially its persistent equation of change with progress. Sasha is a brilliant creation—grave, compassionate, and, despite his disingenuous denials, reflective. When winter arrives and Moses and Lollipop are killed by hunters, Sasha and Dilys have no recourse but to return to the lab and their human captors, sustained by their memories and their hope, as Sasha states, "that Man is not lost."

Donovan's courageous choice of difficult thematic material—which didn't always promise his readers a glibly happy ending—his taboo-breaking use of language and incident, and his unconventionally imaginative treatment of narrative outraged or perplexed many contemporary critics. The controversy that much of his work inspired may have contributed to its gradual eclipse; all his books are now out of print and—with one exception—seem to be little discussed today. That exception, of course, is *I'll Get There*, which has recently been back in the spotlight thanks to the twenty-fifth anniversary of the birth of the modern gay rights movement in 1969, coincidentally the year Donovan's first novel was published. One hopes that this attention might spill over onto the rest of his work; it is too important to be so summarily forgotten.

The Best of the Rest

If Donovan, Hinton, Zindel, and Lipsyte got their start in the sixties, it was the seventies that saw an explosion of new work by many of the other most important writers for young adults, including five of the six subsequent Margaret Edwards Award winners to date (Hinton being the sixth). They are: M. E. Kerr, whose first book, *Dinky Hocker Shoots Smack!* (Harper), was published in 1972; Richard Peck, whose first novel, *Don't Look and It Won't Hurt* (Holt), appeared the same year; Lois Duncan's first serious novel, *I Know What You Did Last Summer* (Little, Brown), came out a year later, in 1973 (she had actually begun publishing in the 1960s, but her early work was, for the most part, forgettable formula romance); then, of course, came Robert Cormier's *The Chocolate War* in 1974; and Walter Dean Myers's first YA title, *Fast Sam, Cool Clyde, and Stuff* (Viking), appeared at mid decade: 1975.

Other important writers who either began publishing in the seventies or whose first significant work appeared then were, as we have already seen, Rosa Guy, Robin McKinley, William Sleator, Alice Childress, Felice Holman, Robert Newton Peck, Sandra Scoppettone, and Barbara Wersba.

To their number must also be added Judy Blume (*Are You There, God? It's Me, Margaret* [Bradbury, 1970]);

Lynn Hall (*Sticks and Stones* [Follet, 1972]), whose first novel, *The Shy Ones*, was actually published in 1967 but even then was a bit of an anachronism, its story of a shy girl who finds herself by working with animals re-calling the theme and tone of Betty Cavanna's 1946 ro-mance, *Going On Sixteen*); Sue Ellen Bridgers's (*Home Before Dark* [Knopf, 1976]); Terry Davis (*Vision Quest* [Delacorte, 1979]); Virginia Hamilton (America's most honored author of books for young readers is very dif-ficult to classify; she began publishing in the sixties with *Zeely* [Macmillan, 1967], but it seems to me that she didn't produce a true young adult novel until *The Planet of Junior Brown* [Macmillan, 1971], and much of her later work blurs the boundaries between children's and young adult books); Isabelle Holland (Holland also writes on the borderline between children's and young adult books; her first title, *Cecily*, appeared in 1967, but it wasn't until 1972 that her *Man Without a Face* established her reputation as a writer for young adults); Harry and Norma Fox Mazer, (*Guy Lenny* [Delacorte, 1971] and *I, Trissy* [Delacorte, 1971], respec-tively); Zibby Oneal actually belongs to the eighties, but her first novel, *War Work* (Viking), was published in 1971.

Finally, at the very end of the decade, came Ouida Sebestyen with *Words by Heart* (Little, Brown, 1979). (Ms. Sebestyen is an inspiration to would-be writers everywhere who might be afraid that their chances have passed them by. Not so, if this late-blooming writer is an example: *Words by Heart* was not published until she was fifty-five years old, and she has published five other novels since!)

The emergence of a serious body of literature published expressly for young adults was finally acknowledged in 1973 by ALA's Young Adult Services Division when, as previously noted, it began considering YA titles for inclusion on its annual Best Books for Young Adults lists.

Young adults themselves were way ahead of the librarians and the publishers. For years they had been hungry for works of literature more demanding than those being published for them and had demonstrated that fact by routinely appropriating adult titles that addressed complex issues relevant to them and which offered multidimensional characters with whom they could identify. How else explain the popularity of such pre-1973 titles as *The Catcher in the Rye, A Separate Peace, The Lord of the Flies, The Chosen, The Autobiography of Miss Jane Pittman, Red Sky at Morning, To Kill a Mockingbird,* and the many others we have already discussed?

Donald Barr, for one, had a different explanation. The then headmaster of the Hackley School, in Tarrytown, New York, mused in a 1986 *New York Times Book Review* article about the reasons for the continuing success of four of these books: *To Kill a Mockingbird, The Catcher in the Rye, A Separate Peace,* and *Lord of the Flies.* To him their popularity was due less to adolescent interest than to the fact that "all four still jostle 'Romeo and Juliet' in middle school and high school reading lists."

"High school students," he went on to assert, "do

not, by and large, choose their own reading but in general the American adolescent is *given* books to read, and less often by his parents than his teachers." [5]

I think there is an element of lingering truth to that assertion—one national book jobber reports, a decade later, that *To Kill a Mockingbird* is still its single best-selling title to teachers and librarians, but *not* to individual teenagers. However, I would also point out that Barr's books were all published between 1951 and 1962—long before there was any kind of significant literature being written and published specifically for young adults. What *was* being published under the patronizing rubric "junior novel" was ever less relevant to the lives of the increasingly sophisticated young people themselves. As S. E. Hinton wrote in *The New York Times*, "Teen-agers today want to read about teen-agers today." [6]

Nat Hentoff wrote about *his* experience of visiting schools in the wake of the publication of his 1965 novel *Jazz Country.* "My visits to those schools were hardly unqualified triumphs. Criticisms were sharp and frequent, both of me and of other writers of books for 12+. There were many more hang-ups in being young, I was told repeatedly, than were even intimated in most of the books they'd seen. I began to read what other writers in the field were doing and agreed with the young critics that little of relevance is being written about what it is to be young now." [7]

Hentoff went on to say, "If a book is relevant to those concerns, not didactically, but in creating textures of experience which teen-agers can recognize as germane to their own, it can merit their attention." [8]

That, I think, is why adult novels—absent any equally significant young adult fiction—"merited their attention" for so long. The same month that Hentoff's article appeared, an associate professor of education at Wisconsin State University reported the results of a reading survey of 420 high school students in Tucson, Arizona. The ten books the kids most often mentioned as influencing their personal and social values were all, once again, adult books: 1. *Black Like Me*, 2. The Bible, 3. *To Kill a Mockingbird*, 4. *Exodus*, 5. *The Good Earth*, 6. *Catcher in the Rye*, 7. *The Ugly American*, 8. *Animal Farm*, 9. & 10. (a tie): *The Lord of the Flies*, and *The Grapes of Wrath*. [9]

It's also noteworthy that three of the four books that Barr wrote about in *The New York Times* appear on the Top One Hundred Countdown (only *A Separate Peace* is missing); surely this must indicate that not only adult teachers but young readers themselves continue to feel these titles have something authentic to say about their lives and, perhaps, their futures.

The same could be said about the best of the realistic young adult fiction that finally began to appear in the late sixties and became such a fixture of seventies literature.

"It started to treat subjects of real depth," a quartet of observers pointed out in 1980. "Profound social and personal problems were examined seriously rather than avoided. . . . Neither subject, nor character, nor literary techniques were forbidden to it, provided only that its primary audience—the teenager—could read it, would read it, and did read it." [10]

Not everyone found this cause for rejoicing. As early as 1973, the poet June Jordan decried the emergence of what she called "this 'be realistic' conspiracy," asserting, "in the name of realism, book reviewers applaud books crammed with a relentless, so-called documentation of pathology flowering from a pivotal, perverted faith in a pathogenic, miserable, and hopeless condition of being which is, allegedly, our realistic condition. . . . I happen to believe, very strongly that what goes down under the name of realism is, 95 percent of the time, pointless, self-indulgent, status-quo-protecting, and irresponsible garbage." [11] (This is more diatribe than criticism, but at least there's no uncertainty about where she stands!)

Eight years later G. Robert Carlsen, defending the proposition "Literature isn't supposed to be realistic," wrote, "The concept of realism seems to have persisted in the birthing of that thing called the junior or adolescent novel. Criticism among American commentators has generally considered only the 'realism' of these works. The last few years have spawned the phrase, 'the new realism,' which means that books treat sex, defecation, profanity, and social problems. Such books have been given wide approbation while the books of the thirties, forties, and fifties have been dismissed as naive or sentimental." [12]

As we are about to see, many readers in the new

decade of the 1980s would join these critics in reject-
ing the new literature of realism, embracing, instead, a
surprising revival of the romance novel.

NOTES

1. Bachelder, Linda, et al., "Looking Backward: Trying to Find the Classic Young Adult Novel," *English Journal*, 69:86 (September 1980).
2. Gottlieb, Annie, "A New Cycle in 'YA' Books," *The New York Times Book Review*, June 17, 1984, p. 24.
3. Nilsen, 2nd ed., p. 88.
4. Townsend, John Rowe, review of *Remove Protective Coating a Little at a Time, The New York Times Book Review*, November 4, 1973, p. 34
5. Barr, Donald, "Should Holden Caulfield Read These Books?" *The New York Times Book Review*, May 4, 1986, p. 50.
6. Hinton, "Teen-Agers Are for Real," p. 26.
7. Hentoff, Nat, "Fiction for Teen-Agers," *Wilson Library Bulletin*, 43:261 (November 1968).
8. *Ibid.*, p. 263.
9. Shirley, Fehl, "The Influence of Reading on Adolescents," *Wilson Library Bulletin*, 43:260 (November 1968).
10. Bachelder, "Looking," p. 86.
11. Jordan, June, "Young People: Victims of Realism in Books and Life," *Wilson Library Bulletin*, 48:140 (October 1973).
12. Carlsen, G. Robert, "Bait: 'Pro'" *English Journal*, 70:8 (January 1981).

CHAPTER FOUR

THE EIGHTIES— THE PENDULUM SWINGS

The Rise of the Paperback Romance

If the laws of physics applied to literature, for every action (read "innovation"), there would be an equal and opposite reaction. I don't know if it was physics or the economics of publishing or an accident of history, but it is a fact that the decade-long emergence of realism, with its relatively unsparing—and unrelenting—focus on life's darker aspects was followed by just such a reaction. That this should have manifested itself as an early-eighties renaissance of forties- and fifties-style romance may, at first, seem surprising until one remembers the conservatively nostalgic climate of a country that had also swept a forties movie star and former host of the fifties TV series *Death Valley Days* into the White House.

Margo Jefferson finds effect in this cause. Writing in 1982, when the romance revival was still in its early innings, she concluded that these emotionally recidivist titles were "grown-up nostalgia repackaged for the young, very like those remakes of the 1950s and 1960s songs done by people in their 30s and 40s pretending to be ten or twenty years younger."[1]

If the adolescent emotional lives portrayed in these new eighties titles were an eerie replication of those already unreal lives found in the pages of the forties and fifties romances, their packaging, at least, *was* different this time around. Consider that while there was a certain sameness to the earlier titles, they were, at least, published as individual hardcovers. The new romances, on the other hand, had little individual identity, being slick mass-market paperback series appearing at the rate of one new title a month under such saccharine rubrics as "Wildfire," "Caprice," "Sweet Dreams," "First Love," "Wishing Star," and on and on.

Publishers had decided that "after years of being deluged with young adult books dealing with the unhappy realities of life, such as divorce, pregnancy outside of marriage, alcoholism, mental illness, and lately child abuse, teenagers seem to want to read about something closer to their daily lives."[2]

Their decision to revive romances was not made unilaterally, however; marketing decisions seldom are. Pamela Pollack asserts, "Mass market paperback publishers gave teens what they 'want' as determined by market research, rather than what they 'need' based on their problems as reflected by social statistics." [3]

In fact, what they wanted in the eighties was what their parents had already been demanding—and getting—for a decade or more: genre romances and bodice-ripper-of-the-month formula Gothic paperbacks. The adult Gothics had hit the racks at least two decades earlier, led by the 1960 publication of Victoria Holt's *Mistress of Mellyn* (Doubleday).

However, it was not until the decade of the seventies, according to Kristin Ramsdell, that "the [adult] romance boom" really began, and while historical romances were especially popular at first, "light, innocent, Category [usually contemporary] Romances were popular as well." [4] This latter type began "trickling down" into young adult publishing about the time that Mr. Reagan's trickle-down theories of economics hit the marketplace.

Both offered what readers have always, not unreasonably, wanted: escape from life's cares and woes. Author Jane Yolen told *Seventeen* magazine that "the trend is a teenager's way of saying 'enough.' Teenagers have seen their adolescence taken away by graphic television shows and movies and books. The return to romance is really a way to return to the mystery and beauty of love, even if only on a superficial level." [5]

"Mystery" and "beauty"? Perhaps. Here's how Pamela Pollack described the daily lives being depicted in these books:

"The heroines—shy, inexperienced small-town

girls—live in happy homes and tend to have names that end in 'ie.' Their primary interest in life is boys; having a steady ensures a place in the high school hierarchy." (Remember that forty years earlier, Angie Morrow, heroine of *Seventeenth Summer*, had said exactly the same thing.) "They are not interested in college or career, and are not involved in the women's movement. They respect their schools' administrators. Their families are not their problem. Their mothers are their role models. Their fathers are shadowy but benign bread-winners. There are no grandparents—in fact, there are few elderly, black or handicapped people to be found. . . . The sixties and seventies have come and gone, their only traces a law-student mother and boy characters who are marginally sensitive and aware." [6]

The predictable adult, hand-wringing response to this was not long in coming: as early as 1981, when the romance boom was only two years old, a coalition of organizations led by the Council on Interracial Books for Children (CIBC) issued a report charging, among other things, that these books "teach girls that their primary value is their attractiveness to boys; devalue relationships and encourage competition between girls; discount the possibility of nonromantic friendships be-tween boys and girls; depict middle-class, white, small-town families as the norm; and portray adults in stereotypical sex roles." [7]

An opposing viewpoint was offered by Eileen Goudge Zuckerman, herself an author of romance series books. Acknowledging that "adjectives like cheap, frivolous and homogenized abound when series fiction for teenagers is the topic for discussion," she goes on to argue that young readers should have the same freedom of choice as their elders—"to read *Moby Dick* one day and *Sweet Valley High* the next."

She reassures anxious parents that kids won't settle for a steady diet of the lighter fare: "Left alone or with some gentle guidance, they'll eventually opt for a wider range and take special delight in the challenge of books for an older, more mature audience. And for slower readers, easier-to-read series fiction can mean the difference between reading and not reading at all." [8]

While Zuckerman's points might be considered self-serving, their spirit, at least, is supported by Susan G. Kundin, who concludes that "formula romance actually deals directly with the major concerns of young people more often than YA problem novels. Compare, for instance, how many girls long for a kiss—as they do in any formula romance—with how many are fleeing from their mother's former pimp, as does Greta in Ruby's *This Old Man* (Houghton, 1984)." [9]

Zuckerman reports having felt empowered by reading about Nancy Drew's series exploits when she was a girl. Apparently eighties readers found equal empowerment opportunities in the then-new romance series. At least, Doris Fong reported on the findings of a 1990 study by Mary Anne Moffitt that seemed to support this idea.

The first of what would soon become a superfluity of romance series was Scholastic's "Wildfire," which debuted in 1979 and sold 1.8 million copies of sixteen titles in one year. In 1980, "noting the popularity of its light 'Innocent Romances' sold through its school book clubs, Scholastic launched its Wildfire Romance series" [10]; Dell's "Young Love" followed in February 1981; Bantam's "Sweet Dreams" in September 1981; Simon & Schuster's "First Love" in February 1982; and so on and on.

Another major difference between these new series and the individual titles of previous decades is that the former were being created for a new retail market; they were not designed to be sold to libraries or schools.

Ramsdell claims that Scholastic's launch of its "Wildfire" series "changed the way materials were marketed to young adults for the foreseeable future. Previously publishers had concentrated on reaching young adults indirectly though the schools and libraries; now they tried selling to them directly, with spectacular results." [11]

Veteran observer of the YA scene Patty Campbell echoed this when she called the rise of the paperback romance series "easily the most significant development in books for teens in the past ten years." [12]

These series and their runaway commercial success signaled the rise of a new retail market for young adult books, though not young adult books as the institutional market had known them. Campbell explains, "The books that are found there [i.e., in the chain bookstores] are of far lower quality and aimed at much younger readers than those that are found on the similarly labeled shelves in public libraries. The whole field has become strangely bifurcated and we seem to be moving in the direction of two separate literatures." [13]

The rise of the chain bookstores was part of a phenomenon that might be called the "Malling of Young America"—the rise of the shopping mall as the home away from home of choice for America's young adults. Richard Peck became the premiere chronicler of this market-driven phenomenon, which was already so universal by the end of the seventies that he was able to offer it up for satire in his novel *Secrets of the Shopping Mall* (Delacorte, 1979).

It was an age when America's adolescents had become America's arch-consumers. Ironically, their supply of pocket money became plentiful at a time when school and public library pockets became empty. The evaporation of federal funding and a national wave of anti-tax initiatives like California's Proposition 13 had left institutions strapped for cash.

Where could hard-pressed publishers turn for a market? Pollack provides the obvious answer: "For the first time paperback publishers are vying for the primary market, teenage consumers themselves." [14]

Announcing a new line of YA paperbacks from Putnam, to be called Pacer Books, then editor in chief Beverly Horowitz explained that Pacer titles would be found in display racks in chain bookstores in shopping malls, "hangout places where kids go on a boring Saturday. You will find Pacer positioned right between the fast-food heaven and the record store. There is a teen-aged consumer force out there, and the only way to reach them is to go where *their* action is." [15]

George Nicholson, then editor in chief of Dell/ Delacorte books for young readers, agreed, explaining that chain bookstores in malls "demystified the traditional bookstore concept for kids. Now they can buy anything they want. They have the power to come in, pay their money, and out they go, without being harassed. No one questions them." [16]

The kids' new purchasing power further empowered publishers with the magnitude of the romance series' sales.

"In 1985, the first young adult novel ever to reach *The New York Times* paperback best-seller list was a 'Sweet Valley High' Super Edition called *Perfect Summer*." [17]

Created by Francine Pascal, the "Sweet Valley High" books—like successful TV shows, which they and many other series resemble, by the way—spawned endless spin-offs: e.g., "Sweet Valley Twins," "Sweet Valley Twins and Friends," "Sweet Valley University," and "The Unicorn Club," "a sensational new spin-off series of 'Sweet Valley Twins and Friends,'" its publisher, Bantam Doubleday Dell, trumpeted in its September–December 1994 catalog (p. 82).

By the end of the eighties there were 34 million "Sweet Valley High" books in print in the U.S. (and this is, remember, only *one* of the Sweet Valley empire of series). [18]

The success of romance series did not, by any

means, subside with the end of the eighties. It continued and, if anything, accelerated along with the emergence of *another*, perhaps even more successful series (commercially speaking): horror novels.

To return to the eighties, though, the romance phenomenon was principally significant not because it marked the reemergence of a once-popular genre, but because it signaled the emergence of a new marketplace—the chain bookstore—and the emergence of a new type of book: the paperback original. Previous paperbacks had typically been reprints of popular hardcovers.

The Multicultural Milieu

What else was happening in the eighties?

Well, despite the resurgence of formula romance fiction, a number of literarily and culturally important new voices actually were beginning to be heard in a spate of serious new fiction that had its roots in the realism of the seventies but transcended its quickly dated topicality by exploring more timeless thematic considerations. I refer here to books by writers like Bruce Brooks, Brock Cole, Chris Crutcher, Cynthia Voigt, and—closer to the end of the decade—Francesca Lia Block, Ron Koertge, and Virginia Euwer Wolff.

Meanwhile, already established voices continued to be heard: major work was published in the decade of the eighties by such stalwarts as S. E. Hinton (*Tex*,

1980; and *Taming the Star Runner*, 1988); Robert Cormier (*The Bumblebee Flies Anyway*, 1983; *Beyond the Chocolate War*, 1985; and *Fade*, 1988); M. E. Kerr (*Little Little*, 1981; *Me, Me, Me, Me, Me: Not a Novel*, 1983; and *Night Kites*, 1986); Richard Peck (*Remembering the Good Times*, 1985; and *Princess Ashley*, 1987); Sue Ellen Bridgers (*Permanent Connections*, 1987); Robert Lipsyte (*Summer Rules*, 1981; and *The Summerboy*, 1982); Virginia Hamilton (*Sweet Whispers, Brother Rush*, 1982); Paula Fox (*One-Eyed Cat*, 1984); and Katherine Paterson (*Jacob Have I Loved*, 1980).

A strong case could be made, thus, for Judy Gittenstein's cheerful 1984 assertion that "young adult literature is the hot new area in publishing today." [19]

Alas, she was speaking from her vantage as the then newly appointed head of Bantam Books, whose "Sweet Dreams" romance series was the chain bookseller B. Dalton's number-one paperback bestseller in 1982—the kind of book "where attention seems to be far more on product than content." [20]

More relevant than Gittenstein's were the comments of legendary editor Charlotte Zolotow, who—by the mid-eighties—had her own imprint at Harper, where she published Zindel, Kerr, Lipsyte, and, at the very end of the decade, Francesca Lia Block. Charlotte Zolotow felt that young adult novels were "becoming more honest and realistic, authors writing out of heart, feeling and genuine motivation." Recalling the early years of young adult literature, she added, "The sheer protectiveness that we felt was necessary in those early days seems ridiculous to me now, when literally any-thing goes. The more original you are in publishing for this age group, the harder it is to be commercially suc-cessful, but good writing survives trends." [21]

Jean Karl, who had founded the children's book department at Atheneum in 1961, said, "Young adults are moving into new areas of their lives, where they need to find books which will provide them with *literary* [emphasis added] experiences that will broaden their view of the world." [22]

This view needed broadening because the world of the 1980s that young (and old) adults inhabited was changing dramatically.

What would become one of the most signifcant of these changes began innocently enough back in 1965, two years before the dawn of the new realism, when the U.S. Congress passed certain amendments to the Immigration and Nationality Act that not only placed a ceiling on immigration from European countries for the first time, but set it lower than the newly estab-lished limits for those of other parts of the world. The result was a major change in patterns of immigration. The percentage of immigrants from Europe began dropping precipitously while that from Asia and the West Indies increased dramatically. In 1940, for exam-ple, 70 percent of immigrants came from Europe. In 1992, 15 percent came from there, while 37 percent came from Asia and 44 percent from Latin America and the Caribbean. [23]

Just as it had taken a decade for adult romances to

trickle down to the YA field, so it would be a decade and a half before publishers began to take cognizance of this new fact of demographic life. (Thanks to hindsight, we now realize that Rosa Guy's *The Friends*, published in 1973, was nearly ten years ahead of its time in its choice of characters and theme.) The 1980s would see the greatest wave of immigration to the United States since the nineteenth century (8.9 million people entered the U.S. legally between 1980 and 1990, and roughly 3 million more illegally).[24] Moreover, most of the new immigrants hailed from such countries as Mexico, the Philippines, Haiti, South Korea, China, the Dominican Republic, India, Vietnam, and Jamaica—all of which had previously seen only modest representation.

And what of literature? Well, a new body of work that was being called "multicultural" had begun to appear, as well, to give faces to these new American peoples.

And not a moment too soon.

According to "Kids Need Libraries," a position paper promulgated by the youth-serving divisions of the American Library Association and adopted by the Second White House Conference on Libraries and Information, "Kids need preparation to live in a multicultural world and to respect the rights and dignity of all people."[25]

A search for those rights had brought yet another huge immigrant swell to our shores: political refugees who came to America not only for economic opportunity but for sanctuary—people from countries like Iran, El Salvador, and Cuba.

The arrival of both new groups of peoples created enormous problems of acculturation for both the new and the established residents, as each tried to cope with innumerable daily crossings of the "borders" of strange languages and often baffling mores.

In this potentially explosive, newly multicultural environment, books had never been more important, for, as Hazel Rochman has wisely put it, "The best books break down borders." [26]

Distinguished editor Margaret K. McElderry says this: "What is of immense importance now, as I see it, is to find writers among the new wave of immigrants, authors who can portray creatively what it is like to adjust to life in the U.S., what their own experiences have been, written either in fictionalized form or as expository nonfiction." [27]

Such writers had already appeared in the world of adult publishing: authors like Gish Jen, Bharatee Mukerjee, Gus Lee, Maxine Hong Kingston, Amy Tan, Sandra Cisneros, David Wong Louie, Bette Bao Lord, Gita Mehta, Frank Chin, and still others.

Who could match their eloquence in the world of young adult literature?

Before we can answer that question, we need to pause for a word of definition. "Multiculturalism" is a portmanteau word, containing in its definition and in its resonant connotations as many concepts as a suitcase does socks.

Sara Bullard explains: "Educators disagree, first,

over which groups should be included in multicultural plans—racial and ethnic groups, certainly, but what about regional, social class, gender, disability, religious, language, and sexual orientation groupings?" [28]

I have been using the term "multiculturalism" to refer to the social and cultural lives of the newly immigrant populations who began arriving here in the wake of the 1965 Immigration Act and of the political strife that infected the global body politic in the seventies and eighties.

However, Bullard's more expansive definition would include indigenous peoples like Native Americans, long-established American people of color, specifically blacks, and other arguably "minority" groups like homosexuals, women, and the physically challenged.

Karen Patricia Smith, in a 1993 article about the concept of multiculturalism and its relationship to literature for young people, argued that "it is . . . necessary, for the sake of coherence, to narrow the scope of one's discussion." [29]

Nevertheless *her* definition might still be described by the currently faddish phrase "big tent": "The term," she says, "will be used to refer to people of color—that is, individuals who identify with African-American, Hispanic, American Indian, Eskimo, or Aleut, and Asian or Pacific Islander heritage." [30]

Among these groups, African Americans were surely the first to find their lives authentically represented in young adult literature: In the wake of the civil-rights movement of the 1960s, a pride of powerful new voices began to be heard as relatively early as the 1970s: Rosa Guy, Virginia Hamilton, Walter Dean Myers, Mildred Taylor, and Alice Childress are only a few of those who began creating a rich new body of literature for young adult readers about the African-American experience. To encourage this creative flowering, the American Library Association, working through its Social Responsibilities Roundtable, established the annual Coretta Scott King Awards in 1969 to recognize outstanding works written and illustrated by black authors and artists.

Similarly, Asian Americans found an early literary representative in Laurence Yep, who began writing about their cultural experience in his second book, *Dragonwings* (Harper), published in 1975. Yep's own experience of growing up as an outsider between cultures had actually found expression—though metaphorically—in his first book, a fantasy titled *Sweetwater* (Harper) published in 1973. Yep continues to be an important voice in young adult literature. One of his most recent novels, *Dragon's Gate* (Harper, 1993), is a historical novel about the Chinese experience of building the transcontinental railroad. It was named a 1994 Newbery Honor Book. Yep has also recently edited *American Dragons* (Harper, 1993), a collection of short stories, poems, and play excerpts by twenty-five Asian American writers, all of whom deal creatively with critical moments in the lives of young adults. In his preface Yep points out the diversity of Asian cultures in America: "Asian Americans," he notes, "come not only from China and Japan but from the many countries around the Pacific rim, including the Philippines, Korea, India and even Tibet. Recently there have been new waves of immigrants, especially from Southeast Asia, countries such as Vietnam, Thailand, Cambodia and Laos." [31]

No one will question the authenticity of Yep's voice or that of the Asian American writers whose work is represented in *American Dragons*. But what about a book like *Children of the River* (Delacorte, 1989) by Linda Crew? Named a Best Book for Young Adults in 1990, this novel about the Cambodian immigrant experience was recently named to the 1994 Top One Hundred Countdown list.

And yet Crew is an Anglo, born in the United States, writing as an outsider about the experiences of an Asian immigrant. Ai-Ling Louie, herself an Asian American, admits, "I have very mixed reactions to this book. Sundara [the protagonist] seems to be a couple of contradictory stereotypes rolled into one: she is both the Suzy Wong and Model Minority figure." [32]

The latter, Louie explains, is a new "myth."

"Asian Americans," she continues, "are seen as overachievers—able to go to the top of their classes in school, to get into the best universities, and to land the most lucrative jobs after graduation. This myth persists despite the studies to the contrary. . . ." [33]

As for that other, more established stereotype, Louie continues: "Sundara seems to be a Suzy Wong, a sexy Asian female who has enchanting powers to charm men. She is highly valued for her looks and will probably pass into Caucasian society easily through her [Anglo] boyfriends. . . ." [34]

It is personally disconcerting to me that I served on the Best Books Committee the year that *Children of the River* was named to the list, and as I recall, neither I nor any of my colleagues articulated any of these concerns.

Louie's comments, however, address one of the more vexing and perplexing issues that has grown up around multicultural literature: what Karen Patricia Smith calls the "insider" versus the "outsider" approach to literature. She explains: "For years, minority populaces have been written about and 'described' by essentially white authors who are outside the cultures about whom they are writing or illustrating. . . . The question posed and often debated is whether or not material written by so-called 'outsiders' is actually valid material." [35]

This is not a new issue: Paula Fox's Newbery Medal–winning book *The Slave Dancer* (Bradbury), published in 1973, was angrily criticized by black author Sharon Bell Mathis in the journal *Interracial Books for Children* for perpetuating what Mathis called "stereotypes about Africa and about Blacks in general." [36]

This is one of those issues that can never be satisfactorily resolved, for at its core it asks an unanswerable question: Can a writer's imagination be powerful enough to create a viable work of fiction about a culture the writer has observed only from the outside?

Richard Peck, for one, believes it can: "Now in the nineties we're told to march to the beat of multiculturalism. This baffles novelists who thought we'd been celebrating the cultural mix of this country well before the textbooks touched on it. . . . Unless—unless a book is to be judged by the race or ethnicity of its author. In which case we are standing at the edge of an abyss. . . . Fortunately, a novel need not brand the race of its characters as a film must. A novel can begin at the next epidermal layer down, to explore what we all have in common." [37]

More recently, the prolific author Jane Yolen has observed, "What we are seeing now in children's books is an increasing push toward what I can only call the 'Balkanization' of literature. We are drawing rigid borders across the world of story, demanding that people tell only their own stories. Not only does this deny the ability of gifted storytellers to re-invigorate the literature with cross-cultural fertilization, but it would mean that no stories at all could be told about some peoples or cultures until such time as a powerful voice from within that culture emerges." [38]

Both Peck's and Yolen's impassioned comments bring us to the brink of another abyss: that aspect of multiculturalism that has come to be called "political correctness"—or what I call "multiculturalism without a sense of humor."

Hazel Rochman is fearless in her indictment of this disturbing movement: *"Multiculturalism* is a trendy word, trumpeted by the politically correct with a stridency that has provoked a sneering backlash. There are P.C. watchdogs eager to strip from the library shelves anything that presents a group as less than perfect. The ethnic 'character' must always be strong, dignified, courageous, loving, sensitive, wise. Then there are those who watch for authenticity: how dare a white write about blacks? What's a gentile doing writing about a Jewish old lady and her African-American neighbors? The chilling effect of this is a kind of censorship and a reinforcement of apartheid." [39]

An example: When Bruce Brooks's book *Everywhere* (Harper) was published in the fall of 1990, it inspired endless debate over the Anglo author's depiction of a black woman, Lucy, who is not only corpulent and outspoken (and, thus, "may remind adults of Hollywood's Hattie McDaniel," according to one otherwise laudatory review [40]) but also passes herself off as a trained nurse when she isn't. To my bemusement, no one I talked with at the time seemed much concerned with discussing Lucy in the context of the book's plot and setting, but rather, most rushed to condemn the book out of hand because her three-hundred-pound size and professional masquerade might perpetuate harmful stereotypes. The point that kept being missed, I think, was that the time and place of the book's setting—the pre-civil rights South—was one in which prevailing segregation would have barred Lucy from getting her nurse's training. The only way she could work in that capacity (to earn enough money for her eleven-year-old nephew's subsequent medical education) was to practice deception.

However, even if Lucy had been an unmitigated fraud, the book should not have been castigated on those grounds alone, for fraud and other crimes are no respecter of race, and the sad truth is that regardless of the race or color of the body its beat sustains, the human heart is sometimes one of darkness. To say otherwise is to sacrifice truth on the altar of propaganda, no matter how well-intentioned that act may be.

Another troubling aspect of multiculturalism and political correctness is their seeming insistence on maintaining the individual identity and integrity of minority cultures; thus, many ethnic populations today seem to consider the word "assimilation" an insult and, accordingly, have hustled the treasured metaphor of America as melting pot off to an early retirement.

"America is now a stir-fry," Tom Gaughan editorialized in the July-August 1991 issue of *American Libraries*, adding—in case we missed the implication—"the ingredients in a stir-fry remain distinct."

This struggle to protect the indissoluble integrity of ethnic and cultural groups has given rise to such extreme attitudes that it—like the problem novel at its loopiest—has begun to inspire satire. Two of the most amusing recent efforts are *Politically Correct Bedtime Stories*, by James F. Garner (Macmillan, 1994) and *The Official Politically Correct Dictionary and Handbook*, by Henry Beard and Christopher Cerf (Villard, 1992), the latter dedicated, with authors' tongues firmly in cheek, to "the former Donna Ellen Cooperman, who, after a courageous yearlong battle through the New York State court system, won the right to be known as Donna Ellen Cooperperson" (p. vii).

Amazingly, political correctness has survived such

satirical broadsides—as well as more reasoned dismemberment by the Pulitzer Prize–winning historian Arthur Schlesinger, Jr., (*The Disuniting of America: Reflections on a Multicultural Society* [Norton, 1992]) and the cheerfully acerbic, plague-on-both-your-houses book *Culture of Complaint,* by art critic Robert Hughes (Oxford, 1993).

The university provided the cradle for this movement and remains the place where it is most hotly contested. On my desk as I write is an article from the November 16, 1994, *New York Times.* It reports the seventy-fifth anniversary of Columbia University's "Contemporary Civilization" course, a part of the university's core curriculum, which grew out of the immediate post-World War I sense "that for better or worse, Wilsonian America had joined the international community and that American soldiers returning from overseas were eager to know more about foreign cultures." [41]

It's ironic that a college course that began as a reaction to American isolationism should now be in jeopardy because of its adherence to traditional classics of Western thought—"a flash point in today's debate on many campuses over multiculturalism."

What this means is that many adherents of politically correct multiculturalism argue that because the great classics of Western literature were written, for the most part, by white European males, they discount the contributions to our modern civilization of non-Western cultures and nonwhite males—and females.

As a result, many in the academy are urging that

these traditional classics be dropped from the curriculum and replaced by other, nontraditional titles. Or, as Paul Gray rather acerbically put it, "The rebellion against Dead White European Male authors has, by now, turned itself into a campus cliché, but that doesn't mean it has gone away. D.W.E.M.s are still being elbowed off reading lists by writers deemed worthy of study solely because of their gender (translation: female), race, ethnicity, or sexual orientation. It is tempting," Gray continues, "to dismiss all this turmoil as academic. One who decidedly does not is Harold Bloom, 64, the occupant of endowed chairs at both Yale and New York Universities, the author of 20 critical works and the editor of hundreds more, and a Vesuvian source of erudition and opinions."[42]

Many of Bloom's opinions about and defense of traditional western literature are to be found in the pages of his newest book, *The Western Canon* (Harcourt, 1994). Among the writers he discusses are such long-dead, white European males as Shakespeare, Dante, Chaucer, Milton, and Cervantes.

Bloom saves *his* particular indignation for those he calls "The School of Resentment," those, he told a *Newsweek* reporter, who attempt "to put the arts, and literature in particular, in the service of social change."

Bloom tells about "a dear friend who teaches English at the University of Chicago [who] told me with great gusto how she had led the fight to replace the stories of Ernest Hemingway with the works of the Chicano-American writer Gary Soto in her introductory course on literature. Now Hemingway, at his very best, is just about as good as Chekhov or Joyce—that is to say, about as good as a short-story writer can be. While Gary Soto couldn't write his way out of a paper bag." [43]

This kind of intemperate overstatement demonstrates that those on both sides of this issue are too easily overcome with emotion to present any kind of reasoned argument. I admit that Soto, a young adult author of increasing importance, is not Cervantes, but surely he deserves better than the dismissive back of Bloom's critical hand. For I believe that in his sensibility and in his simple, straightforward, often colloquial prose, Soto captures the essence of the Hispanic-American experience, an experience that, of all ethnic American experiences, may be the most underexplored in young adult literature.

I'm not quite sure why this should be. Columnists Roberto Rodriguez and Patrisia Gonzalez declare it is because "most of what we (Latino authors) write is considered noise, foreign chatter at best. We are often unable to find a medium for our rich and textured prose—the amalgam of Spanish, English, Indian, and *calo* (street talk). Many publishers not only find our writing unacceptable; they can't read it." [44]

Another reason may be that there is no tradition of creating an indigenous literature for young readers in most Latin American countries—the few books available for them being imported from Spain. (The importing of books from England is, similarly, the reason there was, for years, no national body of children's literature in Canada, Australia, or New Zealand.) And even those few books were (and still are), typically, moralistic and didactic. Isabel Schon, founder and director of the Center for the Study of Books in Spanish for Children and Adolescents at California State University, San Marcos, says, "In Mexico and in other Spanish-speaking countries, they still put out a lot of horribly boring, didactic, moralistic children's books."[45]

Even more reason why a viable literature is urgently needed for this fastest-growing minority group in America, which, some demographers predict, will comprise a fifth of the U.S. population by the year 2050.[46]

Even before then—by 2020—people of Hispanic descent will replace blacks as the nation's largest minority group, numbering 51.2 million, or 15.7 percent of the population (up from 9.7 percent in 1993).[47]

Statistically, Mexicans are the largest national group within the Hispanic aggregate. With a population of eleven million in 1990, they are now the seventh-largest ancestry group in America (up from tenth place and seven million in 1980).[48] Of the 1.8 million Latino immigrants to be granted permanent residence in 1991, 79 percent settled in only seven states (California, Arizona, Texas, Illinois, Florida, New York, and New Jersey). In five of the seven, Mexico was the country of largest national origin among the new residents—by far.

Soto is himself a Mexican American, born in Fresno, California, which provides the setting for three of his best works: *Baseball in April, Local News,* and *Jesse* (1990, 1993, and 1994; all Harcourt, Brace). The only

other author to have created a similarly significant
body of work about the Hispanic-American experience—and to have attracted an equally significant and
enthusiastic young adult readership—is another Mexican American, the poet and short-story writer Sandra
Cisneros, who was born in Chicago, Illinois. Cisneros
is not a young adult writer, however; her lyrical stories
about women residing in the Hispanic quarter of
Chicago or in American/Mexican border towns are
written for an adult audience, but finding little of relevance written directly for them, young adult readers
have embraced her work (*The House on Mango Street*
[Arté Público, 1983]; *My Wicked, Wicked Ways* [Third
Women Press, 1987], and *Woman Hollering Creek* [Ran-
dom House, 1991]) as their own.

I have stressed Soto's and Cisneros's Mexican roots
so that we don't forget that, as important as their work
is, it represents only one type of Hispanic immigrant
experience. S. Shelley Quezada reminds us that "Latin
America embraces more than twenty-one nations."
Noting the cultural complexities of these different
national communities, she explains, "Broad generaliza-
tions about Hispanics are often made in which people
from diverse cultures and backgrounds are lumped together and given any number of supposedly shared
characteristics; at the same time, as an aggregate group
they are also compared with other populations of limited English proficiency which are trying for a place in
American society." [49]

Of course, what she says about Hispanics applies,

as we have seen, with equal force to Pacific cultures, which are too often and too easily lumped together under the generic rubric "Asian."

One recent book that demonstrates the diversity of Latin American cultures while respecting individual differences—as Yep's *American Dragons* did for Asian cultures—is *Where Angels Glide at Dawn* which, edited by Lori M. Carlson and Cynthia L. Ventura (Harper, 1990), contains stories by Latin American writers from seven different countries.

It is not enough for young people simply to have books, however; "Their books," Mildred L. Batchelder points out, "must be in the language they speak." [50]

Not all these young people speak English—in fact, some 32 million people in the U.S. speak languages other than English at home. [51] Indeed, 96 languages are spoken in the Los Angeles public schools alone. [52] At one of these schools, Union Avenue Elementary, 93 percent of the 2,000 students are Latino; a third were born outside the U.S., and "well over half are not proficient in English." [53]

In Los Angeles as a whole, 21 percent of the population under the age of eighteen is foreign-born. [54] In affluent Beverly Hills, 41 percent of the students at the Hawthorne Elementary school, just two blocks from City Hall, have English as a second language. Their first? Not Spanish but Farsi! (Beverly Hills was the destination of choice for a large population of Persian political refugees who fled Iran in the wake of the Shah's fall.)

In the nation as a whole, the number of public school students with little or no knowledge of English increased 50 percent between 1986 and 1991—from 1.5 million to 2.3 million.[55]

The numbers alone are staggering, but Shelley Quezada explains what they mean in human terms: "For both newly arrived and more established Spanish-speaking immigrants, the lack of ability to speak, read, and write English often leaves them living in cultural enclaves. They are often distanced from mainstream society and disenfranchised to the point of feeling that they have no share in what is happening in the world around them."[56]

To resolve this problem, Quezada asserts, "not only do we need quality materials in Spanish, but we must also search out both bilingual and English-language materials which accurately reflect the Hispanic experience and culture."

The intense interest in Spanish-language materials was reflected by the staggering success of the third annual Conference on Books in Spanish for Young Readers. Sponsored by Schon's San Marcos Center, the 1994 conference attracted 93 exhibitors, 18 authors, and 1,500 teachers and librarians from the U.S., Spain, Mexico, and South America.

"The conference," according to the *USBBY Newsletter* of the U.S. Board on Books for Youth, "reflected the current renaissance in the field of books in Spanish."[57]

Perhaps also reflecting this renaissance, a number of U.S. publishers, in the last five or so years, have begun issuing new Spanish-language editions of popular American children's books. Farrar, Straus and Giroux's Mirasol ("Libros juveniles") imprint is just one of these. The publisher's fall 1994 catalog listed translations of such titles as William Steig's *Dominic*, *The Amazing Bone*, and *Brave Irene*; Uri Shulevitz's *The Treasure*, and George Selden's *The Cricket in Times Square.*

Other publishers are doing bilingual editions: Clarion has recently published a beautiful edition of Nobel laureate Juan Ramon Jimenez's classic *Platero and I* (*Platero y yo*) (selected, translated, and adapted from the Spanish by Myra Cohn Livingston and Joseph F. Dominguez).

Of more immediate moment to young adults is 1994's *Cool Salsa: Bilingual Poems on Growing Up Latino in the United States*. Edited by Lori M. Carlson (one of the editors of *Where Angels Glide at Dawn*), the book is published by Henry Holt in its Edge imprint (about which, more in a moment). Thumbing through its pages, one finds work by Soto and Cisneros, of course, but also original work by poets who hail from the length and breadth of Latin America—from Puerto Rico to Bolivia, from Argentina to Venezuela, from Mexico to Colombia and beyond.

Cuban-American novelist Oscar Hijuelos writes in his introduction, "It [*Cool Salsa*] also opens doors to possibilities of thought and feeling in a way no book could do for me when I was growing up, because there were no books that addressed our world back then" (he

was born in New York in 1951). "Hearing one language on the streets, another at home, and a third at
school, I had to find my own words, my own rhythms,
my own story" (remember what Rodriguez and Gonzalez said about multilingualism?). "So have these poets;
each uses his or her own blend of Spanish, English,
and everything in between. But they have the good
fortune of appearing twice, speaking simultaneously in
two tongues; speaking to us with their hearts and their
minds at the same time." [58]

Literature for Understanding and Assimilation

"Assimilation into mainstream U.S. culture can be a painful process for any ethnic group," Quezada observes. [59]

Books can help mitigate the pain and ease the
process of assimilation for immigrants. In the meantime,
however, books are also immeasurably important to "established" Americans who urgently need a crash course
in understanding the new crazy quilt of cultures cover-
ing them in the nineties. Too often cultures do not
meet; they clash. It is sadly ironic that one of the five
"must read" books about Chicano culture, *Bless Me,
Ultima,* by Rudolfo Anaya (TQS Publications, 1972), is
one of the most censored by Anglo watchdogs because it
contains witchcraft (it's the story of a New Mexican
boy's magical encounter with a *curandera,* a healer, and
her owl spirit). As Rodriguez and Gonzalez point out,
"The objections to Anaya's book indicate that those who
would ban it do not understand Latino culture or its

indigenous roots: the practice of healing is part of our indigenous memory."[60]

Sometimes, of course, the pace of change over-
whelms understanding's need for measured reflection.

In 1970 Alvin Toffler coined the now-familiar
phrase "future shock," which he defined as "the shattering stress and disorientation that we induce in individuals by subjecting them to too much change in too
short a time."[61]

Future shock played a smaller part in the first great
wave of immigration, because it was gradual, spread
out over a period of four decades (roughly 1880 to
1920); the second great wave, however, crashed upon
our shores in the space of only one and brought with it
future shock in spades! Too few people deal well with
such rapid change; it induces in them not only disorientation but fear—principally fear of the unknown,
which is why good books about not only the culture
but about the individual human conditions of new
immigrant groups are so important. Without them,
already-established people blindly reject what they per-
ceive as the threat of change—especially when it coin-
cides, as it has in the late eighties and early nineties,
with times of economic distress.

The New York Times confirms that "shifts in public
attitudes [toward immigration] seem to parallel the
changes in economic conditions."[62]

In conducting my research for this book, I have
come across polls conducted independently by *Time,*
Newsweek, and *The New York Times* that show that 60

percent to 73 percent of Americans now feel that immigration is a bad thing and should be strictly limited or decreased. This "feeling" (a word I use advisedly, since I'm not sure how much rational thought went into it) reached its nadir in November 1994, when California voters passed, 59 percent to 41 percent, Proposition 187, an initiative that would eliminate public social services to illegal immigrants—and no matter that the initiative was clearly unconstitutional (and, in fact, a federal judge issued an injunction against its implementation the day after the election). Nevertheless, voters in Arizona and Texas are already talking about trying to implement similar measures in their states. Meanwhile *The Los Angeles Times* reported on November 19, 1994, that California's governor, Pete Wilson, had urged the U.S. Congress to adopt a federal version of Proposition 187.

"In a confident address to the conservative Heritage Foundation," reporter Ronald Brownstein wrote, "Wilson said that the new Congress should either fully reimburse states for the cost of education and medical services to illegal immigrants or seek to end the requirements that they provide such services at all." [63]

Fear and frustration are not limited to the established majority, however: A survey conducted for the National Conference of Christians and Jews in March of 1994 revealed that "minorities held more negative views of [other] minorities than do whites" and are seemingly as quick to embrace negative stereotyping. [64]

Sometimes this is a catalyst to violence, as was the

case in the clashes between African Americans and Koreans that were an aspect of the 1992 Los Angeles riots. More recently, a year-long "war" between black and Latino gangs resulted in fifteen deaths in the Venice, California, area, while in affluent San Marino, California, hard by the stately Huntington Library, two high school students were murdered and seven seriously wounded as a result of warfare between gangs of different Asian nationalities.

"It appears as if the more diversity and burgeoning minority groups we have, the more prejudice we must overcome." [65]

Nevertheless, a June 1993 CBS News/*New York Times* poll revealed a deeply interesting finding: "People are much more willing to welcome immigrants when the issue is couched in personal terms"—the kind of personal terms that good fiction can offer, I would add.[66]

In 1992, Mildred L. Batchelder, who served for thirty years as executive director of The ALA's Association for Library Services to Children, gave a spirited keynote address to the third Pacific Rim Conference on Children's Literature. In her speech Ms. Batchelder saluted the development, since the 1920s, of an international awareness in the field of books for young readers and the use of translated books in this country to promote what she called "world friendship and international understanding." [67]

Recognizing her lifelong commitment to this cause, the American Library Association, in 1968, established the Mildred L. Batchelder Award, which is presented annually to a U.S. publisher of an outstanding children's book originally published elsewhere in a language other than English.

It is disturbing that, as Margaret McElderry noted in her 1994 May Hill Arbuthnot Lecture, "the number of [such] books has drastically diminished in the last fifteen or twenty years. So much so that the Batchelder Award has had fewer and fewer serious contenders. In fact, in 1993, the Batchelder Award committee decided no award could be given." [68]

Ms. McElderry suggested several reasons why this should be: "In part, this has happened, I think," she says, "because our young readers some while ago seemed to lose interest in other countries, other peoples, other ways, tending instead to concentrate on themselves and their peers and life-styles."

Another observer agrees: "American adolescents, for the most part, have little interest in their own traditions and almost none in anyone else's." [69]

Marc Aronson, a senior editor at Henry Holt, offered a more pragmatic reason in a recent phone interview. Aronson reminded me that there is no young adult literature in many foreign countries (as previously noted, puberty may be a universal experience but adolescence is not), and so an American publisher who is looking for relevant material has only adult fiction to choose from, and many of those titles, being experimental in form, are inaccessible to American young adults.

The fiscal impact of all of this on publishers is obvious, as McElderry explains: "Publishers quickly learned that, despite the excellence of a book in another language, if, after the considerable time spent and the expense of arranging for a translated edition, only a relative handful of copies is sold, there is no justification for taking on more books to translate. In the short and long terms, publication is viable only when supported by readership."[70]

To solve this problem, some book publishers seem to have learned a lesson from magazine publishers who, in the last decade, have discovered niche publishing, developing new nongeneral-interest magazines that focus on one relatively narrow subject (often having to do with some aspect of computer technology or leisure-time activity) and are sold to a specific, narrowly defined readership. Some recent examples of this in book publishing would be Children's Book Press in San Francisco and Lee and Low in New York; both are relatively small houses that specialize in multicultural titles. Meanwhile in Houston, Arté Público Books (which published the first edition of Cisneros's *The House on Mango Street*) has announced a new imprint called Piñata Books, dedicated to publishing children's and young adult titles written by U.S. Hispanic authors.

"Piñata Books," the publisher claims in a promotional brochure, "is the first imprint devoted to providing materials for children that authentically and realistically portray themes, characters, and customs unique to U.S. Hispanic culture."

And in Santa Fe, New Mexico, Clear Light Publishers specializes in books portraying Native American cultures. All these publishers seem to be following Ms. McElderry's advice: "to find writers among this new wave of immigrants, authors who can portray creatively what it is like to adjust to life in the U.S." [71]

A mainstream publisher that has had success in doing the same is Henry Holt with its still relatively new Edge imprint, which offers a combination of original work done here in the United States (*Cool Salsa*, for example) and work from abroad (*The Passerby*, by Liliane Atlan, and *The Song of Be*, by Lesley Beake).

The imprint's editor, Marc Aronson—mentioned above—feels there is a viable audience for these "edgy" (his word) titles. He points out that today's kids are increasingly exposed to the world outside America through Benetton ads, MTV, and other media. However, "That world is 'factoids,' headlines, and imagery. How do you get into that world?" he asks rhetorically, answering his own question with one word: "Literature."

More expansively, he adds, "Literature can take you into a world by showing you how people actually see things. Young adulthood is a time of transition; it means coming of age. You become an independent actor out in the world."

Aronson believes that in the Edge imprint, "We're getting very strong writers with something original to say." He adds that many powerful multicultural novels published in the U.S. are not written for young adults. Demonstrating this fact is one of the best titles in the series—in my estimation—*Shizuko's Daughter* (1993) by Kyoko Mori, which began as a piece of short fiction published in the literary magazine *The Kenyon Review.*

Set in modern Japan, the novel focuses on a teenage girl's struggle to deal both with her mother's suicide and her father's emotional distance, which is so great that the girl, Yuki, seems almost to be an exile in her own home. At school she is an outsider, set apart by her academic and athletic achievements and by her desire to be an artist.

Author Mori, now an associate professor of English and Creative Writing at Saint Norbert College in De-Pere, Wisconsin, has said, "I think of being an outsider as a universal theme of young adult life and literature.

"My own interest in that theme," she adds, "is also influenced by my being an outsider to my own culture or cultures."[72]

She explained in a speech to the annual meeting of the U.S. Board on Books for Youth in 1993 that she grew up in a highly westernized Japanese family, came to the U.S. in 1977 to study, and never went back to Japan.

If Mori's theme in her first novel is universal, her treatment of her material is intensely personal and helps the reader to empathetically comprehend the emotional lives of the modern Japanese. Of perhaps greater importance to me as a reader is the fact that Mori made it possible for me to *intellectually* comprehend the lives of her characters; she took me not only into their hearts but into their minds as well, making it possible for me to understand how very different the mind-sets and thought processes of nonwestern people can be from our familiar American ones. Mori's wonderfully thought-provoking book gave me, thus, a much more powerful and memorable experience than the reading of half a dozen nonfiction books about adolescent life in Japan could have given.

Mori is not unique as an Asian who came to America to study and elected to stay and write. Others are Bharati Mukerjee, Anita Desai, and Kirin Narayan.

What Elaine Kendall has said of them can be said, equally well, of Mori: "Like their European predecessors, these writers are concerned with the invention of an American self." [73]

Indeed, Mori has written, "I want to claim the unfamiliar landscape of the American midwest by making internal connections. Though I am an outsider in both the landscape in the midwest and the remembered landscape of Japan, I want to bring them together to create an emotional landscape that is mine. The balance between belonging and not belonging is what I need to write with. I hope there is a metaphor for what I see as the essence of being an outsider as a teenager and as an expatriate." [74] (Readers who may wish to learn more about the landscape of Mori's own life and the roots of *Shizuko's Daughter* are referred to her 1994 memoir, *The Dream of Water* [Henry Holt].)

As we approach the mid-nineties, the issues that we have been discussing continue to be so complex as to baffle our minds and perplex our hearts. In the end,

I believe it is literature—whether imported from other lands in other languages, imported in translation, written in English in this country by immigrants who describe the invention of their new selves here or recall the realities of their former lives in the lands of their national origin—that will prove to be the place of light, the neutral center where all of us can go to find out about each other and, come to think of it, about ourselves as well. "We" need to read about "them" and "they" need to read about "us," and perhaps we will find, thus, that we are all, simply, "we."

NOTES

1. Jefferson, Margo, "Sweet Dreams for Teen Queens," *The Nation*, 234:613 (May 22, 1982).
2. "Wildfire" promotional copy, quoted in Jefferson, p. 613.
3. Pollack, "The Business of Popularity," p. 25.
4. Ramsdell, Kristin, *Happily Ever After*. Littleton, CO: Libraries Unlimited, 1987, p. 8.
5. Kellogg, Mary Alice, "The Romance Book Boom," *Seventeen*, 42:158 (May 1983).
6. Pollack, "Business," p. 28.
7. Ramsdell, Kristin, "Young Adult Publishing: A Blossoming Market," *Top of the News*, 39:177 (Winter 1983).
8. Zuckerman, Eileen Goudge, "Nancy Drew vs: Serious Fiction," *Publishers Weekly*, 229:74 (May 30, 1986).
9. Kundin, Susan G., "Romance Versus Reality." Quoted in Doris Fong, "From Sweet Valley They Say We Are Leaving," *School Library Journal*, 36:38 (January 1990).
10. Ramsdell, *Happily*, p. 10.
11. *Ibid.*, p. 10.
12. Campbell, Patty, "Perplexing Young Adult Books, A Retrospective," *Wilson Library Bulletin*, 62:26 (April 1988).
13. *Ibid.*, p. 26.

14. Pollack, "Business," p. 25.
15. Baldwin, Neal, "Writing for Young Adults," *Publishers Weekly,* 226:18 (October 19, 1984).
16. *Ibid.,* p. 18.
17. Huntwork, Mary M., "Why Girls Flock to Sweet Valley High," *School Library Journal,* 36:137 (March 1990).
18. *Ibid.,* p. 138.
19. Baldwin, "Writing," p. 16.
20. *Ibid.,* p. 17.
21. *Ibid.,* p. 17.
22. *Ibid.,* p. 20.
23. "The Numbers Game," *Time,* 142:14 (Fall 1993: Special Issue).
24. Mydans, Seth, "A New Tide of Immigration Brings Hostility to the Surface, Poll finds," *The New York Times,* June 27, 1993, p. 14.
25. "Kids Need Libraries," *Journal of Youth Services in Libraries,* 3:202 (Spring 1990).
26. Rochman, Hazel, *Against Borders: Promoting Books for a Multicultural World.* Chicago: American Library Association, 1993, p. 9.
27. McElderry, "Across the Years," p. 379.
28. Bullard, Sara, "Sorting Through the Multicultural Rhetoric." Quoted in Karen Patricia Smith, "The Multicultural Ethic and Connection to Literature for Children and Young Adults," *Library Trends,* 41:341 (Winter 1993).
29. *Ibid.,* p. 341.
30. *Ibid.,* p. 342.
31. Yep, Laurence, ed., *American Dragons.* New York: Harper, 1993, pp. xi–xii.
32. Louie, Ai-Ling, "Growing Up Asian American," *Journal of Youth Services in Libraries,* 6:120 (Winter 1993).
33. *Ibid.,* p. 117.
34. *Ibid.,* p. 121.
35. Smith, "The Multicultural Ethic," p. 345.
36. Mathis, Sharon Bell, "*The Slave Dancer* Is an Insult to Black Children," in Donnarae MacCann and Gloria Woodard, eds., *Cultural Conformity in Books for Children.* Metuchen, NJ: Scarecrow, 1977, p. 146.
37. Peck, "Silver Anniversary," pp. 21–2.
38. Yolen, Jane, "An Empress of Thieves," *The Horn Book,* LXX:705 (November/December 1994).
39. Rochman, *Against,* p. 17.
40. Sidorsky, Phyllis G., Review of *Everywhere,* in *School Library Journal,* 36:224 (September 1990).

41. Honan, William H., "Columbia to Celebrate 75 Years of Great Books," *The New York Times*, November 16, 1994, p. B9.

42. Gray, Paul, "Hurrah for Dead White Males!" *Time*, 144:62 (October 10, 1994).

43. Shulman, Ken, "Bloom and Doom," *Newsweek*, CXXIV:75 (October 10, 1994).

44. Rodriguez, Roberto, and Patrisia Gonzalez, "Censorship by Omission: When the Mainstream Ignores You," *The Los Angeles Times*, December 30, 1994, p. B7.

45. Ehrman, Mark, "Separating the *Trigo* from the Chaff," *The Los Angeles Times Magazine*, March 7, 1993, p. 10.

46. Brookhiser, Richard, "The Melting Pot Is Still Simmering," *Time*, 141:72 (March 1, 1993).

47. "Americans in 2020," *The New York Times*, April 22, 1994, p. A7.

48. Brookhiser, "Melting Pot," p. 72.

49. Quezada, S. Shelley, "Bridging the Pacific Rim: Selecting and Reviewing Latin American Children's Books" in Winifred Ragsdale, ed., *A Sea of Upturned Faces*. Metuchen, NJ: Scarecrow, 1989, p. 138.

50. Batchelder, Mildred L., "Learning about Sharing," in Ragsdale, p. 19.

51. "The Numbers Game," p. 14.

52. Dunn, Ashley, "In CA the Numbers Add up to Anxiety," *The New York Times*, October 30, 1994, p. E3.

53. McGuire, Stryker, "Immigrant Schools: The Wrong Lessons," *Newsweek*, CXXII:23 (August 9, 1993).

54. "The Numbers Game," p. 14.

55. Gray, Paul, "Teach Your Children Well," *Time*, 142:69 (Fall 1993: Special Issue).

56. Quezada, "Bridging," p. 138.

57. "Conference on Books in Spanish for Young Readers," *USBBY Newsletter*, XIX:10 (Spring 1994).

58. Hijuelos, Oscar, "Introduction" in Lori M. Carlson, ed., *Cool Salsa*. New York: Henry Holt, 1994, pp. xix–xx.

59. Quezada, p. 138.

60. Rodriguez and Gonzalez, "Censorship," p. B7.

61. Toffler, Alvin, *Future Shock*. New York: Random House, 1970, p. 4.

62. Mydans, "New Tide," p. 1.

63. Brownstein, Ronald, "Wilson Proposes U.S. Version of Prop. 187," *The Los Angeles Times*, November 19, 1994, p. 1.

64. Holmes, Steven A., "Survey Finds Minorities Resent One Another

Almost As Much As They Do Whites," *The New York Times,* March 3, 1994, p. A9.

65. *Ibid.,* p. A9.
66. Mydans, "New Tide," p. 1.
67. Batchelder, "Learning," p. 9.
68. McElderry, "Across," p. 379.
69. Barr, "Should Holden Caulfield," p. 50.
70. McElderry, p. 379.
71. *Ibid.,* p. 379.
72. Mori, Kyoko, quoted in *USBBY Newsletter,* XIX:9 (Spring 1994).
73. Kendall, Elaine, "One Girl's Inventing of an American Self," *The Los Angeles Times,* March 4, 1994, p. E4.
74. Mori, pp. 9–10.

PART TWO

THIS IS NOW

CHAPTER FIVE

THE NINETIES
AND THE FUTURE
A Literature at Risk?

As the new decade of the nineties dawned, Connie C. Epstein, former editor in chief at Morrow Junior Books, reflected on the condition of young adult publishing. Noting reports of "weakening sales for what had come to be called 'problem stories,' " she reported that "some editors, marketing directors, and subsidiary rights directors, discouraged by this downturn, have been wondering whether the young adult novel was ready for burial, and certainly most would agree that the genre is in turmoil." [1]

Four years later, Alleen Pace Nilsen agreed that assessing "the health of the genre" in the nineties was tantamount to "gathering at the bedside of an ailing loved one," though she qualified her diagnosis by specifying that she was referring to "the realistic problem novel" rather than "the entire body of modern young adult literature." [2]

Though it might at first appear that Nilsen's definition of young adult literature is narrower than Epstein's global reference to the young adult novel, I think they are, in fact, talking about the same literary "creature": the mainstream/realistic/coming-of-age/rite-of-passage novel that, published in hardcovers, had traditionally been sold to institutions (i.e., schools and libraries). With the loss of federal funding, taxpayer revolts (beginning with California's notorious Proposition 13), and the American economy's general malaise—all of which were features of the late seventies and a fixture of the eighties—the institutional market declined precipitously. Since hardcover young adult fiction had never become a staple of the retail market that emerged in the eighties in the form of specialty children's bookstores, the commercial potential for serious young adult fiction began to dwindle. I suspect this may be one reason for the phenomenon that Nilsen describes: Major publishing houses, she declares, "have moved from the past practice of bringing out about 80% fiction and 20% nonfiction to doing 80% nonfiction and 20% fiction" [3] (the point being that institutions continue to buy nonfiction to support curriculum needs).

Nilsen also argues that the rampant popularity of daytime talk shows like *Donahue* and *Oprah*, which offer "a daily media glut of stories about the personal foibles and tragedies in which young people get involved . . .

leaves little unexplored territory for authors to mine."[4]

This phenomenon has not been confined to young adult literature. Adam Hochschild, founder of *Mother Jones* magazine, offers a similar observation about adult fiction in the 1990s: "One reason people write fewer traditional realist novels these days," he says, "is that modern readers are jaded. Film, radio, first-person journalism, prying biographers and, above all, TV, have saturated us with reality."[5]

I agree that this is a phenomenon to reckon with, but I strenuously disagree with Nilsen's claim that it leaves "little unexplored territory."

It seems to me that the distorted, sensational, increasingly grotesque take on life that these TV shows offer has almost nothing to do with the real lives of America's young adults. They watch these shows, of course; indeed, they devour them like popcorn in exactly the same way they did the most meretricious "problem novels" of the seventies—for cheap thrills, for entertainment, and for the sake of feeling superior to the novel's hapless protagonists, who have now been translated by television into the equally hapless "guests" (some would say "victims") who appear on the endless, mind-numbing streams of talk and so-called "reality" shows, which seem to be trying to outsensationalize the daytime soaps.

"Television emphasizes the deviant so that it becomes normal," Vicki Apt, a Penn State University sociologist charges. "If you really are normal, no one cares."[6]

Television critic Tom Shales agrees: "These programs may be replacing the soap opera as America's preferred daily fix of titillating escapism . . . but the 'reality' on the daytime talk shows is hyped and twisted and phonied up. The soaps may actually be more realistic."[7]

Another inescapable daily television fix is provided by the increasingly graphic depiction of violence both in dramatic programs and—more and more often—in television's news reports. According to *The New York Times,* "Researchers estimate that the average child will watch 100,000 acts of simulated violence before graduating from elementary school."[8]

Given a statistic like that, who can disagree with David Gonzalez's observation that "there seem to be few havens from the violence that has become an increasingly common part of daily life?"

Gonzalez also reports that America's Roman Catholic bishops, concerned that society "has grown numb to it all," issued a "sweeping denunciation" at their fall 1994 meeting "of 'the culture of violence' that pervades American society."[9]

Such ubiquitous violence ultimately does have a numbing, almost dehumanizing effect on our emotional selves, compromising our capacity to empathize and forcing authors, as Nilsen points out, "to work harder to involve their readers' emotions."[10]

Jaded, numbed, and dehumanized, viewers and readers seem to need ever more visceral doses of violence to jump-start their numbed emotions and sensibilities.

This is one reason, I think, for the phenomenal popularity in the eighties of adult horror novels by Stephen King, Dean Koontz, and Clive Barker and the runaway popularity of the modern "slasher" movies, which, beginning with Sean Cunningham's *Friday the 13th* (1980) and Wes Craven's *Nightmare on Elm Street* (1984), introduced the likes of Jason, Freddy Krueger, and their demonic ilk and which, in their depictions of graphic violence, made Grand Guignol look like the children's hour.

It's noteworthy that teenagers were the chief box-office targets for these movies (as well as being the on-screen targets of the demonic slashers!). Of *Friday the 13th*, film critic Leonard Maltin has noted, with more acerbity, perhaps, than accuracy, "Young folks unexpectedly made this gory, cardboard thriller a box office smash. One more clue to why SAT scores continue to decline." [11]

In fairly short order, the genre moved into young adult fiction, and the paperback horror novel became to publishing in the nineties what romance paperbacks had been to the eighties.

"Adolescents now constitute a booming niche market for the peddling of published gore and violence," Paul Gray explains, noting that Christopher Pike, who is generally credited with starting the stampede to horror with his 1985 title *Slumber Party*, now has 8 million copies of his books in print, while his chief rival, R. L. Stine, boasts 7.6 million copies of *his*. [12] (Ken Tucker of *Entertainment Weekly* magazine, in a reference too good not to mention, calls these two the "Beavis and Butthead of horror." [13])

Both authors know their audience—or perhaps it's better to say are cynical about it: Stine says, "They [his teenage readers] like the gross stuff," adding that his chief challenge is "to find new cheap thrills." Pike agrees: "They want to be scared or they would not pick up the book and read it." [14]

"It's easy to understand why young adult horror is so popular," Tucker adds. "[It's] a combination of youth's eternal desire to shock its elders and a budding interest in all things odd and uncomfortable." [15]

Whatever the root reasons for its popularity with teenagers, there is no doubt why horror is a hit with publishers: It pays the light bill. In 1992, three of the top five paperback best-sellers were by Christopher Pike. Diane Roback of *Publishers Weekly* claims that "with slashers stalking the shopping malls and mummies lurking in the graveyards, the horror genre hit its stride in 1993." [16]

Sales support this notion: Four Christopher Pike titles sold more than 175,000 copies that year, while seven R. L. Stine "Fear Street" titles sold in excess of 100,000 copies.

By 1993 the trickle-down theory had hit horror series just as it had impacted romance series in the eighties, spinning off junior versions for mid-range readers. Stine led the parade in this division with his "Goosebumps" titles for younger aficionados, *ten* of which sold more than 150,000 copies!

Stine's runaway success has not escaped the attention of adult publishers. The October 3, 1994, issue of *Publishers Weekly* reported Stine's being signed by entertainment mogul Brandon Tartikoff for his first adult novel, to be called *Superstition.*

"My goal," Tartikoff noted, explaining his entry into the publishing field, "is to nurture high-concept material that can begin life as hardcover literary [sic!] works and then be developed into compelling properties for film . . ." (p. 16).

Thus we will have come full circle—the horror movies gave Stine a subject; paperback publishing then gave the horrormeister a home; and now paperback books will give him back to the movies—*plus ça change* . . .

Meanwhile, his chief rival, Pike, has already entered the adult lists with *The Season of Passage* (Tor, 1992) and the newly published *The Cold One* (Tor, 1994).

One would like to think that that is *his* problem, but, of course, it is the reader's, too, as is the fact that the horror trend is nowhere near peaking. Consider:

Elise Howard, vice-president of Daniel Weiss Associates, told her audience at the 1994 conference of the Society of Children's Book Writers and Illustrators that every single one of the then twenty-one "Goosebumps," titles had sold in excess of one million copies and that a normal first printing for a title in the series is now 500,000 copies.

Like the romance series, horror fiction is formula driven, produced according to multipage specification sheets that virtually guarantee predictable plots and cardboard characters. Settings are as blandly white, middle-class, and suburban as those of romance novels and are equally devoid of sex (though gouts of blood are always welcome). The threat of sexual violence may be present, however, as young women are once again forced to play the role of helpless victim.

The popularity of genre series is perhaps the most durable phenomenon in the ongoing history of publishing for young readers. They were staples of the twenties and thirties, thanks in large part to the writing factory called the Stratemeyer Syndicate, which churned out Nancy Drew, The Hardy Boys, and other series. Today's writing factories, which are still turning out titles on the creative assembly line as fast as kids can read them, are no longer called syndicates but "packagers," instead. Their typical function is to develop an idea for a series, sell it to a mainstream publisher, and then assemble the talent—including author, editor, and illustrator—necessary to produce the books.

Daniel Weiss Associates, mentioned above, is among the leading packagers, producing ten series per month in "a market-driven style and standard," according to Howard.

Horror may command the headlines, but romance continues to sell briskly too. Sweet Valley books command first printings of 200,000 copies, and in 1993 six of them sold more than 100,00 copies (one is tempted to call them "units," instead of copies, since they are virtually interchangeable in their mass-produced content and format).

According to the Bantam Doubleday Dell catalog for fall 1994, there are now more than 81 million copies of Valley titles in print. And more to come, for, as the catalog crows, "Sweet Valley continues to offer teens all the racy romance, drama, and adventures they're looking for in a series" (p. 90).

And not just American teens, either, since the series is now sold in twenty other countries, according to Howard.

And, like old man river, another BDD romance series, "Sweet Dreams," continues to roll along, too: 221 titles have been published to date, and a new title continues to appear each month.

African-American teens are now represented in a series called "18 Pine Street," which, BDD claims, was "created" by the Margaret Edwards Award winner Walter Dean Myers.

And historical romances are still popular too. Titles in the "American Girl" series for preteens routinely enjoy six-figure sales, and for older teens, Jennifer Armstrong's "Wild Rose Inn" books have been added to BDD's longstanding "Starfire" imprint.

It bears repeating here that—unlike realistic hardcover novels, which were bought by librarians and teachers—these paperbacks are being bought by the teenagers themselves, usually from mall-based chain bookstores or superstores (which are chain outlets with elephantiasis!).

This is tremendously important, because it is now the buyers for the chains—not librarians, not educators, and not psychologists—who dictate how we define "young adults." For them, YAs are now eleven-to-thirteen- or fourteen-year-olds. And since the chains believe that these kid consumers will buy only paperback books, one will look long, hard, and usually fruitlessly for a hardcover YA title in a chain outlet. A result is the continuing growth of paperback series and the increasing importance to editors—when they are considering a manuscript for hardcover publication—of its marketability as a paperback. And since that paperback must be sold to a chain if it is to return a profit, it must be suitable for readers who match the chain's definition of young adults; i.e., eleven-to-fourteen-year-olds. Not surprisingly, this means it must also avoid controversial subjects or themes. For, as George Nicholson, then head of Bantam Doubleday Dell, told Connie Epstein in 1990, the chains will not buy a novel with "anything difficult in it." [17]

And since kids like to read about people like themselves, is it any wonder that the protagonists in young adult fiction have become younger and younger as readers have become younger and younger and are now, typically, of middle school age? And is it any wonder that Richard Jackson, editor of his own imprint at Orchard Books and a major publisher of hardcover young adult fiction, now flatly declares "young adult stops at fourteen?"

It is not young adult fiction that is extinct; it is—so

far as market-force-driven publishers are concerned—
its former fifteen-to-eighteen-year-old readers who
have become the endangered species. I cannot imagine
this situation is going to change any time soon, particularly since, in 1993, hardcover sales were down, for
the first time, to *both* the institutional and retail mar-
kets. The only area to show an increase in sales was—
you guessed it—paperbacks.

Why not, then, launch a renaissance of serious
young adult novels by publishing them as paperback
originals? This tactic has worked with venturesome
adult fiction, especially first novels. But there are problems peculiar to the case of YA fiction. One is that
chains would probably not stock such novels. A second
is that paperbacks tend not to be reviewed, and most
institutions still make purchasing decisions based on
reviews. There is also a certain resistance by libraries
to buying this format—even if it is reviewed—because
it is deemed to be too impermanent. As for authors,
there are problems there, too: for one, there is still a
certain cachet to being published in hardcover (never
mind that one of Nobel laureate Saul Bellow's most
recent novels was published as a trade paperback original). Second, publishers cannot pay a viable advance
to authors for publication exclusively in trade paperback (or so Andrea Cascardi of Hyperion Books told
me recently).

A possible compromise may be a strategy that
Harcourt, Brace began successfully testing several sea-
sons ago: the simultaneous publication in hardcover

and paperback of selected YA titles in a uniform format (the hardcovers are the size of the typical paperback).

Would independent children's bookstores stock both formats? Yes, I was told when I interviewed two leading bookstore owners in the spring of 1994. As a former public library director, I have firsthand knowledge of what is happening in the institutional marketplace, but I was anxious to test the realities of the retail world and to find out if what the media are reporting about the alleged decline of that market is true.

The booksellers I interviewed were Jody Fickes, who is proprietor of Adventures for Kids in Ventura, California, and—at the time of the interview—president of the national Association of Booksellers for Children, and Sharon Hearne, who owns Children's Book World, one of the leading stores in Los Angeles.

Fickes flatly declared that she doesn't believe that the field of young adult literature is dead or dying, and Hearne affirmed the abiding interest of her staff in the field, too. Both stores carry hardcover young adult titles, although Hearne acknowledged that she is buying them more selectively these days, while Fickes told me she has started returning more titles to publishers than she had in the past. (The notion of returns, long established in the adult field, is relatively new to books for young readers, but it's catching on fast. Connie Epstein told the 1994 SCBWI conference participants that returns of 20 percent are now customary; some of these may be rejacketed and sold to institutions, but not all will, and returns can represent significant financial loss to hard-pressed publishers.)

Who *is* purchasing these young adult titles, though? And are those ultimate pop culture consumers of clothes, music, videos, *music* videos, and mountains of eclectic stuff—the kids themselves—among the buyers?

Yes, Hearne and Fickes agree, although both acknowledge that the young adults among their customers formed the bookstore "habit" as children when their parents first brought them to the stores. Fickes points out that over a five- to seven-year period, as the kids grew up, so did the young adult department in her store. She was, in effect, training a whole new generation of book buyers, just as librarians hope to train children to become young adult and, ultimately, adult library users and supporters. This is one of a number of analogies that exist between independent bookstores and libraries—no accident, by the way, since many of the stores were started and are still staffed by former librarians who were forced out of the profession when libraries were first confronted with the economic imperative to reduce the numbers of their staffs in the seventies.

Another analogy is the practice of what librarians call "reader's advisory service" and the booksellers call "handselling," which simply means that the booksellers promote and recommend their own favorite titles to their customers; this explains the gratifying fact that at Children's Book World, the three best-selling titles in hardcover in 1994 were actually serious works of literature: *The Leaving*, by Budge Wilson (Philomel, 1992); *Shabanu*, by Suzanne Fisher Staples (Knopf, 1990); and *Shizuko's Daughter*, by Kyoko Mori (Holt, 1993); and that two of their overall best-selling authors were also serious novelists: Peter Dickinson and Robert Westall.

Word of mouth is also important to stimulating sales, according to Fickes, who adds that today's kids are still as determined as yesterday's not to be the last one on the block to read the new "hot" book, even if it means buying it in hardcover. Some things never change. Sheila Egoff, in her 1979 Arbuthnot Lecture, said that "peer pressure also undeniably plays a part in popularity. Not to have read Judy Blume seems as socially unacceptable as not being familiar with the latest 'in' television show." [18]

Sometimes, though, a hardcover sale is prompted by simple devotion to a favorite author, Gary Paulsen being one example Fickes cited to me.

Good news for both booksellers and publishers is the fact that, for the first time in fifteen years, the young adult population actually began growing in 1992 and its rate of increase is expected to outstrip that of the general population before it peaks at 30.8 million in the year 2010. [19] (Author Janet Bode pegged the 1993 total at 28 million in a speech to "Libraries 2000," the 1993 YALSA preconference.)

In addition to cultivating kids as consumers, Hearne has been struggling, with admittedly little success, to interest high school English teachers in young adult fiction and to persuade them to add young adult titles to their student reading lists, which, she observes, typically contain only classics and titles by such popular contemporary adult authors as John Grisham and Michael Crichton!

Such resistance to young adult literature by English teachers is nothing new. Sometimes it has been based on a misapprehension of what young adult literature is. YA novelist Sylvia Engdahl, for example, pointed out in 1975 that "the nature of junior books has also been radically altered, *a situation of which not all high school teachers are yet aware. Times have changed since publishers labeled insipid mysteries and school romances 'ages 13 up'; both old triviality and the old taboos are disappearing*" (emphasis added).[20]

This old prejudice continued to prevail, however. In 1977 Ken Donelson was ruefully admitting, "I did not come easily or early in my professional life to my enthusiasm for [young adult literature]. In fact I was a college graduate snob about literature."[21]

Donelson has long since become a convert, of course, but unless some way is found to convert enough others so that sales volume becomes sufficient to support the publication of increasingly sophisticated literature for young adults, there will be nothing left to convert anybody *to*.

Which brings us back to the vexing matter of overall sales volume. Both Fickes and Hearne are guardedly optimistic on that score, though they acknowledge that the troubled economy has hurt their industry,

formerly thought to be recession proof. Once numbering as many as 450 stores, independents are beginning
to close their doors all across the country. Children's
Book and Music Center, the oldest specialty children's
bookstore in Southern California (and one of the oldest
in the nation, for that matter) closed in 1993. Eeyore's
in New York City has also closed, and the New
York–based Books of Wonder closed its large Beverly
Hills, California, store in mid-1994.

More troubling to the independents than the
economy is the rise of the chains and superstores that
have cultivated the disquieting habit of moving into
neighborhoods where independents have created a
book-buying patronage and driving out, with their
volume and discounted prices, the established stores.

"I feel independent bookstores are canaries in the
coal mine, and I see a lot of canaries who are sick and
doing poorly these days," best-selling novelist Stephen
King asserted in an interview. "I'm concerned," he continued, "about the effect that price cutters are having
on American popular culture. And, God knows, American popular culture is debased enough without giving
too much economic power to mega-stores that basi-
cally want to reduce diversity to 25 fiction titles, 25
nonfiction titles and 100 record albums, most of which
are by the Beastie Boys."[22]

The five major chains—Barnes & Noble, Borders,
Books-A-Million, Media Play, and Crown—have now
opened 350 superstores (what King called "mega-
stores") throughout the country in the last four years,

"and all are either revolutionizing or bulldozing the book industry." [23]

One cultural commentator, Stephen Games, feels this development has "a special poignancy. The small generalist bookstore," he explains, "is a symbol of our open society. It represents independence and self-reliance. It is sustained by a liberal consensus that sees a moral value and not just a utilitarian value in the diversity of information and ideas." When he goes on to say "profit maximization prevents them from supporting books or areas of interest that may not sell well but expose readers to new ideas," [24] he inadvertently points out a troubling area of commonality between the rise of the bookstores and what I have taken to calling the "conglomeratization" of publishing.

For just as chain bookstores are gobbling up the retail marketplace, so are conglomerates—many of them multinationals—rapaciously gobbling up independent publishers.

As a result, virtually every large publisher in America now belongs to one of nine publishing "groups." (See "Conglomerates at a Glance" in the March 14, 1994, issue of *Publishers Weekly*, p. 38.)

This grouping together of formerly independent publishers has had many deleterious effects, but two appear particularly disturbing. Reporter Sarah Lyall has identified one of these: "An unfortunate side effect of the consolidation of the book business [is that] people with no background in book publishing are now in charge." [25]

The second is suggested by something Frank J.

Biondi said in a recent interview. Mr. Biondi, the president and chief executive officer of Viacom, which recently purchased Paramount Communications and, therefore, its publishing arm, Simon & Schuster, told *The New York Times*, "We're obviously not an eleemosynary institution and we want to make money." [26]

"It's a business, not a charity organization," Judith Regan, who is Rush Limbaugh and Howard Stern's editor, echoes. [27]

Most publishers would feel that money is not to be made by publishing innovative, creatively offbeat, venturesome, risk-taking, and otherwise nonmainstream works of serious literature—particularly if they are by first novelists trying to break into the marketplace. What gets published instead, according to an anonymous New York editor, "are products, they are phenomena, but that doesn't mean these things are books. Publishers today are manufacturers." [28]

The resolution of this problem may lie—as in the case of multicultural titles—with niche publishing. The Society of Children's Book Writers and Illustrators recently reported that "many small publishers are also reporting strong sales as they carve out profitable niches in the market." [29]

Another positive factor, according to author Sue Alexander, Chair of the SCBWI Board of Directors, is "the 'whole language movement' in schools, which [has] encouraged traditional publishing, the kinds of books that libraries and schools look to for enrichment." [30] (The whole language movement encourages the replacement of textbooks in the classroom by relevant fiction and nonfiction trade titles.)

What impact has all this had on the actual number of young adult books being published, though? Has it increased? Has it decreased? Has it remained constant? It's very difficult, actually, to find statistics to answer these questions, since the numbers of books the trade media report as being published and sold are usually aggregate figures; they lump young adult and children's books together into one generic "children's books" category. The closest one can come to confirming what is usually handwringingly described as a precipitous decline is to look at the number of titles being reviewed, a total that *has* been steadily declining for at least three years, although even here we must exercise caution, since some of the earlier figures may have been inflated by the inclusion of adult books cited as suitable for young adults or by round-up reviews of paperback series. At any rate, according to the *Bowker Annual*, a total of 2,186 young adult books were reviewed in 1990 by *Booklist* magazine (the only review medium whose statistics are regularly listed). In 1991 the total dropped dramatically, to 1,199; the downward spiral continued in 1992, when only 891 titles were reviewed, and again in 1993, when only 447 titles were reviewed.

Another decline that hardly needs corroboration, since it is now so widespread as to be a given, is the declining purchasing power of libraries and schools and the declining number of professionals specially trained to meet the needs of young adults and to select materials for the collections that serve them.

According to "Services and Resources for Young Adults in Public Libraries," a 1988 survey sponsored by the National Center for Education Statistics, fully 25 percent of public library patrons are young adults, but only 11 percent of America's libraries have young adult specialists on staff. At 67 percent of the remaining libraries, staff called "generalists" or "adult librarians" are pressed into service—usually unwillingly and probably without any special training or experience. Of the libraries responding to the survey, 84 percent have "some sort of collection specifically designated for young adults."[31] One wonders who selects the materials for these collections.

According to another survey, however—this one conducted in 1992 by the Young Adult Library Services Association of its members—"respondents . . . expressed frustration with the many barriers to [information] access that are directly related to funding—e.g., *outdated collections* [emphasis added], a substandard technology base, inadequate facilities, and a dearth of qualified staff. Many felt that during budget crises, YA funding was cut first. Others termed the loss of library funding 'a national epidemic.' "[32]

Thus far, we have heard from booksellers and librarians about the current condition of young adult literature. What about editors? To find out what they are thinking, I invited five industry leaders to share their views with participants in the 1994 YALSA preconference at Miami Beach.

The five were: Marc Aronson of Henry Holt; David Gale, Simon & Schuster; Richard Jackson, Orchard Books; Robert Warren, HarperCollins; and Linda Zuckerman, Browndeer Press/Harcourt, Brace. Two of these editors, Jackson and Zuckerman, have their own imprints.

Consensus on some points was predictably elusive; however, there *did* seem to be general agreement that young adult publishing is still alive, though hardly robust—somewhere between "Rest in peace" and Mark Twain's sardonic "The report of my death was an exaggeration!" (*New York Journal,* June 1, 1897).

Zuckerman was probably the least sanguine about the future of young adult literature, saying, frankly, "I think young adult literature is dying." She explained that—presumably because of market forces—there is only a limited amount of time and risk that publishers are willing to take with new authors. Accordingly, the young adult field will continue to narrow, focusing on series and the work of a handful of established authors—those hundred whose work appears on the 1994 "Best of the Best List." (Sue Alexander, already quoted, refers to this phenomenon as the emergence of a "star" system in publishing.)

There was, however, unanimous agreement among the Miami Beach five that the field is becoming more tightly focused in another way: Despite the fact that the annual Best Books for Young Adults list is aimed at the entire twelve-to-eighteen-year-old spectrum of adolescence, publishers *are*, indeed, now targeting the

twelve-to-fourteen-year-old end of the range. In fact,
as also previously reported, Jackson flatly stated that,
in publishing parlance, "young adult now stops at
fourteen." Accordingly, almost nothing is being published for the genre's traditional fifteen-to-eighteen-
year-old readership ("this strange no-person zone,"
Aronson dubbed it).

George Nicholson, while still at Bantam Doubleday Dell, had hoped to redress this imbalance by introducing a new imprint, to be called Vintage New
Fiction, which would feature protagonists between the
ages of eighteen and twenty-three. Unfortunately, he
left the company before he could put this into place.[33]

Gale, who worked for Nicholson at BDD, was
alone among the panelists in saying that he actively
searches for books for older teenagers, though he acknowledged that he must be careful of manuscripts
that contain too much sex or violence, since he might
lose the increasingly conservative school market with
such a title (and, as previously noted, he might also
lose any hope for chain bookstore sales). Gale also acknowledged that novels don't sell particularly well in
today's market; accordingly, fewer are being published,
and too many of those, he alleges, are "problem novels" of the sort that were being published twenty-five
years ago. As for books for older readers: They are, he
says, "nonexistent" in bookstores (i.e., chains and superstores).

Underscoring the increasing importance of paperback sales, several editors acknowledged that a major

factor in their decision to publish a book in hardcover is its demonstrated potential for paperback reprint sale. Warren rhetorically asked, "Do paperback sales drive the market? Yes."

Since this panel appeared at the same conference that was busily developing the "Top One Hundred Countdown" superlist, the editors were asked about what impact or influence the annual Best Books list has had on young adult literature.

Most agreed that inclusion on the list is enormously prestigious and helpful to an author's career—particularly to a beginning author—but has little immediate impact on sales, since, by the time a book appears on the list, it has already gone into paperback. Gale added ironically that inclusion is especially important to institutions, where the market is the softest.

Warren felt that more multicultural and cutting-edge titles need to be included, and Zuckerman echoed this, calling as well for more "Best" lists—for risk-taking titles, for "sleepers," for excellence in design, and the like.

Aronson had the last word on this subject when he called the Best Books list "the keeper of the flame during a time of transition."

The final overall word was from Warren, and happily, it was an optimistic one: Speaking for all editors and publishers, he pronounced, "We're not publishing a genre; we're publishing an author. And," echoing Charlotte Zolotow, "a good book will always, always be published."

A Generation at Risk

Ironically, all this discussion about the future viability of young adult literature comes at a time when America's young adults themselves are at risk—indeed, I think it is no overstatement to say that they are the most at-risk generation in our nation's history.

Let me explain why.

In 1992, while preparing to teach a Texas Woman's University graduate seminar on social change and the public library, I began clipping newspaper and magazine articles that, I felt, could be loosely described by the generic rubric "Youth at Risk." The clipping became a habit that continued long past the teaching experience and has now produced a collection large enough to fill an entire filing cabinet. The sheer number of the clippings is dismaying—hundreds of articles about every conceivable societal and personal problem plaguing, taxing, and threatening the development and, indeed, the very lives of today's adolescents.

To actually read these clippings and to begin to comprehend the kind of world they describe is not simply dismaying, it is horrifying. Even when you acknowledge that many of these reports are culled from the media and so a certain latitude must be allowed for—well, *exaggeration* in the interest of a good story, the world depicted is still one of almost unimaginable risk and terrible, stultifying fear—fear of poverty, fear of parental divorce or being homeless, fear of guns, drugs, and even death.

Such fears are well founded. Consider:

One in five young adults was living in poverty in 1992: That's 14.6 million, up 5 million since 1973. And each day 2,700 babies are born into poverty, almost insuring that the problem will be perpetuated.

As for divorce: Twenty percent of American adolescents now live in a single-parent home (30 percent if they're Latino and fully 50 percent if African-American).[34]

And some of them don't have a home at all. Each year as many as 1.3 million teenagers run away, not—like Toby Tyler—to join the circus, but instead to escape home lives that are often unendurably hellish.[35] Part of that private hell is manifested in the form of parental abuse. Some 1,700 kids are abused by their parents each day. In 1993 this totaled 3 million cases of child abuse, according to the National Committee for the Prevention of Child Abuse, a rate 50 percent higher than in 1985.[36]

Presuming they do stay home, here's a cheerful picture of the typical school day they might expect: At least 100,000 students now carry a gun to school each day; 160,000 skip classes for fear of physical harm—with good reason, since 40 are hurt or killed by firearms each day, while 6,250 teachers are threatened with bodily injury and 260 are actually physically assaulted.[37] Small wonder that 2,000 students not only skip but actually drop out of school daily.[38]

Violent death has become a daily part of too many lives. Between 1987 and 1991, juvenile arrests for *murder* increased by 85 percent, and 30 percent of those arrests involved not only a perpatrator but a victim under the age of eighteen.[39] In 1991 a staggering total of 2,702 fifteen-to-nineteen-year-olds were murdered— an average of one mortality every 3½ hours.[40]

"Criminals are getting younger, victims are getting younger," Wesley Scogan, a professor of political science and urban affairs at Northwestern University in Evanston, Illinois, says. "It's a combination of bravado, hopelessness, access to firepower and the allures of the drug market."[41] (Illicit drug use among adolescents increased significantly in 1992 and 1993, according to the U.S. Department of Health and Human Services, the increase being "driven by a dramatic rise in the use of marijuana and more of the stimulants and inhalants."[42] In 1994 the University of Michigan's Institute for Social Research reported that nearly half of all high school seniors have tried illicit drugs—an increase of 3.2 percent over 1993.)[43]

No wonder at least twenty states in 1994 moved to prosecute more violent juveniles as adults, "thereby allowing courts to impose longer sentences." They will have no shortage of cases to try. In addition to the homicide rate discussed above, cases of aggravated assault increased 95 percent and the violent crime rate for persons under eighteen increased 57 percent between 1983 and 1992.[44]

When violence becomes self-expression, every kind of interaction, even sexual, becomes tainted. Four or five teenagers have now experienced some form of sexual harrassment at school,[45] while forcible rape cases rose by 27 percent, to 5,400, in 1992.[46] The Justice Department reports that "girls younger than 18 are victims of more than half the rapes reported to police (though they constitute only 25 percent of the female population) and the younger the victim, the more likely the attacker is a relative or an acquaintance."[47]

These are all such desperate problems, it can come as no surprise that teenage suicide rates have climbed 200 percent in the last four decades.[48] One in ten teenagers tries suicide these days, and enough succeed to make it the third-leading killer of fifteen-to-twenty-four-year-olds in America.[49]

How can we solve problems of such magnitude? How can we even comprehend them? Well, if knowledge is power—or, as we would say today, "empowering"—there is no shortage of powerful nonfiction that describes the shape and scope of these problems. Many of the best of the nonfiction titles take us a step further by letting us hear, through interviews, the authentic voices of the young people themselves who are at risk or who live at the narrower margins of society. I think, for example, of books like *Voices from the Future: Our Children Tell Us about Violence in America* (Edited by Susan Goodwillie [Crown, 1993]); Susan Kuklin's *Speaking Out: Teenagers Take on Race, Sex & Identity* (Putnam, 1993); Judith Berck's *No Place to Be: Voices of Homeless Children* (Houghton Mifflin, 1992); and S. Beth Atkin's *Voices from the Fields* (Joy Street/Little, Brown, 1993).

But good as these books may be, we need more than

they can give us. We need more than information; we need . . . *wisdom*. And for that we must have fiction—*young adult* fiction, that is, which is written for and about adolescents and the mind-boggling problems that now plague and perplex them. Not a formula-driven fiction that begins and ends only with the problem, though, but a new kind of problem novel that is as real as headlines, yes; but enriched by the best means literature can offer—an expansive, fully realized setting; a memorably artful narrative voice; complex and fully realized characters; and unsparing honesty and candor in use of language and treatment of material—a young adult fiction, in short, that takes creative (and marketing) risks to present hard-edged issues of relevance so that it may offer its readers revelation and, ultimately, that elusive wisdom. More about such books and some examples in the next chapter.

NOTES

1. Epstein, Connie, "A Publisher's Perspective," *The Horn Book*, LXVI:237 (March/April 1990).
2. Nilsen, Alleen Pace, "That Was Then, This Is Now," *School Library Journal*, 40:30 (April 1994)
3. *Ibid.*, p. 30.
4. *Ibid.*, p. 32.
5. Hochschild, Adam, "War and Peace, Part II," *The Los Angeles Times Book Review*, August 7, 1994, p. 11.
6. Roan, Shari, "Next! When Abnormal Becomes Normal," *The Los Angeles Times*, September 6, 1994, p. E1.
7. Shales, Tom, "Talk Shows Are Now a Peephole on our Neighbors, Family and Friends," *The Los Angeles Times TV Times*, September 4, 1994, p. 10.

8. Kolbert, Elizabeth, "Television Gets Closer Look As a Factor in Real Violence," *The New York Times,* December 14, 1994, p. A13.

9. Gonzalez, David, "Catholic Bishops Grapple With a 'Culture of Violence,' " *The New York Times,* November 26, 1994, p. 9.

10. Nilsen, "That Was Then," p. 33.

11. Maltin, Leonard, *Leonard Maltin's Movie and Video Guide 1992.* New York: Signet, 1991, p. 420.

12. Gray, Paul, "Carnage: An Open Book," *Time,* 142:54 (August 2, 1993).

13. Tucker, Ken, "Nameless Fear Stalks the Middle-Class Teen-Ager," *The New York Times Book Review,* November 14, 1993, p. 27.

14. Gray, "Carnage," p. 54.

15. Tucker, "Nameless," p. 27.

16. Roback, Diane, "Hollywood and Horror," *Publishers Weekly,* 241:S14 (March 7, 1994).

17. Epstein, "Publisher's," p. 238.

18. Egoff, "Beyond," p. 196.

19. Kunz, Tom, "Word for Word/Teen Magazines," *The New York Times,* April 24, 1994, p. E7.

20. Engdahl, Sylvia, "Do Teenage Novels Fill a Need?" in *Writers on Writing for Young Adults,* edited by Patricia E. Feehan and Pamela Petrick Barron. Detroit Omnigraphics, 1991, p. 13.

21. Donelson, Kenneth L., "YA Literature Comes of Age," *Wilson Library Bulletin,* 52:241 (November 1977).

22. Streitfeld, David, "Pop Culture," *The Washington Post Book World,* November 13, 1994, p. 15.

23. Peyser, Marc, "Reading Frenzy," *Newsweek,* CXXIV:71–2 (November 14, 1994).

24. Games, Steven, "Superstores, Narrow Choices," *The Los Angeles Times,* October 16, 1994, p. M5.

25. Lyall, Sarah, "Publishing Chief Is Out at Viacom," *The New York Times,* June 15, 1994, p. C14.

26. ———. "Viacom Acts to Calm Fears over Dismissal of Snyder," *The New York Times,* June 16, 1994, p. C1.

27. Shapiro, Susan, "Going for the Lion's Share," *The New York Times Magazine,* July 17, 1994, p. 24.

28. *Ibid.,* p. 24.

29. *SCBWI Bulletin,* April/May 1994, p. 1.

30. Alexander, Sue, "Putting Changes in Context," *The Sampler,* Summer 1994, p. 3.

31. Chelton, Mary K., "The First National Survey of Services and Resources," *Journal of Youth Services in Libraries*, 2:226–7 (Spring 1989).
32. Latrobe, Kathy Howard, "Report on the Young Adult Library Services Association's Membership Survey," *Journal of Youth Services in Libraries*, 7:238 (Spring 1994).
33. Epstein, "Publisher's," p. 238.
34. Carnegie Corporation on Adolescent Development, *A Matter of Time*, abridged version. New York: Carnegie Corporation, 1994, p. 8.
35. Hull, John D., "Running Scared," *Time*, 144:94 (November 21, 1994).
36. Vogel, Jennifer, "Throw Away the Key," *The Utne Reader*, 64:56 (July/August 1994).
37. "Every School Day," *Time*, 141:23 (January 25, 1993).
38. Vogel, "Throw Away," p. 56.
39. Kantrowitz, Barbara, "Wild in the Streets," *Newsweek*, 122:43 (August 2, 1993).
40. *Ibid.*, p. 43
41. "Youth Crime, Workplace Violence Rising, Studies Say," *The Los Angeles Times*, July 25, 1994, p. A15.
42. Cimons, Marlene, and Ronald J. Ostrow, "Illicit Drug Use by Youths Shows Marked Increase," *The Los Angeles Times*, February 1, 1994, p. A1.
43. Ostrow, Ronald J., "Nearly 50% of 12th Graders Linked to Drug Use," *The Los Angeles Times*, December 13, 1994, p. A34.
44. Brownstein, Ronald, " '94 Candidates Agree on 1 Goal," *The Los Angeles Times*, October 10, 1994, p. A5.
45. Shogren, Elizabeth, "Survey Shows 4 in 5 Suffer Sex Harassment at School," *The Los Angeles Times*, June 2, 1993, p. A10.
46. "Youth Crime," p. A15.
47. "Report Cites Heavy Toll of Rapes on Young," *The New York Times*, June 23, 1994, p. A8.
48. Waters, Harry F., "Teenage Suicide: One Act Not to Follow," *Newsweek*, 123:49 (April 18, 1994).
49. *Ibid.*, p. 49.

CHAPTER SIX

A TIME FOR RELEVANCE—
AND REVELATION
Into the Heart of Darkness

"Relevance"—when applied to literature—is a word that has been in disfavor for some time now, smacking, as it does, of the too topical, the too pessimistic, the problem-driven, the dreary, the earnestly didactic, and the preachy.

Here's what Natalie Babbitt had to say about it: "Hope, joy, beauty, and most of all, humor, have been relegated to the wings of this new fiction, and the *Zeitgeist*, becomingly costumed as *relevance* [emphasis added], is attempting to carry the full weight of the performance. *Zeitgeist* by itself, it seems to me, makes a pretty thin show."[1]

Nevertheless, in view of the magnitude of the real-life (and real life-threatening) problems discussed in the last chapter, it is perhaps time to reintroduce it to our literary vocabulary, along with some consideration of that also out-of-favor phrase "problem novel."

In 1984 Ann Durell, then vice-president and publisher of children's books at E. P. Dutton, said, "There will always be a place for the problem novel because, as long as writers for young adults show kids a mirror into themselves, problem novels will come as the inevitable consequence."[2]

The challenge for today's writers is to find a way to create literature out of problems, to marry art and relevance. It is a challenge that all writers of compassion and conviction inevitably face whether they're writing for adolescents *or* adults. Timothy Foote, chair of the fiction committee for the 1994 National Book Awards, said of the 240 novels submitted for the judges' consideration, "too many of them came out of the news rather than from felt experience."[3]

Babbitt has expressed the same thought: "I have this deeply held conviction," she said in the 1989 Anne Carroll Moore Lecture, "that you can't write a decent book if the subject or theme is prescribed from the outside, by something beyond your experience and your own truths and passions."[4]

How do good writers deal with this bad problem? Consider the case of consummate professional Richard Peck, whose landmark novel *Remembering the Good Times* (Delacorte, 1985) was one that was prescribed from the outside—by the increase in teenage suicide and the author's compassionate, adult concern about it.

Reflecting on the genesis of this novel, Peck writes, "We lose a young person to suicide every ninety minutes, that we know of. I had a lot of painful learning to do to put me in this picture: research in the California and New York state-wide suicide-prevention programs, and among suicide-hotline volunteers."[5]

It was such research, for example, that drove his decision to make the protagonist a boy (he learned that three times as many boys as girls commit suicide), and more research led him to create a suburban setting and an environment "that presses the young to succeed without imposing the necessary skills and disciplines for success."

"But," Peck wisely adds, "he [Trav, the self-destructive character] couldn't be a personality printout or a list of clinical symptoms, and a novel has to be more than a warning."

To avoid this trap, Peck wrote a novel that not only warns about suicide but also celebrates the life-affirming qualities of a friendship among young people, Trav, Kate, and Buck.

He further enriches their story by dramatically introducing interrelated themes of change and violence and shows how these phenomena flourish in the suburban community where the friends live—an impersonal town so new that its developers are still carving it out of a pastoral landscape and uprooting the past in the process.

The past is memorably personified in the character of Kate's great-grandmother, Polly Prior—a character who has a *prior* life in other Peck books, not as an old woman but as one of his most popular heroines: thirteen-year-old Blossom Culp. Peck admits as much: "Of all the elderly characters in my novels, Polly Prior is the best I can do, and she is Blossom Culp grown old."[6]

Polly becomes part of the circle of friends that circumscribes the three teenagers. She is their link to the past not only because she lived it but because she owns an ancient pear orchard near the house that she shares with Kate and Kate's mother. The now-played-out orchard provides, as well, a symbol for the past and a refuge for Kate, who goes there when she's troubled.

Polly is blunt, outspoken, and shrewd, but not shrewd enough to see the trouble that lies ahead for Trav—no one is, not even insightful Kate. But Peck is very good at foreshadowing—for the reader—Trav's ultimate act of self-destruction, sprinkling the narrative with hints of what is to come. Buck reports these without fully comprehending their significance—until it's too late.

For example, when Kate and Buck visit Trav's new home and see his room for the first time, they are surprised that along with the expected trappings of the overachiever, it's filled with "a lot of things that he'd had as a younger kid, quite a lot younger."

"Trav saw me being surprised at this little nest from the past," Buck notes. "He shrugged."

"They [parents] tear up your roots. They get more and more successful, and they just expect you to walk away from everything" (p. 46).

Peck artfully shows that it is not only Trav but all

three of the friends who live in an environment that does only one thing well—violently tears up roots to make way for the kind of change that masquerades as progress.

The horse farm where Kate and Buck first meet, for example, is soon replaced by a shopping mall. The school administration abolishes the junior high system, replacing it with a middle school, so, as Kate points out, "instead of being big ninth-graders at Slocum JHS, we're going to be lowly freshmen in the high school."

"You're making this up," Buck protests, adding a telling comment: "I hate change" (p. 69).

Like it or not, however, change is a normal condition of being for adolescents. And thus, if the school system and the local landscape are changing, so is the landscape of the kids' bodies: Buck reports, "I was beginning to develop, at least physically, but nothing seemed to be the right size. Every morning I woke up, I had to check me out to see who was there" (p. 33).

Other things are changing less agreeably: As the environment becomes more impersonal, violence begins "oozing in around the edges" (p. 100). Buck's father loses his best friend when the man is killed in a senseless hold-up of the service station he owns, an event that foreshadows Buck's loss of *his* best friend through an equally senseless (though self-imposed) act of violence.

Violence and change are most artfully paired, however, when Polly decides to sell her pear orchard, thus destroying the last remaining link with the past, and Trav chooses the clearing in the soon-to-be-destroyed orchard as the place where he will destroy himself.

This may sound heavy-handed in my retelling of it, but Peck manages it so artfully that there is an aesthetic inevitability about it.

Headline-grabbing problem is skillfully transformed into complex theme and fleshed out with multidimensional, unforgettable characters. Moreover, the book is beautifully written, full of memorable lines and moments.

One example may suffice: Buck loses a fight with a local bully (one of the first instances of the violence that will become so thematically important). The bully wears "year-long overalls and a sweat shirt. It looked like the sleeves of it had been bitten off by wild beasts" (p. 54).

Despite these many strengths, there are flaws; in fact, one of them involves that bully just mentioned: When he begins threatening a vulnerable young female teacher, it is, improbably, Kate (who has earlier said she hates violence) who arranges a particularly violent punishment for the bully; the implied "lesson" is that one answers violence with violence, and surely this is not the message that Peck intended.

Another flaw involves voice: Sometimes it is too clearly Peck who is telling the story and not his first-person narrator, Buck. This is especially the case when ex-teacher Peck's anger at a school system, and a school *administration,* that demonstrate almost willful incompetence at meeting students' needs takes over the narrative voice. It is surely Peck, for example, and not Buck who says of the bully, "He'd been promoted. They [the school administrators] don't like to scar any of us with failure" (p. 77). It is also Peck, not Buck, who says, "Puberty scrambles your brains" (p. 27). And the classic example: "The administration is into group dynamics like seating configurations and room size. They learn these things at seminars" (p. 171).

Occasionally the teenage characters seem too old for their years (one must keep reminding oneself that they are only fourteen and fifteen), and sometimes they seem a bit *too* good to be true: Buck, for example, far from being the alienated adolescent, aspires to be just like his father when he grows up, and Kate agonizes over being ashamed of her mother.

One almost hates to raise such objections, since there is so much to admire about this fine and important book. It successfully dramatizes a vital issue and will, one hopes, inspire some much-needed discussion among adolescents and between them and caring adults. It is, arguably, the best book by a writer who, after all, was the second to be honored with the Margaret Edwards Award for the body of his enduring work. And it does what the most important works of fiction must do: It offers a personal vision; it is not a landscape, but what I might call an "idealscape," Peck's version of a world where a boy aspires to be like his father; where a girl struggles to understand her mother and involve her great-grandmother in her life; where elderly people are valued and, in return, serve as valuable purveyors of wisdom; and where teenagers *and* octogenarians can be friends and companions who care about each other.

In these aspects it is, I suspect, Peck's vision of paradise.

Robert Cormier's *We All Fall Down* (Delacorte, 1991), on the other hand, offers a vision of hell and, as clearly as any of his other books, demonstrates the truth of British critic John Rowe Townsend's assessment: "Robert Cormier is a powerful but deeply disturbing writer." [7]

Disturbing because the evil world he describes looks alarmingly like the real one we all inhabit and read about in our morning papers and see depicted daily on the TV news.

Cormier's book begins the way Peck's ends: with an act of senseless violence. In Cormier's case it is not a suicide but, instead, the trashing of a suburban house by four teenage boys and the near-trashing of a life: When fourteen-year-old Karen Jerome makes the mistake of arriving home unexpectedly and catches the vandals in action, they first try to rape her and then, when they fail at that, push her, in frustration, down the cellar stairs.

They escape; she winds up comatose in the intensive-care unit of the local hospital.

The leader of the self-appointed wrecking crew is a high-school senior named Harry Flowers, an upper-middle-class son of privilege whose father is a famous architect. Two of the other three, Randy and Marty, are Harry's "stooges." Their unmotivated, violent behavior makes no sense to reasonable readers, and most people would find equally incomprehensible their complete lack of remorse for what they have done. After the trashing and the assault on the fourteen-year-old girl, they adjourn to a nearby restaurant and argue—not about the immorality of what they have done, but about the relative merits of ketchup and mustard as condiments.

Luis J. Rodriguez wouldn't wonder, though: "Sociopathic behavior," he has written, "exists within the framework of a sociopathic society." [8]

Or a loveless one . . .

There is a fourth trasher, remember: He's a high-school junior named Buddy Walker, who lives in a "terrible house that was his home" (p. 26), "a house where nobody loved anybody else anymore" (p. 31). His parents are divorcing. His father, indifferent to his children (Buddy has a younger sister named Addy), has moved out (to live with his new girlfriend, perhaps), and Buddy's mother is left emotionally devastated, too numb to notice her children's needs.

The night after the father abandons his family, Buddy meets Harry and, with his encouragement, gets drunk for the first time in his life. In short order Buddy realizes he can find solace of sorts in a gin bottle. For him the alcohol is like a friendly piece of sandpaper, which he can use to smooth the rougher edges of reality, the "hate and the ache" (p. 26).

In fact, he's drunk when he joins the others in vandalizing the house, but he alone feels guilty.

Jane Jerome, the older sister of the girl who has

179

been assaulted, also feels guilty. Earlier that evening she and Karen had argued, "the usual stupid argument." It reached its emotional peak when Jane had shouted at her younger sister, "Will you please go have an accident?"

"What had happened to Karen was much worse than an accident, of course, worse than being struck by a car. It was savage, brutal, personal" (p. 5).

Cormier has said that *We All Fall Down* is "about an act of violence and its effect on two families"[9]—Jane's and Buddy's. And it does seem that Jane's—a traditional, nuclear family consisting of mother, father, and two daughters living the good life in suburbia—is an institution under siege. Buddy's is already beyond nuclear and is now just so much life-threatening fallout.

To dramatize the psychological effects of the act of violence, Cormier tells the story in the third person from Buddy's and Jane's respective points of view.

To their two he adds a third point of view, that of "the Avenger," a mysterious character who is obviously a psychopath, whose pathology offers counterpoint to the sociopathy of Harry and his stooges.

The Avenger is an unobserved witness of the trashing, and he makes it his business to avenge the house—and Jane, with whom he is secretly infatuated.

The subplot involving the Avenger adds an element of thriller to the novel and provides an opportunity for Cormier to strew a few red herrings in the reader's path with regard to the true identity of this character, who tells us only that he is eleven years old and that he has committed two murders previously—he has killed a sadistic school classmate and, subsequently, his retired police-officer grandfather, when the man threatened to uncover the truth about the first murder.

Cormier has said that he writes "cinematically," [10] and that technique is clearly evidenced in this book, which intercuts points of view and proceeds scene by scene, not chapter by chapter (in fact, there are no chapter breaks). This technique is well suited to building suspense, particularly as the reader becomes more involved with the Avenger and the inevitable speculation about who he is and how he will exact his revenge. In addition to building suspense, this character also provides a kind of psychic relief. Since he is clearly insane, his actions become more comprehensible and less disturbing than the equally violent—but morally incomprehensible—actions performed by the superficially "normal" kids.

The Avenger serves a third but more subtle purpose, too; he ultimately turns against Jane and, in a scene that in some ways is uncomfortably close to an R. L. Stine or Christopher Pike "moment," captures her and, having tied her up, threatens to kill her.

She does not allow herself to be victimized, though; "her anger buoyed her, gave her hope and confidence."

"*I am sixteen years old and I am not going to die this way,*" she thinks (p. 171).

This angry determination is made more powerful when coupled with her intelligence: "Think, she urged herself. Outthink him."

And ultimately she does, saving herself in the process.

Buddy, on the other hand, is clearly a victim. On a superficial level he is victimized by Harry, who even boasts to Jane, "I took advantage of his crappy life. That's why he got drunk and came with us to your house" (p. 190).

But on a deeper level, the reader understands that Buddy is a victim of his parents' disregard for his feelings in their decision to divorce. Essentially Buddy is a victim of child abuse, a casualty of his parents' emotional incapacity, a dysfunction that echoes that of Harry and his stooges.

Harry, though he is clearly intended to personify evil in the same way that Archie does in *The Chocolate War* (numerous references are made, for example, to his "evil" grin), is probably a victim, too: When the police apprehend him, his father quickly agrees to make restitution and Harry is placed on probation. "My father helped me out," he taunts Buddy. "My father loves me. He wrote the check and asked no questions" (103).

But love is more than writing a check and looking the other way; and though Harry doesn't, the reader implicitly understands how ironic that statement "he loves me" is intended to be.

Love is an important *explicit* element in this book too: In fact, as Cormier has said, "this new novel has what I think of as my first love story in it. And although I didn't anticipate it, the book has that element in the midst of all this violence. There's that sort of a tenderness to it, I think."[11]

Buddy becomes as obsessed with Jane as the Avenger does, following her to the mall where they meet, accidentally, and fall in love. For a time the relationship offers a kind of salvation to Buddy, but he ultimately falls victim to his own weakness: He is afraid to tell Jane that he has been one of the trashers, and when she finds out—in the worst possible circumstances, from the Avenger—the relationship is doomed.

One suspects that it would have been doomed anyway. For it dramatizes what Cormier described to interviewers Geraldine DeLuca and Roni Natov: "Once an author has established the people and the situations, there's an air of inevitability about it that can't be tampered with."[12]

In the case of Buddy and Jane, this inevitability leads, naturally, to the destruction of their relationship and to the loss of any hope of Buddy's redemption. In the haunting last scene of the book, Jane and Buddy meet, once again by accident, in the mall. Buddy is now a lost soul, drinking again and lying about it, lying about and denying the reality of his life: "Things are fine at home," he tells Jane. "I mean, my mother and father are definitely getting divorced but it's a friendly divorce. Addy is doing fine, and my mother's doing fine, too. . . . I don't drink anymore. I'm concentrating on my studies . . ." (p. 192).

" 'Good,' she said. *He was obviously lying.*

"She stepped on the escalator and slowly ascended,

not looking back, leaving him down below" (p. 193, emphasis added).

It is obviously no exaggeration to equate "down below" with Buddy's personal hell, and Jane's ascension with—not heaven, exactly, but the possibility of a happy future.

For her, at least, it is a cautiously optimistic ending. For Buddy . . . well, Buddy is fatally flawed, incapable of making the moral choice, and so he is destroyed.

This is a heavy burden for young adult fiction to bear.

What John Rowe Townsend has written of Cormier approaches this issue: "In Robert Cormier's novels," he states, "violence takes complex and alarming shapes. . . . It can be strongly argued that fiction for young people should not present an unduly rosy view of the world, but Cormier's novels seem to me to err the other way—to suggest that decency is a loser, that evil is great and will prevail. . . ." [13]

The point that needs to be made here is that Cormier's fiction is not necessarily *for* young people, in the sense, at least, that it is written specifically for them. Cormier has made the point repeatedly in interview after interview that he eschews such labels.

"I just write novels," he told one interviewer in 1983, "and I don't try to aim toward a 14-year-old boy or girl. And frankly I don't sit there saying, 'Will this upset them?' because I couldn't care less. When a writer has to worry that way about his audience, that's death to all creative impulses. And yet I know the kids are out there. I always had in my mind an intelligent reader who likes me and will forgive me my trespasses and errors and go along with me. And thank goodness, that intelligent person often turns out to be 14 years old."[14]

This sets him apart, I think, from a writer like Richard Peck, who *does* very clearly write for a young adult audience, an audience he has studied very carefully. To the point where he can even state, categorically, "Young people don't want to read about characters their age. They want to read about people who are two years older."[15]

That Cormier's work is published as young adult fiction has less to do with the audience for which it is written than with the age of the people who populate its pages. Cormier claims that *"The Catcher in the Rye* was a door-opener for me. It made me see that adolescence could be something very dramatic to write about. It is such a lacerating time. . . . Most of us carry the baggage of that adolescence with us all our lives. And I think that's why a lot of young adult novels jump over the borders of the genre and can be read by other people."[16]

Not a *lot* of young adult novels, actually—but Cormier's, certainly.

Questions of intended audience aside, what sets Cormier apart, what makes him such a significant writer, I think, is that all his work is informed by an overarching, personal vision; it is summarized by the very title of the book we have been discussing: "We all fall down."

Cormier explains the derivation of the phrase (and

hence the title) in a scene between Harry and Buddy. The two boys are watching a group of younger children playing ring around the rosy, all the while innocently chorusing, "Ashes, ashes, we all fall down."

"Stupid," Harry snorts, adding, "those little girls don't know what they're doing. . . . It's what kids sang back in the olden days when the Black Plague was killing millions of people" (p. 59).

The plague, thus, provides the symbolic underpinning for this book about the death—not of the body but of the spirit. The plague could also symbolize evil, which, to Cormier, is equally contagious, contaminating human existence and, if untreated, causing death.

Good and evil are *the* essential considerations of every Cormier novel. And while the author may acknowledge his debt to J. D. Salinger (and call writers like Hemingway and Thomas Wolfe his heroes), it is surely another "adult" writer, Grahame Greene, to whom he is most clearly indebted. As Greene was, so is Cormier a Roman Catholic whose beliefs, guilts, and questionings enrich all his themes and all his fictions. It's obviously manifested in *We All Fall Down*, where polarity after polarity visits the book's theme: good and evil; guilt and innocence; sins of omission and sins of commission; love as agent of redemption and hate as agent of damnation and engineer of violence, free will and determinism—on and on.

In this, Cormier also resembles Brian Moore, another important adult writer who owes a debt to Greene. When Moore won the 1994 Robert Kirsch Award (presented annually by *The Los Angeles Times*), an anonymous judge wrote, "Like Greene, Moore has written novels of the kind Greene called his 'entertainments'—serious thrillers which . . . have a marked psychological and moral interest" (Sound like *We All Fall Down,* too? I think so.) "though," the judge continues, "the bulk of his fiction, like Greene's, is concerned with the most profound and reverberating moral questions, such as the dilemmas of Catholic faith, of the uniquely isolated individual in a hostile society, of passionate but unrequited love. When I think of the problem of the serious writer in our time, who works in the shadow of mass catastrophes that threaten to overwhelm the imagination, I think of Moore and his ability to find a context and a scale for the individual life through which he can engage the great questions of politics, faith, and conscience, and I am grateful that he lives among us."[17]

As for me—I think of Cormier, and I am equally grateful that *he* lives among us too.

NOTES

1. Babbitt, "Between," p. 141.
2. Baldwin, "Writing for Young Adults," p. 18.
3. Baker, John F., "1994 National Book Awards," *Publishers Weekly,* 241:26 (November 21, 1994).
4. Babbitt, Natalie, "The Purpose of Literature: Who Cares?" *School Library Journal,* 36:151 (March 1990).
5. Peck, *Mall,* p. 98.

6. *Ibid.,* p. 79.

7. Townsend, *Written for Children,* p. 284.

8. Rodriguez, Luis J., "Rekindling the Warrior," *The Utne Reader,* 64:58 (July/August 1994).

9. Sutton, Roger, "Kind of a Funny Dictionary: An Interview with Robert Cormier," *School Library Journal,* 37:31 (June 1991).

10. DeLuca, Geraldine, and Roni Natov, "An Interview with Robert Cormier, *The Lion and the Unicorn,* 2:133 (Fall 1978).

11. Sutton, "Kind of," p. 31.

12. DeLuca, "Interview," p. 114.

13. Townsend, *Written for Children,* p. 283.

14. Graeber, Laurel, "Robert Cormier," *Publishers Weekly,* 224:98 (October 7, 1983).

15. Peck, *Mall,* p. 69.

16. Sutton, "Kind of," p. 31.

17. Miles, Jack, "The Epiphanies of Love and Loss," *The Los Angeles Times Book Review,* November 13, 1994, pp. A, G.

CHAPTER SEVEN

SEX
AND OTHER
SHIBBOLETHS

YA Comes of Age

It is possible, I think, to view the history of young adult literature as a series of inspired exercises in iconoclasm—of taboo busting, of shibboleth shattering: Cormier's lifting the veil on evil, Hinton's acknowledgment of class warfare in these supposedly egalitarian United States, Childress on heroin abuse, etc.

The one area of life that has been most stubbornly resistant to such taboo breaking is, surely, human sexuality. Nothing new in that. America was started by Puritans, after all, who viewed sexual expression as something to be denied and suppressed. And this attitude has been a hardy perennial ever since. *New York Times* television critic John J. O'Connor puts it a bit more acerbically: "It's hardly news," he says, "that

America is inhabited by large numbers of Puritanical hysterics." [1]

Hysterical or more reasoned, such Puritanism, God knows, has long flowered in the garden of young adult literature.

The great Margaret A. Edwards herself acknowledged this, writing in her 1969 book *The Fair Garden and the Swarm of Beasts*, "Many adults seem to think that if sex is not mentioned to adolescents, it will go away. On the contrary it is here to stay and teen-agers are avidly interested in it. There are excellent factual books on the market, but the best novels on the subject go beyond the facts to the emotional implications of love." [2]

She goes on to discuss eight exemplary novels*— all of them published for adults—and concludes, "All of these have something to say about love that cannot be learned from informational books. Too many adults wish to protect teen-agers when they should be stimulating them to read of life as it is lived."

Since the early 1980s, this reticence has assumed life-and-death proportions through the appearance of AIDS and its nearly incomprehensible corollary that love kills.

Before we talk about AIDS, however, we need to look at the cautious and halting evolution of young adult literature's attitude toward and treatment of sex.

The first important novel to deal with teenage sexuality was surely Henry Gregor Felsen's *Two and the*

---

* *Of Human Bondage, Wuthering Heights, The Cruel Sea, Love Is Eternal, Winter Wheat, Gone with the Wind, Bridge to the Sun,* and *Three Came Home.*

Town (Scribner's, 1952). Though simplistic by today's standards, it was at least fifteen years ahead of its time in its treatment of premarital sex, pregnancy, and forced marriage.

Consider: High school football star Buff gets dark-haired loner Elaine pregnant, and they are forced by Elaine's father to marry. When a baby ("little Buff") is born, big Buff enlists in the U.S. Marine Corps to escape this new burden. In the Corps he learns how to be a real man and take responsibility for his family. He returns home after a high-school football injury conveniently provides a *deus ex machina* for early separation from service and is now determined to be "happy with his wife and little Buff."

A possibility of a happy ending is held out to the reader, but in the meantime the two young characters have been thoroughly punished for their indiscretion by a censorious society, personified by their family and friends. Such "punishment" was, of course, a *de rigueur* staple of popular culture, particularly in the post–Hays Office world of motion pictures.

Despite its carefully cautionary element, Felsen's book was quite controversial in its day. Mrs. Edwards recalls that "the book came off the press in the fifties, a few weeks before the American Library Association met in New York City. There was to be a preconference on young adult work in the public library, and I was to sit on a panel where I expected the book to be questioned.

"Sure enough, [the book] came up for discussion and the panel seemed agreed it 'was not up to Felsen'

[I presume she means not up to his usual standards], which simply meant they thought it too hot to handle. I came to the book's defense saying we had no other book that dealt honestly with this problem . . . and asked what they would give to a young person who wanted a book on this subject. One of the true-blue ladies drew herself up and announced, 'I would give him [note the sex of the presumed reader] *The Scarlet Letter!*" [3]

Shades of the Puritans . . .

The Puritans didn't have a great deal to worry about for the next fifteen years, until 1967, in fact, when the next important milestone on the road to literature's sexual liberation appeared: Ann Head's *Mr. and Mrs. Bo Jo Jones* (Putnam). At that, there was no immediate cause for concern, because the book was first published in hardcover as an adult novel. However, within a year it "was offered to high school students through paperback teenage book clubs" [4] and quickly became a harbinger, along with *The Outsiders* and *The Contender*, of more realistic fiction to come. Its influence and enormous popularity are evidenced by the fact that it has appeared on two of the four retrospective best of the best lists.

Bo Jo is not dissimilar to *Two* in bare plot outline: Two teenagers, July and Bo Jo (July is the girl, Bo Jo is the boy), are swept away by passion, she becomes pregnant, and they elope.

This time, however, the couple's families, especially July's, attempt to break up the marriage. Her father

runs the local bank, while Bo's is a construction foreman. Parental interference is the least of their problems,
however. The two quarrel over money and friends and
their baby dies; they break up but in the end are reunited and go off to college together. In the context of
what has preceded it, the happy ending may be more
imposed than inevitable, but as a work of fiction, the
book is much more fully realized than *Two and the
Town* and is probably responsible for a host of imitators.
In fact, W. Keith Kraus reports that in 1970—only
three years later—"four of the five top books sold
through Xerox Educational Publications' teenage book
clubs were about sex and pregnancy."[5]

The same year that *Bo Jo* was published for adults,
Zoa Sherburne's *Too Bad about the Haines Girl* (Morrow)
was published for young adults. This time the teenage
girl who gets pregnant does not marry the father but
turns, instead, to her parents for help with her problem.

In 1966, a year before *Bo Jo*, Jeannette Eyerly's *A
Girl Like Me* (Lippincott) appeared. This time it's not
the protagonist who gets pregnant but a teenage friend,
Cass Carter, who brings shame to her family and is
sent off to a Dickensian home for unwed mothers. At
the twelfth hour the young father, the wealthy Brew-
ster Bailey Winfield III (yep, that's his name) appears,
volunteering to do the right thing at last, but Cass
nobly refuses, having decided to give the baby up for
adoption "by somebody who'll love him, even if it
turns out to be a girl—a girl like me."[6]

Abortion as an option in resolving a teenage

pregnancy was first dealt with in 1969 by Paul Zindel in his *My Darling, My Hamburger* (Harper). The indefatigable Jeannette Eyerly was not far behind. Her take on this topic, *Bonnie Jo, Go Home* (Lippincott), appeared in 1972 and presented, Norma Klein has noted, "such a negative, dark view of abortion that it would scare the wits out of almost anyone"[7] (not unlike her previous take on teenage pregnancy).

All these books had, for good or ill, one thing in common: All were primarily concerned not with the act but with the consequences.

Not so Judy Blume, whose *Forever* (Bradbury, 1975) is a celebration of the sexual act itself. As a result it has been one of the most sought-out (by kids) and most censored (by adults) of all the books about the "S" word.

Not only do Blume's protagonists, high school seniors Katherine and Michael, have sex, they (shudder) *enjoy* it, and the reader gets to watch the explicit action! ("This time Michael made it last much, much longer and I got so carried away I grabbed his backside with both hands, trying to push him deeper and deeper into me—and I spread my legs as far apart as I could—and I raised my hips off the bed—and I moved with him, again and again and again—and at last I came" [pp. 149–50].)

Whew!

Norma Klein, whose own novels offered a similar cinema verité take on teenage sexuality, notes that "*Forever* was the first—I hope not the last—book to show teenagers it was all right to have sexual feelings, to be unashamed of this very natural physical and emotional reality. It showed them that love, even when it doesn't last forever, is still an important part of growing up."[8]

The trouble, however, is that it's *not* love that is the part being written about here; it's sex, as a rite of passage, that Katherine—like her best friend, Erica—can't wait to experience and to have done with. As a result it too often seems that Blume has not written a novel but a scarcely dramatized sex manual to help them achieve that end.

Blume is careful, for example, to show Katherine (and the reader) how to employ the necessary protection to insure that she does not get pregnant. And to demonstrate what happens when you don't take precautions, she introduces a promiscuous friend for her protagonist: Sybil, who "has a genius I.Q. and has been laid by at least six different guys" (p. 9).

Of course, it will be Sybil who becomes pregnant. Just like Cass a decade earlier in *A Girl Like Me*, she chooses not to have an abortion but to carry the baby to term and then to give it up for adoption. Blume does underscore how much else has changed, however, by having Sybil announce, from her hospital bed, "I'm getting an IUD so I won't get pregnant again because I've no intention of giving up sex" (p. 179).

This only reinforces the notion that, in the worst tradition of the single problem novel, it is the *issue* of sex that drives the action—and motivates the characters—

not vice versa. The characters, in fact, are little more than cardboard conveniences, bodies—like Sybil's—that can be manipulated by the author to perform the obligatory acts.

Forever is not a novel, it is a tract—wonderfully well-intentioned, but a tract nevertheless.

Blume has the same good intentions that Katherine's grandmother does when she sends the girl "a whole bunch of pamphlets from Planned Parenthood on birth control, abortion, and venereal disease" (p. 128).

But unfortunately Blume's message is as blatantly telegraphed as that of the pamphlets. Consider that, a page later, Katherine reports, "That night I got into bed early and read all the pamphlets. When I'd finished, I thought, well, I can start a service in school, I know so much, which might not be a bad idea, considering there is a girl in my gym class who, until this year, never knew that intercourse was how you got pregnant, and she's already done it!"

To insure the availability of all the clinical information necessary to make the connection between cause and effect, Blume devotes an entire subsequent chapter to Katherine's visit to a Planned Parenthood clinic.

Readers will not have to make a similar visit, since Blume makes sure they know everything they might have learned from such a field trip—all about venereal disease, premature ejaculation, birth-control devices, periods, vaginal specula, etc., etc.

Aside from the overly clinical content and didactic

tone of the book, Blume, as author, makes some bad choices. For one, she chooses to have Michael fondly name his penis "Ralph." This has the unfortunate effect of sending an already embarrassed reader off into gales of uncontrollable giggles every time "Ralph's" name is mentioned—or whenever "he" puts in one of his frequent appearances.

Worse than that, though, is Blume's introduction of a boy named Artie whose role is to function as Erica's boyfriend. Artie is a brilliantly talented actor, but he is less—er, *talented* when attempting to perform the sex act. Finally a frustrated Erica tells Katherine, "When he took me home from the party and kissed me goodnight on the cheek I came right out and asked him, *Artie, are you queer?*" (p. 64).

Reasonably enough, Katherine asks, " 'What'd he say?' "He said, 'I don't know, but I'm trying to find out.' "

Erica, of course, decides that it is incumbent on her to help him find out, and when Artie continues to fail at his appointed function, he tries to hang himself. He fails at this, too, and his parents institutionalize him.

And that's the last we see of Artie.

I trust Blume did not intend it, but the message here seems to be that if you are gay (and other evidence suggests that Artie is) and thus are unable or unwilling to have sex with a willing girl, you are doomed either to kill yourself or to be declared insane and be institutionalized. Whether intended or not, this second alternative was not much more attractive than those being offered by the slender body of young adult books about homosexuality that had begun appearing in the early seventies—all of which seemed to decree that if you were gay, all you could look forward to was a life of despair or an untimely death, though usually in a car crash instead of by suicide. This point was equally true of adult books of the same era.

Last, Blume fails to make any convincing equation between sex and love, though to give due credit, she does try. Unfortunately, the effort is too often more of the didactic "tell 'em" variety than the more novelistic "show 'em" school.

Consider this conversation between Erica and Katherine from early in the book:

" 'I've been thinking,' Erica said, 'that it might not be a bad idea to get laid before college.'

" 'Just like that?'

" 'Well . . . I'd like to be attracted to him, naturally.'

" 'What about love?'

" 'You don't need love to have sex.'

" 'But it means more that way.'

" 'Oh, I don't know. They say the first time's never any good anyway.'

" 'Which is why you should at least love him,' I said.

" 'Maybe . . . but I'd really like to get it over with' "(p. 36).

Clearly Blume hopes to create a dramatic dialectic here between two opposing views of love. Unfortunately, we have already seen what effect Erica's view will have on Artie.

Katherine's more romantic notion would seem to present Blume's own point of view. As may be inferred from the above exchange, *Forever* is told in the first-person voice of the protagonist, Katherine, and since she is a reliable narrator, the reader is expected to identify with her.

As the book unfolds, she and Michael pledge their undying love, promising to love each other, well, *for-ever*—though even the dimmest reader will understand, fairly early on, that the title is intended ironically.

Of course, kids need to understand that even their most deeply felt passions may turn out to be transient. The sex act is quickly over and so, occasionally, may be the love that has accompanied it. Unfortunately, the device Blume chooses to dramatize this compromises the validity of her presumed theme that love is a necessary companion to sex: Against her wishes, Katherine is sent off to work at a summer camp as a tennis instructor while Michael goes off to another state to work for the summer.

Within a month Katherine has fallen head over heels for another camp counselor, an "older man" (he's a senior in college), and so much for (and so long to) her pledge of undying love to Michael.

Katherine may lamely say, on the final page of the book, "I wanted to tell him that I will never be sorry for loving him, that in a way I still do—that maybe I always will. I'll never regret one single thing we did together because what we had was very special" (p. 220).

But unfortunately her actions have not demonstrated this. Most readers will wonder if she ever loved Michael, since she so quickly, without any more motivation than meeting another boy, ends the relationship. (The death of her grandfather is offered as the catalyst for her decision to approach the other boy for the comfort of sex, although she is rejected: "He untangled himself from me and said, 'Not like this . . . not with death for an excuse' " [pp. 206–7]).

What Katherine tells the reader in justifying her actions seems to be not her but the author talking: "Maybe if we were ten years older it would have worked out differently. Maybe. I think it's just that I'm not ready for forever" (p. 220).

What *is* she ready for? At book's end, she arrives home (following this meditation) and receives a message from her sister; it's the last line of the book: "Theo called."

Theo is the new boyfriend, of course, though obviously not forever. . . .

As a reader, I might feel more kindly disposed to Katherine as a character if Blume had devoted more time and space to developing motivation for her actions. That she didn't validates what Robert Cormier, in a 1978 interview, pointed out about young adult literature in general: "To me a lot of young adult novels read—and I suppose this is an awful thing to say—but they read like outlines for novels. They're not fully developed."[9]

Too much of Blume's book is devoted to page after

page of nondramatic dialogue; we hear her characters talking endlessly but we don't see enough of their *doing*—beyond the sex act, that is—and we don't see enough of their world, either, to be able to evaluate the validity of their responses to it. I suspect Blume is aware of this and tries to explain it away by having Katherine say: "About school I have two things to say. One, senior year is a bore, except for activities and history, and two, everyone is just marking time until graduation and all the teachers know it.

"About my other friends, *which I also haven't mentioned,* I already know that after graduation we won't be seeing much of each other" (pp. 122–23, emphasis added).

I am reluctant to offer such relatively harsh criticism of Blume's book, because I agree with Norma Klein when she said, "I would like more, not less, explicit sex in books for teenagers."[10]

Not to include sex in books for young adults is to agree to a de facto conspiracy of silence, to imply to young readers that sex is so awful that we cannot even write about it. I applaud the courage of Judy Blume's candor, which shattered the conspiracy of silence, making it possible for the writers who came after her to deal more maturely with one of the most important parts of life—well, if not *of* life, then certainly *to* life, since we would have none of it without the act of sex. Though until Blume spoke out, most teenage readers might have been forgiven for continuing to believe that it was not sex but the stork that brought babies. . . .

I think *Forever* also made it possible for young

women to consider questions of choice—not about abortion, to which the word *choice* has now been inextricably linked, but about sex: They can choose—despite all the importuning and pressure of their partner—*not* to be physically intimate, a theme that informs Norma Fox Mazer's later novel *Up in Seth's Room* (Delacorte, 1979).

It is also thanks to Blume that later writers had the liberty of beginning the important work of writing about other, less savory aspects of sex—notably its perversion by the interjection of violence in the forms of rape and sexual abuse, even of incest.

A year after *Forever* was published, another important novel by Richard Peck appeared; this one, *Are You in the House Alone?* (Viking, 1976), was about rape and was written with the author's signature sense, sensitivity, and insight. The continuing viability of Peck's view of this persistent problem has been evidenced by his book's being singled out for special recognition when the author was presented the Margaret Edwards Award in 1990; it was also chosen for the 1994 Top One Hundred Countdown list.

One of the last taboos to fall in the sexual arena was not rape but the issue of incest. When I interviewed much-honored author Virginia Hamilton less than a decade ago and asked her if there was any subject that could not be addressed in literature for young adults, she hesitated only a moment before replying, "Incest, I suppose."

That is no longer the case. In fact, not one but

three excellent novels treating this issue were published in 1994: Francesca Lia Block's *The Hanged Man* (Harper); Cynthia Voigt's *When She Hollers* (Scholastic); and Jacqueline Woodson's *I Hadn't Meant to Tell You This* (Delacorte). (Two other novels dealing with the same issue were published in 1992 and 1993, respectively: Ruth White's *Weeping Willow* [Farrar] and Cynthia D. Grant's *Uncle Vampire* [Atheneum]. Both of these were named to the Best Books list the years of their publication.)

Although these three newer titles are quite different from one another in their treatment of the issue of sexual abuse, all have in common the art their gifted authors employed to transform what could have been a simple journalistic reporting of the facts of this excruciatingly painful problem into powerfully artful literature instead.

Woodson, for example, creates a beautifully realized small-town setting for a novel that is not only about incest but about racial prejudice, broken families, and the redeeming power of friendship, which transcends considerations of race and class. The story is told in the first-person voice of Marie, an affluent African-American girl who defies social convention, peer pressure, and parental opposition to befriend a poor, unkempt white girl, Lena Bright, who is a natural outsider in the suburban Ohio community of affluent blacks where they both live.

Their friendship is tested, however, when Lena reveals that she is being sexually abused by her father.

At first, Marie refuses to believe her friend: "I don't want to hear it, Lena. . . . You're probably lying. Nobody really does that kind of stuff. Not to their daughter."

" 'Yes, they do,' Lena said weakly. 'But it don't matter, right? 'Cause you can't do anything about it if it's your father' " (p. 55).

This terrible sense of helplessness is the true horror of the situation. According to U.S. Justice Department statistics, one in five rape victims under the age of twelve is raped by her father. [11] Robin Abcarian, a columnist for *The Los Angeles Times*, notes that the "overwhelming number of cases [of incest] involve fathers and daughters." And yet "it is still very rough going for children who make accusations of incest. Often, they are put into foster care, subjected to years of court battles and forced therapy, and may even wind up in the custody of the very parent they claimed abused them." [12]

Once Marie accepts the truth of what Lena has told her, she reflects on this same feeling of powerlessness: "We were helpless, Lena and me. It was like someone gave us our dumb lives and said, 'Sorry, this is the best we can do.' . . . How come this stupid world couldn't just let us go through life being little girls? Why did people have to come along and mess things up for us?" (p. 78).

Ultimately, all that Lena can do to escape her father's continuing abuse is to run away . . . and to keep running.

There is something *Marie* can do, though: She can

tell Lena's story. Some years later she wakes from a dream of her long-gone friend and writes, "This morning when I woke up from that dream, I knew I would tell it. It seemed like Lena was saying, '*It's okay now, Marie. Go ahead and tell it. Then maybe someday other girls like you and me can fly through this stupid world without being afraid.*

"So I should start at the beginning.

"And tell the world" (p. 13).

The power that "telling the world" affords to stop such abuse is the theme of Cynthia Voigt's novel *When She Hollers.* To underscore that theme, I think, the title is purposely incomplete, inviting the reader to finish it by adding a phrase: "When she hollers, *let her go.*"

In this case it is not the protagonist Tish's real parent but her adoptive father who is abusing her. But that makes the abuse no less soul destroying. In one of the most painful moments in this almost unbearably sad book, Tish shouts, "I SHOULDN'T BE ASHAMED NOT TO BE DEAD!" (p. 170).

The violence of the loveless act which is being performed on her is also underscored by Tish's decision to begin carrying a knife with her, what she calls her "survival knife." Violence, as always, breeds violence.

But, of course, it is ultimately her cutting words, not her knife, that will help her survive: When she finally finds the courage to tell her story to a lawyer (whose name, "Mr. Battle," also has symbolic weight), he says, "We have reason to hope."

And the author follows with this observation: "That was better news than Tish had heard for all of her life" (p. 171).

Tish does more than tell the attorney her story, however; she courageously determines to return to her "father's" home, to confront him.

And preparing to do this, she realizes that outside his domain "he didn't dare act the way he let himself act when he was in his own house" (p. 176). Because the truth has given her perspective, she now realizes how very small that space is compared with the whole great world outside its walls. She imagines how tiny that house is in comparison to the world. "Everything," she thinks, "except for that tiny little dot *wasn't* his" (p. 176).

This idea, as much as the truth she has spoken to the attorney earlier, has empowered her, and so "she wrapped her hand around that idea and held it out in front of her, like a knife" (p. 177).

Both Voigt's and Woodson's books are beautiful in their passion and in their righteous anger at the horrors the world visits on young women.

Francesca Lia Block's *The Hanged Man* is equally angry but beautiful, as well, in its language, its imagery, and its arresting ambiguities—in its *art*, in short.

Unlike the other two, Block's novel is told in the first-person voice of the victim herself, a young woman named Laurel, like the California canyon that soars above the mean streets of Hollywood and that provides the green-flowering, semirustic setting for Block's celebrated Weetzie Bat novels. This time, however, "the

sky is swollen and dirty" (p. 128) and the lush green-
ness is overripe and verging on decay, though Laurel
herself, refusing to eat and living on coffee and ciga-
rettes, is wasting away—trying to starve her emotions
as well as her physical body.

Part of the bleak darkness of Block's vision comes
from the black void at the heart of her character's life,
a space that—in a proper world—would be filled by
the light of love. But through the violence of his physical abuse the father, who dies of cancer as the book
begins, seems to have murdered his daughter's heart, to
have destroyed any opportunity for joy and fulfillment
to flower there. "I will be thin and pure," she thinks,
"like a glass cup. Empty. Pure as light" (p. 14).

He has also murdered her womanhood—she no
longer has her period—and has left her obsessed, as
her mother is obsessed with cleaning and purifying.
Both teeter on the brink of madness, a condition of being that blurs the line between dream and reality; the
mother, for example, sees white moths everywhere and
thinks they are the spirit of her dead husband.

This particular image invokes the spirit of Gabriel
García Márquez and the magical realism that enriches
the Weetzie Bat books, although Block told me in a recent interview that there is more of the authentic
fairy-tale ethos in this book than of magical realism—
the grim fairy tale, that is, full of darkness, danger, violence, and passion. There are echoes, too, of Angela
Carter's *The Bloody Chamber and Other Adult Tales*
(Harper, 1979) and its infusion of masculine abuse and

sexuality into the world of fairy tale. Consider that Laurel says, "I feel like Hansel and Gretel" (p. 13). Her mother calls herself a gypsy witch, and the daughter thinks of both her and the mother of a friend as being witches (the equation of the witch with womanhood, nature, and wildness is also an operative factor here, according to Block; note, too, that later in the book Laurel describes herself and her friend Claudia as "riding the tree like witches on brooms" [they're sitting astride the branch of a eucalyptus tree] [p. 101].) Laurel's bedroom is in a castlelike tower into which her lover climbs at night like the swain in Rapunzel, perhaps; a clown at Venice Beach paints Laurel's dreams on her face; Laurel makes love in the ruins of the magician Houdini's house; she divines the truth about people by equating them with characters from the magical tarot deck and sees herself as the Hanged Man, a figure that symbolizes renunciation and self-deprivation (she denies herself food, remember) and is suspended in illusion (p. 102).

Is the illusion magic or madness? At one point Laurel thinks, "All the magic we believe in is becoming madness. Delirium" (p. 116). This is surely a reason that Laurel's friend Claudia abuses drugs—to find her own sense-delighting delirium. But in the process she visits even more unreality on Laurel's life. What is ultimately real in Laurel's life? Is her lover Jack real or is he a dream of her dead father or is he the killer who is roaming the hills, breaking into houses, raping women, and cutting their throats? (There is an equation, by the way, between this killer and AIDS, which Laurel thinks of as "a nightmare demon coming in through bedroom windows" [p. 141].). Has her mother been driven mad by her silence about and, thus, tacit complicity in her husband's offense, or is it Laurel who is mad and misinterpreting her mother's actions? Is the recurring figure of a tiger a real animal, or is it the embodiment of Laurel's memory of her abuse that is clawing her to pieces?

Ultimately for Laurel, as for Voigt's Tish, confrontation is liberation: Laurel's lover Jack forces her to confront the truth of what her father has done to her. Or perhaps—another ambiguity—she has imagined this entire episode; we remember that earlier she has said to her friend Claudia, "I wish you could climb in my mind with me" (p. 109), and significantly, in this context, Jack's confrontation happens at night after *he* has climbed into her bedroom/mind; once Laurel has faced the truth, she finds that he has mysteriously gone, and she does not see him again thereafter, though she dreams of the tiger and discovers that it has Jack's eyes. In her dream she releases the tiger and watches it *limp* away—its power to hurt her has been vanquished.

Laurel's redemption derives from more than confrontation, however; it also stems from her new commitment to art. On the last page of the book she realizes, "I want to paint. I want to paint things that make people feel their pulse. . . . I will paint a Tarot deck—my own" (p. 137). She will create herself anew.

Again, Block told me that at the end of *The Hanged Man* "there is no warmth of love—only the redemption of art." She also reminded me that Laurel's father had been a gifted artist who gave up his art, and that act became his essential damnation—and that of his wife and ultimately of Laurel, too. After all, as Claudia has pointed out to Laurel, the Hanged Man is in hell, condemned to eat his own waste. Self-poisoning. More importantly, however, the character also symbolizes resurrection.

Only by purging herself of the decay that fills her—essentially the abusive acts that her father has performed on her—and embracing the transforming power of art is Laurel able to rise from hell and also to resurrect herself and her womanhood. Waking from her dream, she finds that she is bleeding, her period has been restored, "the way it's supposed to be" (p. 136).

These are complexly mature and subtle ideas and themes, and I think they are as much the reason as the powerfully dark material itself for the relatively cool critical reception this book has received—in contrast to Voigt's and Woodson's more accessible titles, which have garnered universal critical acclaim.

It's a pity, because *The Hanged Man* is actually a more mature work of literature than the other two in its imaginative and poetic use of symbol and image and in its artful employment of ambiguities to invite thought, speculation, rereading, and the rewards of new discovery. The book speaks not only to victims of incest but to an audience of all older young adults, people for whom too few books are being written and published.

Such considerations aside, all three of these books are of unquestionable thematic importance and should be read because they shed light on a problem that, for too long, has been shrouded in darkness. Since incest is not a subject its victims can easily talk about, too many of them must live in self-imposed isolation and, like Tish, in unbearable shame. Books can't solve the problem, but at least books can give human faces to its victims, to let real-life kids know that they are not alone, to show them a means of resolution, and, above all, to give them hope. Lena, Tish, and Laurel are survivors. They may not live happily ever after, but they are alive and they have each found the strength to stop the abuse, whether the perpetrator is a continuing presence in their daily lives or the memory of an act that lives, with equally debilitating force, in their minds.

Chris Crutcher, one of the best of the current crop of young adult authors and a practicing family therapist who works with child-abuse victims, expresses a similar thought from both professional perspectives. "I believe stories can help," he writes. "Stories can help teenagers look at their feelings, or come to emotional resolution, from a safe distance. If, as an author, I can make an emotional connection with my reader, I have already started him or her to heal. . . . *I am not alone* is powerful medicine." [13]

Silence = Death

Our society's lack of thoughtful, reasoned dialogue regarding sexuality has forced too many teenagers into painful isolation and, increasingly, into the possibility of an untimely death. For as Francesca Block wrote in *The Hanged Man*, "Sex can kill you" (p. 14).

She is referring, of course, to the sexually transmitted disease AIDS, which has captured newspaper headlines for a decade and a half but which has gone almost unacknowledged by young adult literature. Despite the fact that the disease has been rampant since 1981 and 400,000 Americans have contracted it and 250,000 have died from it through 1994, fewer than a dozen novels about it have been published for young readers, and most of those few seem to suggest that only your teacher can contract it—or your uncle (you know—the one who owns the antique store). (I have no personal animus against antique-store owners, only against authors who have chosen that profession as a "code" for homosexual.)

The outspoken Norma Klein once observed, "What is shameful in life is concealment and distortion and evasion, not truth." [14]

More recently Matt Fuller, an HIV-positive volunteer for the People with AIDS Coalition in New York, wrote, "The time for denial is past. Our reluctance to discuss sex, disease, and death has already permitted AIDS and those of us living with it to slip to the recesses of collective consciousness while everyone else

moves on to the next human tragedy of the week. I am
less concerned with making others feel comfortable
than I am with trying to save lives, including my
own." [15]

We may try to make teenagers comfortable by pretending that AIDS does not exist or that it can afflict
only adults or can be contracted only by receiving
tainted blood from transfusion while in the hospital.
But the reality is otherwise. AIDS *does* exist, and as of
December 1994, it has become the leading cause of
death among Americans between the ages of 25 and
44, according to the Centers for Disease Control and
Prevention. [16] It is contracted through the transfer of
body fluids—blood or semen—usually through having
unprotected sex or by sharing contaminated needles to
inject drugs (in the early days of the epidemic, it *was*
sometimes contracted through receiving contaminated
blood by transfusion, too, of course, but thanks to more
careful screening of blood supplies, that almost never
happens in this country today). Sadly, it can also be
transmitted by pregnant mothers to their children in
utero.

AIDS was first identified in 1981, but it was not
until 1986 that the first young adult novel about the
disease appeared: M. E. Kerr's *Night Kites* (Harper).
Ironically, almost a decade later, it remains one of the
best. The story is told in the first-person voice of seventeen-year-old Erick Rudd, whose twenty-seven-
year-old brother, Pete, has AIDS and has come home
to die. Pete is gay, and despite the fact that in those

early days of the plague approximately seventy-five percent of AIDS sufferers *were* homosexual, it was courageous and innovative of Kerr to acknowledge that in her fiction. In fact, in her Margaret Edwards Award speech, she admitted, "While I wrote this book, I thought I was committing a form of professional suicide . . . [but] it seemed to me that *not* to have a homosexual be the AIDS sufferer would be a way of saying I'll recognize the illness but not those who have it . . . a sort of don't ask/don't tell proposition, where the reader can know the nature of the plague without having to deal with those personalities who threaten the status quo."[17]

Fortunately she was wrong about the suicide—although she acknowledges that she is still admonished by high school principals not to discuss this book when visiting classes—but she got everything else wonderfully right, and *Night Kites* remains a model of the realistic novel, which, through sensitive treatment of subject and the creation of believable, sympathetic characters who behave believably, can deal with a serious social issue without being didactic. Kerr's courage—and that of her editor, Charlotte Zolotow—have made it possible for other authors to write about this horrible disease and all the good people it plagues—not only the disease victims themselves but their families, too. For as long as this disease exists—and who could have believed it would have lasted this long?—its impact on friends and families also needs to be addressed.

Two books published in 1994 do this with unsparing

honesty and integrity: Theresa Nelson's beautifully written and moving novel *Earthshine* (Orchard) explores the impact of the slow and painful death of twelve-year-old Slim's father, Mack, on the girl *and* on the father's lover, Larry, a sweet-tempered bear of a man. Nelson does a brilliant job of conveying the reality of these characters and of how they manage—and sometimes fail to manage—to deal with the inexorable dying of the man who is the central figure in both of their lives. At one point, overcome with anger and frustration, Slim heatedly tells Larry she wishes it was he who was sick and not her father. Larry's heartbreaking answer is, "I wish I were, too. Dear God, I wish I were, too" (p. 118). In the end they are reconciled, and though Slim admits she still wouldn't know what to call Larry if she had to fill out "another of those forms for school," she realizes that *"friend* is true, but it's not enough. He's my family, that's all I know" (p. 177).

Nelson pulls no punches in showing the reality of the debilitating effects of the disease on Mack's AIDS-wracked body, but she manages to lighten the book's bleakness with welcome moments of humor, most of them deriving from Mack himself, who is irresistibly funny and makes brave jokes even in the face of death. There is humor, too, and an engaging honesty in the first-person voice Nelson has created for Slim to tell the story. Although that voice sometimes sounds too mature for a twelve-year-old, it is so artfully done that the reader gladly suspends the occasional disbelief.

Like Pete in *Night Kites,* Slim's father, Mack, is gay,

but Nelson demonstrates that AIDS is blind to both sexual preference and to gender. Slim, at first against her will, becomes part of a support group of kids who are also living with PWAs (Persons With AIDS). There she meets eleven-year-old Isaiah, whose mother is infected with the disease and whose father has already died from it. Because the mother is pregnant, the reader learns that babies can be infected in utero. Mercifully this one isn't, but more and more babies are being born with the disease as the percentage of heterosexual AIDS infections continues to increase. It is now estimated that about 30 percent of those born to HIV-positive mothers end up infected themselves. [18]

Though at first comprising no more than 25 percent of AIDS cases, heterosexuals have now drawn even with or passed homosexuals in the number of cases reported (the rate of their infection increased by 130 percent in 1992–93 alone), and as a consequence increasing numbers of children are losing their mothers to the disease: By the year 2000 it is estimated that as many as 125,000 children will have suffered this loss. [19] (One of their stories is told in another 1994 novel: Barbara Ann Porte's *Something Terrible Happened* [Orchard].)

Mack dies at the end of Nelson's book; that is the sad inevitability of the incurable disease. But the birth of Isaiah's healthy baby sister leaves Slim—and the reader—with cause for hope.

Deborah Davis's first novel, *My Brother Has AIDS* (Atheneum, 1994) has little of the art of *Earthshine*, but it is an important contribution to the small body of AIDS fiction in its even more unsparing look at the effects of the disease on those infected. In this case it is the protagonist, thirteen-year-old Lacy's twenty-five-year-old brother Jack who, like Pete in *Night Kites*, is gay and comes home to die. There are other similarities between the two novels, especially the determination of Lacy's parents to keep their son's illness a secret; but the difference here is that the younger sibling, Lacy, bravely—and believably—elects to reveal the truth about her brother's illness in an oral report at school. In the end, Davis's novel is probably too much problem and too little novel, as plainspoken and information-driven as its title, but it has the integrity of truth and provides an excellent introduction to the reality of the disease and, more than *Earthshine*, to people's abiding fear and still too-frequent loathing of those who are infected, particularly when they happen to be gay, too. In a moving passage Lacy's father admits his adult shame that as a boy he had beaten up a schoolmate for no other reason than that—like Lacy's brother—the boy had been gay.

Whether gay or straight, an increasing number of the newly infected have one thing in common: They are young adults. Half of the 6.5 million people worldwide who have been infected with AIDS since 1981 contracted the disease when they were between fifteen and twenty-four. And "adolescents are the leading edge of the *next* wave of this epidemic," according to Dr. Karen Hein, director of the Montefiore Medical Center in New York City.[20]

In an even newer development, girls are now most frequently the victims. According to data presented at the 1993 International Conference on AIDS, in the general U.S. population there are two reports of new HIV infection for every new AIDS case; among teenagers there are ten; among boys the ratio is eight to one, but among girls it is twenty-two to one.[21]

Though they were written before these statistics became available, three books dramatize the plight of young women who have become infected—by unprotected sex in each case. They are:

What You Don't Know Can Kill You by Fran Arrick (Bantam, 1992); *Until Whatever*, by Martha Humphreys (Clarion, 1991); and *It Happened to Nancy*, ed. by Beatrice Sparks (Avon, 1994).

In appointing Patricia Fleming to the post of Director of AIDS Policy in November 1994, President Clinton specifically asked that she prepare a report on the problem of AIDS infection in teenagers. Nevertheless, Fleming acknowledged in an interview that "it would be especially difficult to gain support among lawmakers for prevention and education programs promoting safer-sex practices, particularly those targeting adolescents, one of the fastest growing populations of infected Americans."[22]

This is particularly disheartening since, according to *Newsweek* magazine, "AIDS experts see their best hope in prevention."[23] And, in fact, in June 1993 the National Commission on AIDS called for "greatly expanded prevention programs for the nation's youth, saying that educational efforts must directly address issues of sexuality and abstinence, condom use and availability."[24]

Further underscoring the importance of education is the fact that few of America's adolescents have met anyone with AIDS or seen a friend of their own age become infected, sicken, and die. As Charles Kaiser, a forty-three-year-old journalist who is writing a history of gay life in New York, has observed, "They haven't had the shock treatment my generation has had."[25]

If the federal government is not prepared to support such education, what about local schools? According to *Newsweek*, "School programs offering explicit information and free condoms meet fierce, often unyielding, opposition."

"Schools don't want to talk about sex," agrees Frances Kunreuther, Executive Director of the Hetrick-Martin Institute (formerly the Institute for the Protection of Lesbian and Gay Youth) in New York.[26] This was vividly demonstrated when the New York City School Board voted, in February 1993, not to renew the contract of its then chancellor, Joseph Fernandez, after he succeeded in making the city the first to distribute condoms in public schools. His successor, Ramon C. Cortines, obviously got the message: According to the *The New York Times* of March 23, 1994, "Prompted by the distribution of explicit literature on gay sex at a student conference, [Cortines] is reorganizing an AIDS clearinghouse for high school students and placing it more directly under his control" (p. B12).

A month earlier, across the continent, in Glendale,

California, the Unified School District canceled the performance of a play at Hoover High School because "it dealt with safe sex and condom use." Sponsored by Kaiser-Permanente, a huge California HMO and previously approved by the school's parent-teacher-student association, the play was deemed by school officials to be contradictory to the district's family-life policy, which promotes abstinence as the only option in sex education.[27]

When silence becomes official institutional policy, it is up to literature to speak out. Unfortunately, the body of literature about AIDS remains dismayingly small. In addition to the six titles listed above, the only other AIDS-related novels I can find are *Be Still My Heart*, by Patricia Hermes (Putnam, 1989) (a teacher's husband gets AIDS through a blood transfusion and paranoid parents clamor for her firing); *Rumors and Whispers*, by Marilyn Levy (Fawcett, 1990) (parents—who have already disowned their gay son—try to force their daughter to drop an art class when her gay teacher contracts AIDS); *Good-bye Tomorrow*, by Gloria Miklowitz (Delacorte, 1987) (a teenage [heterosexual] boy is infected by a blood transfusion); and *The Mayday Rampage*, by Clayton Bess (Lookout, 1993) (two teenagers, a boy and girl, print hard-hitting stories about AIDS in their student newspaper; the girl subsequently contracts the disease when she—rather improbably—has unprotected sex).

There are also three books for mid-range readers: *When Heroes Die*, by Penny Raife Durant (Atheneum,

1992) (a seventh-grade boy is devastated when a favorite uncle is revealed to be gay and contracts AIDS);
Real Heroes, by Marilyn Kaye (Harcourt, 1993) (an
eleven-year-old boy is devastated when a favorite
teacher is revealed to be gay and tests positive for HIV).
In the third, AIDS is not the primary focus but provides
a subplot for Morris Gleitzman's delightful and compassionate *Two Weeks with the Queen* (Putnam, 1989).

AIDS also plays a significant part in Ron Koertge's
wonderful young adult novel *The Arizona Kid* (Little,
Brown, 1988), which we will discuss later, and Barbara
Ann Porte's *Something Terrible Happened* (Orchard, 1994).

Albert Whitman has published a picture book for
grades K–3 titled *Losing Uncle Tim* (by Mary Kaye Jordan, illustrated by Judith Friedman, 1989) and, in 1994,
Be a Friend (edited by Lori S. Wiener), a nonfiction
collection of drawings and personal comments by
thirty-five kids with AIDS.

Ryan White: My Own Story (Dial), the as-told-
to–Ann M. Cunningham autobiography of the most
famous young person with AIDS, was published
posthumously in 1991.

One of the best of the nonfiction presentations of
the particulars of AIDS is *100 Questions and Answers
about AIDS*, by Michael Thomas Ford (New Discovery,
1992).

Even the best nonfiction, however, lacks the emotional power to involve the reader empathetically, to
command the heart, which is, after all, a more powerful persuader than the mind can hope to be.

And yet, over fifteen years into the plague, no more than ten young adult novels have appeared. And of that ten, only four feature adolescents with AIDS. Perhaps as perception catches up with the reality that AIDS is an enormous—and ever-growing—problem for the entire young adult population, more fiction will follow to give faces to the growing numbers of them who are becoming infected. One can only hope so. Their lives depend on it.

Still Trying to Get There

Another group of young adults who have gotten too little exposure in young adult fiction are America's 2 million gay and lesbian teenagers. (This figure is from a 1994 Louis Harris poll reported by *The New York Times*.[28])

Since the first gay-themed young adult novel appeared in 1969 (John Donovan's *I'll Get There: It Better Be Worth the Trip*), no more than sixty-seven novels with gay themes or characters have appeared—surely a shamefully small number to give faces to so many who are as much at risk as those exposed to AIDS: The killers here, however, are not only AIDS but also ignorance and fear, which manifest themselves as hatred of homosexuals and foster the kind of social opprobrium that leads to spiritual death and even suicide. One in ten teenagers now attempts suicide, and 30 percent of *those* do so because they cannot deal with being homosexual—a hugely disproportionate number, since probably no more than 6 to 7 percent of adolescents are gay (figuring 2 million out of 28 million).

Many others choose to drop out in less drastic ways: *The New York Times,* reporting the testimony of homosexual students before the Massachusetts legislature, noted, "What made the lobbying so compelling was the stories of the students' anguish. They told of being spat upon and called names, of being physically threatened and attacked, of feeling isolated and alone. Some had dropped out of school." [29]

In a national context, "some" become "many." Kevin Jennings, a gay Massachusetts teacher and editor of *Becoming Visible,* described as the first gay history book for secondary schools, claims that 28 percent of gay high school students are dropouts. Why? "Homophobia causes that," he tersely replies. [30]

Frances Kunreuther of the Hetrick-Martin Institute agrees. "There's still an enormous amount of pain that these kids have to go through. The fact is, gay-bashing is up." [31]

With so much fear, with so much ignorance, with so many lives at risk, why have there been so few gay books for young adults?

Well, I've already quoted M. E. Kerr on her concern that she was committing professional suicide when she wrote about a gay AIDS patient in 1986. Imagine the climate of concern seventeen years earlier, in 1969 when John Donovan's *I'll Get There: It Better Be Worth the Trip* was published by Harper & Row.

Michael Thomas Ford reports how Bill Morris,

now a HarperCollins vice president and a member of its library marketing staff, recalls the event: "Everyone was very frightened. In fact, we went to such great lengths to make it 'acceptable' to the general public that the book got more attention for the fuss we made than for anything that was in it." [32]

One understands the concern; for that time, the very inclusion of such a taboo subject was revolutionary, but read twenty-five years later, the book's treatment of the subject seems so circumspect that it is hard to imagine anyone taking offense. As previously noted, Davy, the thirteen-year-old protagonist, and his friend Altschuler kiss each other, and several days later, when Altschuler spends the night at Davy's apartment, the two boys do something together that Davy calls "it."

"That's how it happened," he reports the next morning (p. 152).

Subsequently Davy's beloved dog Fred is run over by a car, and inevitably the boy—and the empathetic reader—infer that this is a cause-and-effect punishment for doing the now obviously awful "it."

At the end of the book the boys talk about this "queer" business and agree "the important thing is not to do it again," and further, "if we made out with some girls, we wouldn't have to think about, you know, the other . . ." (p. 188).

Talk about the love that dare not speak its name!

These lines are quoted out of context, of course, but even in context it seems to me that they convey guilt and shame and the unrealistic expectation that all one has to do is to do "it" (oh, that word!) with a member of the opposite sex and, voilà!, one will be healed, whole, and heterosexual.

A reader would draw the same conclusion from the first lesbian novel, Rosa Guy's *Ruby* (Viking, 1976), for despite Ruby's passionate devotion to her friend Daphne and despite the fact that their friendship becomes a "love affair" (p. 172) and finds physical expression in "lovemaking" (p. 124), when Daphne capriciously decides to end the affair, Ruby is clearly prepared simply to forget her lesbian rite of passage and turn to an old boyfriend, Orlando, as a prospective new lover. And when we next encounter her in *Edith Jackson*, the third novel in Guy's trilogy, there is no suggestion that she is anything but the heterosexual girl we had first met in *The Friends*, the book that precedes *Ruby*.

At least Ruby doesn't die. In each of the four gay-themed books that precede it (*I'll Get There*; Isabelle Holland's *The Man Without a Face* [Lippincott, 1972]; *Trying Hard to Hear You*, by Sandra Scoppettone [Harper, 1974]; and Lynn Hall's 1977 *Sticks and Stones* [Follet]), either the gay character or someone (or, in the case of Fred, some*thing*) close to the gay character dies—usually in a car crash. Clearly one can be excused for thinking that early gay literature featured the worst drivers this side of my grandmother!

Scoppettone commented on this aspect in 1983: "The ending of *THTHY*, in which one of the homosexual boys dies, was misconstrued by many people.

Perhaps this was my fault; I should have made the reason for this clearer. My intention was to show that he died trying to be something he wasn't (heterosexual) [he has taken a girl out on a date] and *not* because he was a homosexual." [33]

I think Scoppettone's comment smacks of the wisdom of hindsight; the inescapable fact is that the boy does die—violently. But gay characters are *still* dying—violently—these twenty and more years later, most recently in Bette Greene's rather shrill novel *The Drowning of Stephan Jones* (Bantam, 1991), although the cause of death here—gay bashing—is at least more *au courant.*

Alas, when a book features gay characters who not only do *not* die but continue to be nourished and supported by a loving relationship, the author may be the one who gets "punished" by having her or his work censored. The most recent case in point is Nancy Garden and her 1982 lesbian novel *Annie on My Mind* (Farrar, Straus).

The current controversy surrounding this title began in October of 1993, when a copy of the book was burned by religious fundamentalists in front of the Kansas City, Missouri, school district headquarters.

Three months later, the book was removed from the nearby Olathe, Kansas, school libraries at the order of the district superintendent. As a result, Garden told me in a September 1994 interview, four district students and their parents, in concert with the American Civil Liberties Union, filed a lawsuit to reinstate the title.

While waiting for the case to come to trial in the fall of 1995, Garden visited Kansas City on a book-signing and speaking tour and reports "the reception was wonderful. One of the most gratifying things is that the kids have been great. They really get what is going on. They understand the First Amendment is being hacked away."

The court ultimately agreed. On November 29, 1995, U.S. District Judge Thomas Van Bebber ruled that the Olathe School District violated the First Amendment when it removed *Annie*, and ordered the book restored to the library shelves.

Though the judge's decision is clearly a victory for freedom of speech, to beleaguered gays it must seem that *any* mention of homosexuality is still perceived by would-be censors as advocacy. (Or "recruiting," the favorite buzzword of the moment for fundamentalists and political conservatives. An example: when the Los Angeles School Board declared June 1994 "Gay and Lesbian Pride Month," the Rev. Louis P. Sheldon, founder and chairman of the Traditional Values Coalition, wrote a letter to Los Angeles area pastors declaring, "We must protect our children and youth from this homosexual recruiting."[34]) For, in fact, the number of attempted censorings of gay-themed books is growing. According to Garden, the director of the American Library Association's Office for Intellectual Freedom, Judith Krug, states that the number of reported challenges to such books grew from 40 in 1991 to 64 in 1992, and to 111 in 1993.

Through June of 1994 a total of 56 reports had been received. [35]

In fact, according to the ALA, the topic of homosexuality was the leading cause of book challenges in 1993. And the single most censored book of 1993 was not an adult title or even a young adult book but a children's book, titled *Daddy's Roommate*. Written and illustrated by Michael Wilhoite and published by Alyson Publications in 1990, *Daddy's Roommate* is a sweet-spirited celebration of diverse families (two gay men share parenting duties) and of love, "the best kind of happiness," as the book simply but memorably puts it.

That such a gentle little book could inspire such passionate detractors—angry parents kept 230 students out of Juneau, Alaska, public schools on October 25, 1993, to protest its inclusion in school libraries—is distressing, as is the fact that the third-most-censored title of 1993 was a book with a similar sweet-spirited theme: *Heather Has Two Mommies*, by Lesléa Newman, illustrated by Diana Souza (Alyson, 1989).

Librarians who have courageously stood up against such censorship efforts are to be commended and encouraged, but the kids themselves are often the most stalwart supporters of such books against would-be censors. Ford reports, for example, that Kansas high school students protested the banning of *Annie* by checking thousands of books out of their school libraries to show how bare the shelves would be if all the titles that might be open to censorship were removed.

Meanwhile, student advisory board members at the Boulder, Colorado, Public Library have written a program called "Don't Read This" to protest censorship and have performed it on a number of campuses, despite the fact that at least four schools have canceled performances, giving the students a firsthand experience of being themselves censored. [36]

And Steve Case, one of the student plaintiffs in the *Annie* case, told the Associated Press "as an informed student, I cannot stand by and allow this flagrant act of censorship to remain unchecked." [37]

As Garden said, "They [students] really get what is going on."

What is going on in publishing, I think, is that there are still too few books on this subject—so few, as Ford points out, that when in 1994 a mainstream house, HarperCollins, published *Am I Blue? Coming Out from the Silence*, a collection of original short fiction about gay youths, "its appearance [was] still newsworthy 25 years after Donovan's book first broke through the 'gay barrier.' " [38]

Whether this paucity is attributable to publishers' fear of censorship, as Ford seems to believe, is a moot point. Garden, for one, thinks that it is equally a matter of editors not receiving enough publishable submissions—although this could be interpreted to mean that it is the authors themselves who are responsible for the lack through self-censoring of their own work.

Whatever the root cause, the result is the same: insufficient books. And more importantly, insufficient *good* books. For it is not enough simply to publish a book because it deals with gay themes or depicts gay characters. The books also need to be honest and candid in their treatment of the subject—unlike the titles that appeared in the seventies, which were discreet to the point of circumspection. But even more importantly, they also need to succeed as *literature*, and too few do. Most either are problem novels or they define their characters by their sexual preference alone.

Although there is almost no critical literature dealing with the body of gay-themed young adult fiction (in my research for this book I found no book-length studies of the subject and no more than five magazine articles), the little that exists is not nearly tough-minded enough, excusing literary deficiencies on the grounds that if there is so little available, anything must be better than nothing. One very valuable exception is Christine A. Jenkins's "Young Adult Novels with Gay/Lesbian Characters and Themes 1969–92: A Historical Reading of Content, Gender and Narrative Distance" (*Journal of Youth Services in Libraries*, 7: 43–55 [Fall 1993]).

In her thought-provoking and painstakingly thorough study, Jenkins makes the very interesting point that in "both the earlier and the more recent novels, most gay/lesbian people are white and middle-class," and no doubt accordingly, "most books take place within a white, middle-class community" (p. 45).

Demographic diversity is as lacking in these books as it was in the mainstream young adult fiction of the forties and fifties! If anyone doubts that homosexuality crosses all lines of race, economic condition, and geography, let him or her read *Two Teenagers in Twenty*, edited by Ann Heron (Alyson, 1994), in which more than forty young gays and lesbians from all across the country, from every walk and way of life, tell their own real-life stories.

In assessing the fictional accounts of gay lives, Jenkins makes another arresting observation: "One aspect of the novels' portrayals that has changed strikingly is the distance between the protagonist/narrator and the novels' gay/lesbian content" (p. 50). In other words, the narrator in the current crop of books tends to be heterosexual; the gay/lesbian character(s) is/are a close relative or friend.

Jenkins astutely points out that "this trend works both to broaden and to narrow the scope of gay/lesbian YA fiction" (p. 50).

Ford, describing the situation in 1994, puts it this way: "And although there have been more gay characters in YA books from mainstream publishers, their roles have been limited." [39]

That is the negative aspect of the phenomenon, perhaps. More positively, this phenomenon may suggest that we are approaching the point that Garden identified when she told Ford, "until we get to the point where gay characters just *are*, we won't be where we need to be." [40]

Two good examples I can think of from recent literature that illustrate that point are, first, Jacqueline Woodson's *The Dear One* (Delacorte, 1991), in which the best friends of the protagonist's mother are a couple who have a warm, loving, and supportive relationship, and—oh, yes—they happen to be lesbians. (Woodson's book is also one of the few that also depict gay people of color, by the way). Second is Paul Robert Walker's *The Method* (Harcourt, 1990), in which a friend of the protagonist's comes out to him and, happily, is not rejected. ("Are we still friends?" the gay friend asks. And the reassuring answer he receives is "You know we are.")

There have been several books, as well, that attempt to dramatize the point that it should make no difference whether a person is gay or not and accordingly maintain an ambiguous posture regarding the sexual identity of the character in question. Two examples of this are *Elliott and Win,* by Carolyn Meyer (Macmillan, 1986), and *Twelve Days in August,* by Liza Ketchum Murrow (Holiday, 1993).

While I applaud the good intentions represented here, I think that at this point in the evolution of gay-themed literature, it is still important that the sexual identity of a character be specified. One would hope that this would not be a Sturm und Drang matter and that, as in the Woodson book, the homosexuality of the characters would be simply acknowledged and accepted. Nevertheless there are still too few gay characters to be coy about the issue of "Are they or aren't they?"

Gay kids, like any others, need to see themselves represented in literature; they need positive role models too, just like any other kids.

And so regarding the increasing number of books employing what Jenkins calls "narrative distance," it is important and welcome, I think, that the homosexuality of the secondary character(s) *is* usually of central relevance to the life of the narrator. Often it involves a case of a young adult's having to come to terms with the coming out of a parent or other relative or of being put in the position of having to deal with the already established homosexuality of another relative.

Interestingly, too, these books are often among the most successful literary treatments of the subject. Among these I enthusiastically count Ron Koertge's *Arizona Kid*, in which sixteen-year-old Billy goes to spend a summer in Arizona with his uncle Wes, who is just like anybody else—only handsomer, smarter, funnier, more successful and, oh, by the way, gay. Then there is *Jack*, by A. M. Homes (Macmillan, 1989), in which the eponymous teenage protagonist must deal—with wit and believable anxiety—with his father's coming out.

The Arizona Kid and *Jack* also have in common their almost revolutionary—and long overdue—infusion of humor into their treatment of this subject.

One example speaks for itself: in *The Arizona Kid*, Billy asks Uncle Wes, " 'Will you not get mad at me if I ask you something else?'

" 'Who knows?'

" 'Do you kiss these guys?'

" 'Sometimes.'

" 'Yuk.'

" 'Do you kiss Cora Mae? [Uncle Wes asks]'

" 'Well, sure.'

" 'Yuk,' he said" (p. 151).

And most recently there is *Deliver Us from Evie*, by M. E. Kerr (Harper, 1994). Once again, the protagonist is not the gay character but, in this case, a fifteen-year-old boy named Parr Burrman, whose older sister, Evie, is lesbian, is outed (with Parr's complicity) but manages, courageously and at great personal cost, to survive and to maintain her loving relationship with her partner, Patsy.

As Hazel Rochman wrote in her enthusiastic *Booklist* review, "We've come a long way from the stories of homosexual love that end in disaster. No car crashes here. No sin. No victims. Evie has to leave home, and she misses the farm; but then she and Patsy get an apartment in New York City, and they fly to Paris and Rome. Patsy drives a fancy car, and it doesn't crash."[41]

As she did in *Night Kites*, Kerr has once again tackled a particularly thorny subject in *Evie*—not only the consideration of homosexuality but also one of its more awkward aspects: sexual stereotyping. It's hardly a secret that many heterosexual people have stereotypical images of how gay people look and behave—gay men have dyed blond hair, wear fluffy sweaters, and own poodles (which they dress up for "walkies"); lesbians look like cowboys and drive tractors. Well, Evie is a lesbian and she *does* look like a cowboy (or like the singer k. d. lang who, since she came out, has probably provided many people a ready-made image of how a

lesbian with style and panache looks) and she *does*
drive a tractor—and can repair it too.

M. E. Kerr wrote about the evolution of her own
personal attitudes toward such stereotyping in her
foreword to Roger Sutton's *Hearing Us Out: Voices from
the Gay and Lesbian Community* (Little, Brown, 1994):
"In our EEGO [East End Gay Organization] group
we talked, too, about how very early into our self-
acceptance, we could not yet tolerate those among us
who 'looked it.' I remember one of the first appearances of male and female homosexuals on an afternoon
TV talk show in the 1970s. We sat waiting for it to
begin, holding our breath and hoping the men wouldn't
be too nance, the women too butch. It took a while to
grasp the meaning of gay pride, and that it did not
mean looking and acting as straight as possible" (p. ix).

The marvel of *Deliver Us from Evie* is that Kerr has
made the same point without ever turning her artful
narrative into a didactic tract—or, even worse, *an old-
fashioned problem novel!*

Would her book—or Koertge's, or Homes's—have
been better, more immediate, more powerful, if the
protagonists had been gay and had told their own stories in their own first-person voices? Perhaps, although
a case could be made that narrative distance is necessary in cases like these for perspective. Another recent
novel with lesbian characters, Stacey Donovan's *Dive*
(Dutton, 1994), for example, shows how claustrophobic
a first-person treatment of emerging sexuality can be
(the protagonist, fifteen-year-old Virginia, falls in love

with Jane, a new girl at her school). (An interesting footnote is that Donovan is the niece of the late John Donovan, author of that first gay-themed book, *I'll Get There: It Better Be Worth the Trip*.)

A more practical consideration is that having a heterosexual narrator may increase the chances that straight kids will read the book. It's possible that having only gay, first-person narrators and having books in which homosexuality is always *the* central theme can ghettoize the issue and the characters, just as isolating gay kids in alternative schools or sponsoring gay-only proms can ghettoize *them*.

Routinely including gay characters in young adult books may ultimately have the same positive, cumulative effect that their increasing visibility on television promises. John J. O'Connor, a television critic for *The New York Times*, made this point recently: "A few years ago, gay groups were complaining, justifiably, that they were tired of seeing homosexuality portrayed on television as a problem. They wanted to see themselves integrated into ordinary situations. They wanted to be depicted as being as demographically diverse as heterosexuals."

Amazingly, given its inherent bottom-line-driven self-censorship, television may have come farther than young adult literature has toward achieving this. Ideally, what O'Connor goes on to write about television might soon be said, with equal force, of literature: "With ever more gay and lesbian images easing into television's universe, easy demonizing may be a thing of the past."[42]

In the meantime we can underscore the importance of the fact that all the books we have discussed at least show that gay people—teenagers and adults—can survive; that they can be happy and successful and lead lives of fulfillment in loving relationships.

What the best of them also demonstrates is captured, I think, by Francesca Lia Block's *Weetzie Bat* (Harper, 1989). But of course, this book demonstrates many things with marvelous art and insight; one is the technical matter of point of view: It is not told in the first-person voice of the gay character (Dirk), nor of the gay character's friend, the eponymous Weetzie Bat. Rather it is told from the omniscient point of view— from that of the author, if you will. And it is obvious to any reader that the author not only knows her characters intimately but that she loves and respects them deeply.

Accordingly, *Weetzie Bat* epitomizes what all of the most successful and satisfying books about homosexuality have in common: They deal with it not in terms of sex or even success but in terms of love—and acceptance and respect.

For me the single most moving moment in twenty-five years of gay-themed young adult literature is also the simplest. And it occurs in *Weetzie Bat,* when Weetzie's boyfriend, Dirk, comes out to her. Here's how it happens:

" 'What were you going to tell me?' Weetzie asked.

" 'I'm gay,' Dirk said.

" 'Who, what, when, where, how—well, not *how,*'

Weetzie said. 'It doesn't matter one bit, honey-honey,' she said, giving him a hug.

"Dirk took a swig of his drink. 'But you know I'll always love you the best and think you are a beautiful, sexy girl,' he said.

" 'Now we can Duck hunt together,' Weetzie said, taking his hand" (p. 9).

In Weetzie's wonderfully hip argot, "Duck hunt" means to search for your true love. And, *mirabile dictu,* both Weetzie and Dirk succeed. Weetzie finds her Secret Agent Lover Man and Dirk finds his—*Duck,* a boy his age who is actually named Duck.

And they all live—well, here's what Weetzie thinks at the book's conclusion as she looks at the circle of her loved ones surrounding her, "all of them lit up and golden like a wreath of lights: I don't know about happily ever after . . . but I know about happily, Weetzie Bat thought" (p. 88).

Nancy Garden knew about happily too. In the penultimate moment of her landmark novel *Annie on My Mind,* one of her characters utters an unforgettable line that, years later, still shines with illuminating truth: "Don't let ignorance win. Let love" (p. 232).

NOTES

1. O'Connor, John J., "Is the BBC Too Adult for Amercian Viewers?" *The New York Times,* December 29, 1994, p. B5.
2. Edwards, Margaret A., *The Fair Garden and the Swarm of Beasts: The Library and the Young Adult.* New York: Hawthorn, 1969, p. 72.

3. *Ibid.*, p. 82.
4. Kraus, W. Keith, "Cinderella in Trouble Still Dreaming and Losing," *School Library Journal*, 21:18 (January 1975).
5. *Ibid.*, p. 19.
6. *Ibid.*, p. 21.
7. Klein, Norma, "Thoughts on the Adolescent Novel," in Feehan and Barron, p. 24.
8. *Ibid.*, p. 23.
9. DeLuca, "An Interview," p. 135.
10. Klein, "Thoughts," p. 25.
11. "Report Cites Heavy Toll of Rapes on Young," *The New York Times*, June 23, 1994, p. A8.
12. Abcarian, Robin, "Incest: Sexual Politics or a Matter of Therapy and Recovery?" *The Los Angeles Times*, November 27, 1994, pp. E1, E6.
13. Crutcher, Chris, "Healing through Literature" in Donald R. Gallo, ed., *Authors' Insights*. Portsmouth, NH: Boynton/Cook Publishers, 1992, p. 39.
14. Klein, Norma, "Books to Help Kids Deal with Difficult Times" in Feehan and Barron, p. 231.
15. Fuller, Matt, "Marked Man," *The Advocate*, 669:6 (November 29, 1994).
16. Harrison, Eric, "AIDS Is No. 1 Killer of Young Americans," *The Los Angeles Times*, December 2, 1994, p. A8.
17. Kerr, M. E., "1993 Margaret A. Edwards Award Acceptance Speech," *Journal of Youth Services in Libraries*, 7:29–30 (Fall 1993).
18. Lee, Felicia R., "AIDS Toll on Elderly: Dying Grandchildren," *The New York Times*, November 21, 1994, p. A11.
19. *Ibid.*, p. A11.
20. Stolberg, Sheryl, "Girls Seen More at Risk as AIDS Hits Adolescents," *The Los Angeles Times*, June 6, 1993, p. A8.
21. *Ibid.*, p. A8.
22. Cimons, Marlene, "Clinton Stresses Priority, Names AIDS Policy Chief," *The Los Angeles Times*, November 11, 1994, p. A32.
23. Cowley, Geoffrey, "What If a Cure Is Far Off?" *Newsweek*, CXXI:70 (June 21, 1993).
24. Cimons, Marlene, "Aim AIDS Prevention at Youth," *The Los Angeles Times*, June 3, 1993, p. A9.
25. Gelman, David, "The Young and the Reckless," *Newsweek*, CXXI:60 (January 11, 1993).
26. *Ibid.*, p. 60.
27. "Safe Sex School Play Canceled," *Frontiers*, February 25, 1994, p. 25.

28. Roane, Kit R., "Two White Sport Coats, Two Pink Carnations," *The New York Times*, May 22, 1994, p. Y12.

29. Rimer, Sabra, "Rights for Gay Students in Public School," *The New York Times*, December 10, 1993, p. E2.

30. Merrett, James, "High School Confidential," *Frontiers*, May 20, 1994, p. 45.

31. Tsang, Daniel C., "State of the Young Gay," *Frontiers*, May 20, 1994, p. 39.

32. Ford, Michael Thomas, "Gay Books for Young Readers: When Caution Calls the Shots," *Publishers Weekly*, 241:24 (February 21, 1994).

33. Scoppettone, Sandra, "Some Thoughts on Censorship: An author symposium," in Feehan and Barron, p. 391.

34. Dunlap, David W., "Minister Stresses Anti-Gay Message," *The New York Times*, December 19, 1994, p. A8.

35. Garden, Nancy, "Lesbian and Gay Kids' Books under Fire," *Lambda Book Report*, 4:11 (November/December 1994).

36. *Ibid.*, p. 13.

37. "ACLU Sues for Return of Book Removed from School," *Frontiers*, April 8, 1994, p. 19.

38. Ford, "Gay Books," p. 24.

39. *Ibid.*, p. 27.

40. *Ibid.*, p. 27.

41. Rochman, Hazel, "A Fine Romance," *Booklist*, 91:125 (September 15, 1994).

42. O'Connor, John J., "In TV Entertainment, a Heightened Gay Presence" *The New York Times*, November 23, 1994, p. B6.

CHAPTER EIGHT

WHY WE READ, AND OTHER IMPONDERABLES

Young Adult Literature for Young Adults

As should be clear by now, young adult literature is as restlessly mutable as Odo, the shape-shifting character on *Star Trek: Deep Space Nine*, endlessly changing shape, form, mode, theme, and topic in response to changes in the culture (especially the popular culture), in reader interest, and in market demands and dictates.

The question remains, is it all worth it? In the final analysis, do we really need a literature for young adults? Well, *I* think so, but there are those who would disagree.

In a hard-hitting critical essay titled "Between Innocence and Maturity," Natalie Babbitt flatly declared, "Teenagers do not need a fiction of their own: they are quite ready to move into the world of adult fiction." [1]

Babbitt made her declaration in 1978. Four years later, *New York Times* film critic Vincent Canby made a similar point in an article about the new realism in films for adolescents. Regarding the movie version of S. E. Hinton's novel *Tex*, he wrote, "It's well-executed 'young adult' fiction, a term that carries self-criticism within it. Young adults should not have to be babied into reading decent prose. If they are of a certain intelligence, they should be able to read good stuff—Salinger, Vonnegut, Algren, Dickens, Dreiser, Zola, Hemingway and possibly even Joyce." [2] (Presumably this means young adult literature is bad stuff!)

These are both bold statements, but read in context they betray the fact that each is based on a misapprehension—that the fiction being provided for young adults is exclusively the kind of simplistic problem novel "dominated" by moral instruction of the "hellfire and brimstone" type (Babbitt) and further distinguished by an absence of hope and humor and written to order specifically for teenagers.

Babbitt was still wrestling with this issue eleven years later. In the 1989 Anne Carroll Moore Lecture, she responded to those who call for a literature that addresses "the current societal problems of America's children" by declaring, "It is an order that leads the writer away from the general to focus on the particular—to write directly to the present needs of one segment of the child population, to think specifically of the audience, to find motivation outside his or her own life. It is an order that could be filled far more effectively and efficiently by social workers and psychologists than by writers of fiction." [3]

Unfortunately, many of those who have written

about or taught literature over the course of the last four decades have unwittingly reinforced Babbitt's reservations by focusing less on the literature (except for its utilitarian potential as a bridge or a ladder) than on the developmental and psychological needs of the books' presumed audience, the teenagers themselves.

Hazel Rochman was quite right when she observed that "in our necessary emphasis on young adults' developmental needs, especially their need to separate from childhood, we have reduced the complex, mysterious literary experience to a therapeutic model."[4]

That word "model" invites inevitable thoughts of *formula*, too. And again, it seems to me that the endless focus that observers of young adult literature have put on mechanical listings of its "characteristics" invites authors to follow a similar recipe-model; something like this:

Take one teenage protagonist (fifteen or younger—usually younger); give her/him a story to tell in her/his first-person voice. Keep the number of other characters to a bare minimum and develop their identities sketchily (no room for complexity, you know). Limit the story's time span to a year or less. Fold in an undistinguished setting in a sentence or two and don't refer to it thereafter. Add a lot of pop culture references and brand names. Stir briskly—no time for reflection or introspection—using lots of dialogue and a simple, unadorned, straightforward, colloquial style. Keep it short—no more than 200 pages; kids have short attention spans, you know. Hang the plot on a problem that can—after lots of hints of impending doom—be resolved satisfactorily by the protagonist without adult interference. The experience will change the protagonist forever—and for the better, please. Because downbeat endings are definitely not welcome. Cook until half-baked.

The insidious effect of stressing such "characteristics" is to retard innovation and originality, to quash creativity, and to discourage the writing and publication of anything that does not fit into these molds. Worse, it is based on a lack of respect for the innate abilities of adolescent readers. This focus on defining characteristics has an equally discouraging effect on the criticism of such so-called "literature."

Hear John Rowe Townsend: In his Arbuthnot Lecture he said, "Once establish a formula and you open the door to bad and pedantic criticism by people who rely on rules instead of perceptions." [5]

Recognizing this, British novelist and critic Aidan Chambers in a 1978 essay bemoaned the lack of what he called "a critical apparatus" for the explication and serious evaluation, according to literary principles, of young adult literature. [6]

There are a number of reasons such an apparatus has not been developed. One is that, for many years, there was no perceived need for it. Margaret Edwards, writing in 1969, said, "Fiction written especially for the teen-ager does not need to be judged by the standards set up for adult novels." [7]

Mrs. Edwards doesn't explain why, but I suspect her reason could be found in Patty Campbell's later explanation of why there is a body of critical literature about children's literature but none about young adult literature: "The juvenile reviewer is interested in the inherent value of a particular book as an enduring work of art. The YA reviewer must instead focus on the book's inherent value for the teenage reader at this very moment in time."[8]

The focus, thus, is on its timely utility, not its enduring art. And so it has always been here in the U.S. Imagine my pleasant surprise, therefore, to find that phrase "critical apparatus" employed by an American critic ten years before Chambers used it—pleasant until I read the purpose proposed for it: "But the need, *in the context of the curriculum*, is for a useful and comprehensive critical apparatus which will allow teachers and librarians to do the job they are uniquely qualified to do: judge the merits of individual books which might be *useful* in the classroom and in the school library."[9]

The fundamental problem with the utilitarian approach is that it demands too little either of the body of literature or of the critic, who, in my opinion, needs to be a kind of literary Luddite, tearing down the mechanistic view of literature and celebrating, instead, literature as art—not for its own sake but for the sake of addressing, with aesthetic relevance, the real lives of its audience.

In addition to his later call for a critical apparatus, Chambers (not Dunning, note) also admitted that while he hopes, à la Babbitt, that young adult readers will reach into "the mainstream of literature" as soon as possible, he continues to believe "that most people will reach into it more vigorously, more willingly, and with deeper understanding of the pleasures it offers if they have encountered on the way a literature which is *for* them . . . and which is written and published with as much dedication and skill as the best of the mainstream work." [10]

This attitude dignifies not only the literature but also its readership, which is prepared to bring skill and dedication to its apprehension and appreciation of the work.

While Babbitt remains unconvinced of the need for a separate literature for young adults, she at least respects the audience for it, rather grudgingly advising those who insist upon writing YA fiction to "accept the fact they are in reality writing for adults—very young adults no doubt but intelligent, critical, skeptical, and very quick to spot a phony." [11]

I wouldn't disagree with that. In fact I've already pointed out that some of the most enduring young adult novels—*The Catcher in the Rye, The Chocolate War, The Moves Make the Man,* and *Weetzie Bat* among them—were actually written as *adult* novels. Or perhaps it is better to say they were written without particular reference to *any* audience but, instead, in a way that satisfied the artistic needs of the story. Cormier, at least, continues to ignore any consideration of audience when he writes. Block—in her originality—and Brooks—in his intelligence—also refuse to write according to prescription, although Brooks admits that writers, himself included, "find ourselves tempted toward the most pernicious of deeds: to make it easy. We are so afraid that children will be put off reading by books containing plot twists or vocabulary or emotional resonances that are 'beyond' or 'above' them; we are so afraid that the quiet act of piecing together letters and words and sentences and paragraphs will be boring . . . that we interpose ourselves between them and the best words, sentences, ideas. We need to recognize that what we value most in reading is, essentially, its difficulty. It challenges the imagination to go beyond the immediate and familiar, to create something new. This means work. Good work, but work nonetheless. Why, then, do we so often try to protect our kids from the challenges of such difficulty?" [12]

The answer is, as I have suggested, that we too often fail to respect them and their abilities. If, as author Chris Lynch has said, "YA is looked at as the B-team of literature," [13] that is surely because young adults themselves are considered the B-team of society—the bargain basement of age groups: discounted, misunderstood, ignored, and patronized. We conspire with those who patronize, I think, when we routinely discount kids' intelligence and capacities, accepting the specious but popular "wisdom" that a generation raised on MTV, thirty-minute television series, and video games must have the patience and attention span of a hummingbird that has just drunk twelve cups of coffee. In time, that becomes a self-fulfilling prophecy, and we begin calling for an MTV literature, too—stripped down, souped up, oversimplified, discontinuous, robbed of substance and complexity, and above all short, short, short! And when a writer dares to create a complex work of art that requires close reading or, God forbid, rereading—a book, for example, like Bruce Brooks's *What Hearts* (Harper, 1992)—it is criticized for its "highly contemplative style" that lacks "the immediacy necessary to grab all but the brightest readers."[14]

The result is the current rush to dumb down literature.

"It's not something people want to talk about, the dumbing down of literature," Mary Warner Marien, a fine-arts professor at Syracuse University told *The Los Angeles Times* recently. "You create intolerance for difficult language and for difficulty itself."[15]

This dumbing-down inevitably leads to the kind of gratuitous but now-routine sniping that otherwise distinguished adult critics like Doris Grumbach indulge in. Writing recently in *The New York Times Book Review*, Grumbach snippily dismissed an adult biography by saying it "comes very close to the stripped-down, simplistic style of a young-adult book."[16]

If we continue to treat teenage books "as beyond serious interest, as a bastard and unwanted hybrid," can we wonder that "those who are equipped with the training, skills, and knowledge to build the critical approaches that might help" are frightened off, not wanting "to be thought academically retarded"?[17]

This is not to say that a measure of literature's quality is how much it makes the reader sweat, but it is to invite some consideration of the *purpose* of literature—if, indeed, it has one—as well as the reasons for reading it.

Purposeful Literature, or Books as Tool Kit

The most frequently cited purpose of young adult literature, as I've already pointed out, is to serve as a bridge from children's to adult literature.

"Teen novels," Edwards declared in 1954, "are not ends in themselves but are intended as tools in the development of the reader." [18]

Or as she puts it elsewhere, "The teen-age novel served the purpose of helping teens make the transition to adult reading."

Forty years later Hazel Rochman—one of our finest contemporary critics—wrote of "some wonderful contemporary books that have the power to stimulate and delight and *to serve as a bridge* [emphasis added] to the best adult literature." [19]

Aidan Chambers takes this point a necessary step further: "I came to see that teenage literature was not simply about bridging . . . it could do what any literature that is whole does: grow to satisfy writers and readers in multifarious ways, responding to its own history, to other arts, and to the needs of its own time." [20]

I interpret "the needs of its own time" to imply the provision of contemporaneity and relevance to its treatment of real-life issues and challenges. As for writers: Their challenge, of course, is to do this *artfully* so that young adult literature, like any real literature, can provide "enrichment, both in the sense of giving pleasure and in the sense of broadening experience and developing taste." [21]

In terms of broadening experience, literature must

provide exposure to mainstream *and alternative* social and personal values—to offer implicit models for a code of conduct, if you will, from which young readers can select strategies for how to live a moral life. Or as Baskin, Carter, and Harris put it, literature "trains the reader in the conventions of meaning peculiar to the society, giving the members of the group a common conceptual framework." [22]

Such training was formerly offered by centering institutions like the church, the family, and the school, but as these have lost their moral force and suasion, it falls increasingly to literature to provide such models by creating lives that readers might wish to replicate—or avoid, as the case may be.

In *The Fair Garden and the Swarm of Beasts*, Margaret A. Edwards adds another aspect, saying young adult books' "most important contribution is to supplement [young peoples'] experience, to intensify their lives." [23]

Michael Angelotti would later call this the "therapeutic function" of young adult literature; i.e., "helping kids discover the universality of adolescent experiences through vicarious reading experiences which offer alternatives to their lives and deepen their understanding of themselves and of the world." [24]

Natalie Babbitt, with whom we began this chapter, offers another view: "Maybe, after all," she says, "there is one single purpose for literature—one foremost purpose, anyway. Maybe the giving of pleasure is the purpose. I find I could care about that. The purpose of literature is to give pleasure to the reader." [25]

But *not*, I think, the whole purpose.

Three Reasons for Reading

In his *Notes Towards the Definition of Culture*, T. S. Eliot offers three "permanent" reasons for reading: 1. the acquisition of wisdom, 2. the enjoyment of art, 3. the pleasure of entertainment. [26]

John Rowe Townsend stresses the aspect of enjoyment: "I will say that what is offered by literature as such is, above all, enjoyment: enjoyment not only in the shallow sense of easy pleasure but enjoyment of a profounder kind: enjoyment of the shaping by art of the raw material of life and enjoyment, too, of the skill with which that shaping is performed; enjoyment in the stretching of one's imagination, the deepening of one's experience, and the heightening of one's awareness; an enjoyment which may be intense even if the material of the literary work is sad or painful." [27]

Townsend is writing about books for young readers, of course, but Eliot makes no distinction between them and books for adults. Nor would I. To me, all three of Eliot's reasons should be perfectly viable permanent reasons for the reading of young adult literature. They can also serve as a viable shorthand and de facto critical apparatus for evaluating young adult books: i.e., do they offer wisdom—or knowledge, at least, which is the beginning of wisdom; are they artfully written; are they successful in aesthetic terms; and are they entertaining; do they amuse; heck, are they just fun to read? We sometimes get so concerned with the nutritional value of literature that we forget it should taste good, too. And while I spent a lot of time and energy in an earlier chapter conjuring up sociological, psychological, and cultural reasons for the popularity of series/genre fiction, the most enduring one may be the simplest: Kids find them fun to read.

Few works of genre fiction provide much in the way of the enjoyment of art, however, since their focus is story and not style. Fewer still offer enough substance for the acquisition of wisdom. But unfortunately, this could be said of too much of young adult literature in general, the principal reason being, I suspect, that too little has been demanded of it and of those for whom it is written.

In 1969 Edwards wrote, "Style that distinguishes a book as literature is very rare. Though it is to be cherished when found, it is not essential. [!] ... It is far more important to awaken in young people a social consciousness than to insist that they appreciate style."[28]

Whether you agree that style is unessential, one reason for its rarity in young adult literature is the conventional use of the first-person adolescent voice as narrator. For this device encourages the colloquial, the declarative, the conversational, and *dis*courages adventurous diction or syntax, imagery, figurative language, rhythmic or aesthetic expression. Reader empathy seems to demand the sacrifice of literary style.

Without style, what is left for the critic to address? Structure, perhaps, but here again convention demands the use of a simple, straightforward, linear form: The reader starts at point A—the beginning—and, without looking backward or straying from the straight and narrow plot path, moves directly to point B and then on to C, D, and however much farther the author thinks his reader's patience and endurance will take him—not *very* far, typically. One exception to this convention is the novel that is told from the perspective of the still-teenage narrator looking back at some life-changing incident or period that happened in the past—but seldom more than one or two years earlier (a good example is Richard Peck's *Remembering the Good Times*).

As for substance, Katha Pollitt has complained of the current view of literature as "medicine" (Angelotti, again, calls this the "therapeutic function" of literature).

Pollitt explains by paraphrasing those she criticizes: "The chief end of reading is to produce a desirable kind of person and a desirable kind of society."[29]

No wonder that Townsend has noted, "It appears to be widely believed that literary merit is a kind of ornamentation: the turrets and twiddles that decorate a building, rather than its essential structure."

He goes on to argue, quite cogently I think, "I cannot accept this view. To me it seems that a book is a whole: its style and form are as integral to it as its content and values, and indeed these various aspects are not entirely separable."[30]

There are too few writers whose work demonstrates this integrity and offers wisdom, art, and enjoyment. One such writer is Bruce Brooks, and since his abilities and talents are so rare, it might be instructive to briefly consider, here, the body of his work to date:

The publication of his much-acclaimed first novel, the 1985 Newbery Honor Book *The Moves Make the Man* (Harper), established Brooks as a commanding new presence in the world of books for young readers. As one critic put it, "Armed with talent and techniques, [he] strode into the world of children's and young adult fiction as if on stilts." [31]

And yet, as one of his own characters observes in another context, "talent and technique [alone] could not create power." What makes Brooks such a powerful writer are not only his gifts of talent and technique but also his matchless ability to create highly intelligent, complex characters; to invest them with strong, idiosyncratic voices; and to successfully develop his books' unfailingly ambitious yet subtly stated thematic concerns. These typically include: a fascination with process, with analyzing and understanding how things work—whether they are sports, music, or the human heart—in order to capture their essential truth; his characters' need to control and manipulate both that truth and other people; and, finally, a closely reasoned examination—without violating the works' fictional form—of the sometimes symbiotic, occasionally dialectical relationship of lies and truth, of emotion and thought, of intellect and love.

If these sound like ambitious considerations for the sometimes fragile framework of young adult literature to bear, they are. The point is that Brooks, more than any other writer of his generation, has tested and expanded the parameters of the genre, perhaps because he respects the intelligence of his "hardworking readers who are ready to be inspired," [32] perhaps because, in his writing, he refuses to be confined by traditional limitations, or perhaps because he recognizes the potential power of literature, as it deals with large issues, to enrich and expand lives.

Brooks also loves a challenge. In his first two books, he chose to write, respectively, in the first-person voices of Jerome Foxworthy, a thirteen-year-old African-American boy living in the then recently desegregated south, and of Sibilance Spooner, a sixteen-year-old white girl who is a musical prodigy, one of the three or four finest cellists in the world. At the same time, his narrative strategies in these two books required the integration of considerable expository material about basketball and music into his fictional form. That the narrators' voices are authentic in their believable verisimilitude and that the integration of exposition and fiction is seamless are measures of Brooks' skill as a writer.

In his third book, *No Kidding* (Harper, 1989), he dared to distance his challenging material from the reader by not writing in the first but in the more remote omniscient authorial voice and by setting his book in a bleakly dystopian future world where 69 percent of the adults are alcoholics. His fourth book, *Everywhere* (Harper, 1990), was a novella, a marvel of subtle economy, which—though marketed for a mid-range readership and certainly accessible to that audience—managed nevertheless to reveal large and haunting truths for all ages about the healing power of love.

His fifth book, *What Hearts* (Harper, 1992), another Newbery Honor title, was a departure in form that shook up the structural conventions of young adult fiction—neither novel nor novella but a collection of four interrelated short stories, in which the reader follows the maturation of a boy named Asa from age seven to early adolescence. (The book's seven-year time span is another departure for a form that, as previously noted, usually confines its action to one year or less.)

Like Jerome in *Moves* and Sib Spooner in *Midnight Hour*, Asa is preternaturally intelligent. Like Sam, the protagonist of *No Kidding*, he has been forced into an unnatural adult maturity by the circumstances of a mother's illness. Like Bix, Jerome's friend in *Moves*, whom he closely resembles, Asa has, at best, an uneasy relationship with a domineering, unsympathetic stepfather.

As this brief summary suggests, Brooks has great sympathy for young people who are outsiders, whether by virtue of their intelligence or by virtue of their domestic (or in the case of Jerome, societal) circumstances. Almost all his characters come from broken homes, and many of them are further challenged by the mental illness or alcoholism of a parent. Given this context, it is no wonder that control or manipulation of the truth or of other people should be a consistent thematic consideration of the author's (and a personal concern of his characters)— from his very first book, in which Bix Rivers resolutely refuses to learn the fake-out, duplicitous moves of basketball, to the last, in which Asa invents the imagined reality of dramatic baseball games. To lie may be to control the truth or other people's perception of it, to bring some order to a chaotic personal world, or, simply, to survive, but in extreme cases it is also, as Bix understands, to invite the alternative reality of madness, which is also an exercise in ultimate solitude.

For Brooks and his characters, redemption can sometimes be found in the giving up of control, as in the case of Sam, perhaps his most controlling character, who in his self-imposed maturity has betrayed his essential adolescent self but finally finds that self when his mother practices her own deception and Sam is released to say, poignantly to her, "Can I be myself . . . can I just be your boy?" (p. 199).

More often, though, it is found in a character's discovery of love, which, in its sweet simplicity, is the perfect complement to the complex intelligence that serves to define so many of Brooks's characters when the reader first encounters them. To give expression to words of love is not only, for Brooks, an exercise in honesty but an act of completion, a rejection of isolation—as most obviously manifested in the character of Asa but also in that of Sib and her discovery of love for her father and certainly in the case of the healing love of the young narrator for his ailing grandfather in *Everywhere*.

Bruce Brooks is that rarity in the world of books for young readers—a novelist of ideas. But he is also a rare stylist whose writer's razzle always dazzles, thanks to his uncanny ear for voice and his gift for powerful imagery and unforgettable simile and metaphor. His style is wonderfully on display in his recent collection of personal essays, *Boys Will Be* (Henry Holt, 1993). His voice here is a marvelous juxtaposition of cool elegance, unaffected hipness, unabashed sesquipedalianism ("the rich bouquet of exuded sebaciousness"), and swell conversational slang (TV's "warpo" effects). It also offers memorable turns of phrase (war as "humanity's greatest strategic horror"), absolutely apposite use of adjectives, alliteration, and a quite wonderful employment of series, be they adjectives, adverbs, or nouns.

Aside from the satisfactions of its author's stylish voice, what unifies a collection that is delightfully disparate in subject is its subversive celebration of intelligence and integrity; the essays actually invite readers to think, to question a lot of the easy "givens" of their young lives, and to muse about what are usually imponderables like morality, ethics, and the meaning of maturity. The form allows Brooks more latitude than his fiction does to share some ire, outrage, and genuinely righteous indignation about such awfulness as bullies and the failure of adults to trust and respect kids. The honesty and integrity of his beliefs shine from every page. Ultimately it is his own luminous intelligence that brings light to the sometimes dark complexities of who we humans are and why we behave as we do. In everything he writes, he demonstrates canny understanding of the workings of the human heart and how it can challenge the intellect to develop dazzlingly subtle and inventive strategies for survival. For me he is the young adult author nonpareil.

Another powerfully gifted new writer for young adults is Francesca Lia Block, who, as we have seen in the case of her novel *The Hanged Man,* invests her work with thematic weight. But she also bestows two other literary gifts both on her readers and on the reviewers and critics of her work: the most richly realized settings in contemporary young adult fiction, and brilliant originality in 1. her choice and treatment of material, and 2. her literary style and tone, which are perfect matches for that material in poetic imagery, unselfconscious wit, and offbeat whimsicality.

In her first novel, *Weetzie Bat,* Block wrote a modern fairy tale about punk life and culture, set in a Los Angeles that, to outsiders, must have seemed like a magically imagined netherworld but that, to those who live here, is as thoroughly real as a trendy Melrose boutique or a raucous West Hollywood club or a flower-covered Venice bungalow. Her characters speak a hip argot that sounds so authentic, it invites sociological or linguistic study but that, in fact, has been wholly created by the author.

Her characters have their roots in the motion picture business or the world of rock music or the Pacific Coast surf culture—all of which, to outsiders, must also seem like magical fairy-tale kingdoms but which have real-world universality in the pursuit, by those who live there, of love and the nurture of nature. In fact, stripped of the trappings of their closely observed settings and the charming eccentricities of their characters' "slanguage," all Block's books are, at heart, love stories, but with an idiosyncratic, added factor: For her there is an inevitable equation between love and *magic.* As one of her characters, Witch Baby, muses in *Missing Angel Juan* (Harper, 1993), "Maybe magic is just love."

In fact, Block told me in a 1993 interview, "Magic and love—that's the equation, finally. I've seen it in my life and I believe that out of love there emerge transformation and transcendence. Every time I write about it, I discover new things—there are so many expressions of it."

When I pointed out to her that love finds expression in most of her books through the interactions of extended and very nontraditional families as well as through magic, she observed, "I was an only child. I had a loving but small family and sometimes I felt isolated from the outside world. I think as I got older, I started finding people who are really my brothers and sisters and uncles. It's made me so much stronger and that's what happens in my books, too."

Though Block's unconventional and large-hearted acceptance of love in all of its various forms—heterosexual and homosexual—has infuriated some adult critics, young readers embrace her attitudes. She may, for example, be the only young adult author whose work is celebrated by a teen "zine" (*Weetzie Bat, the Zine*, published by two fans in Stamford, Connecticut), and Marjorie Ingall, book review editor of the teen magazine *Sassy*, wrote in a letter to *Publishers Weekly* that "*Sassy* readers love Francesca Lia Block because she offers a distinctive voice and emotional honesty." [33]

Block and her characters also love the earth, and humanity's mistreatment of the environment brings them as close to despair as they ever come—perhaps because for them the earth is a living being. In *Missing Angel Juan*, Block, meditating on the L.A. landscape, writes that from Weetzie's house "you can see a few blue pools like the canyon's eyes and waves of palm, eucalyptus and oleander like the canyon's swirly green hair."

Part of this respect for the earth derives from Native American tradition—personified in the recurring character of Coyote—which provides particular thematic underpinning to *Cherokee Bat and the Goat Guys* (Harper, 1992) (note the significance, in this context, of Cherokee's name), and part of it derives—as we have seen in *The Hanged Man*—from the ancient tradition of Wicca, and the earth-rooted role of woman as witch. Not surprisingly, then, Block's favorite character is not Weetzie but her "almost daughter" Witch Baby, who is the product of an early indiscretion between My Secret Agent Lover Man and Vixanne (Vixen?) Wigg.

When I asked Block why she chose to tell *Missing Angel Juan* in Witch Baby's first-person voice (the first time she has employed this device), she answered, "I really wanted to get inside this character because I feel more connected to her than any of the others. She keeps developing on her own. I wanted to give this story more life by using her language. I tend to like first person best, anyway, coming from a poetry background, and I feel that, using it, I can go deeper in some ways."

Indeed, in this book, she did go deeper—she descended into the very earth itself, symbolized in a real-world way by New York City's subways, but culturally as well, in her story's unstated invocation of the Orpheus legend.

As we've already noted, much of Block's work is enriched by its association with fairy tale, myth, and magic. She has told me that her late father, the screenwriter and artist Irving L. Block, used to tell her many of these stories when she was a child, and obviously that experience had a powerful formative influence on her imaginative life as a writer. It also explains, I think, her attraction to the Latin American tradition of magical realism. (In *The Los Angeles Times* she has even described her work as "pop magic realism." [34]) When I asked her about this aspect of her work, she explained, "I'm drawn to two elements: the magical and the very—almost grittily—realistic. They appear together in almost everything I do. But it's hard for me to say that I'm a magical realistic writer and put myself thereby in the company of my favorite writer, Gabriel García Márquez, especially since I'm coming from such a different culture. The word 'pop' softens that comparison, I think."

Her two adult fantasies, *Ecstasia* (ROC, 1993) and *Primavera* (ROC, 1994), are the most purely magical/fantastical of her books, but the work that most clearly marries the grittier aspects of the real world and the mythical/magical is *Missing Angel Juan*, in which the character Witch Baby goes to New York in search of her lover, the musician Angel Juan, who has earlier gone to Manhattan to find himself and to make his own music.

In this novel—her best since *Weetzie Bat*—Block discovers a radically new setting, New York City, where the canyons' man-made faces are constructed not of exotic flowers and green-leafed trees, as in Los Angeles, but of steel and concrete, both as cold as a corpse.

"Flowers look like they're wondering what they are

doing in this city," Witch Baby observes, where "the light is chilly and the color of lead," where "men [are] crumple-slumped in the gutters like empty coats" and "kids . . . look harder than everybody pretends kids look."

It would be an oversimplification, though, to imply that New York City is simply an impersonal, frozen hell to Weetzie's summertime Los Angeles heaven. After all, Witch Baby quickly finds a loving friend and guide there in the wistfully charming ghost of Weetzie's father, the late Charlie Bat, whose old apartment she is staying in. Her elderly neighbors—and "almost uncles"—are a devoted gay couple named Meadows and Mallard, an older analogue to Dirk and Duck.

"I've had this bond with gay men all my life," Block told me, "and my life and my work are so interconnected that while I don't consciously think I'm going to put gay characters into my books, they're a part of my life; they're my friends, and so they're naturally in my work. But I'm also interested in breaking down barriers and if my work reaches people who aren't familiar with the gay world and if it helps them become familiar with that world and with gay people, then I think that's great."

Despite the coldness of the City, there is warmth and beauty in the relationship between Meadows and Mallard and, indeed, in all the love that Witch Baby sees manifested around her. But still unable to find Angel Juan, she feels her own loneliness "attacking all of her cells like a disease." The smell of death is in the air, and when Witch Baby first descends into the underworld of the subways in search of her musician lover, there are strong evocations of Orpheus's own descent into the underworld in search of *his* lover, Eurydice (although the roles are reversed here). A later, even more dramatic descent reinforces this notion, while adding to it the nightmare quality of another underground: Alice's Wonderland, where a psychedelic tea party is in progress, attended by mysterious, soulless mannequins and a menacing "demon ghoulie ghoul," the book's antagonist, who is improbably named Cake.

Ultimately, if *Weetzie Bat* was about finding love, *Missing Angel Juan* is about letting it go, for only by refusing to possess the beloved, Witch Baby learns, can you truly know love.

Like *Weetzie* and Block's other, earlier novels, *Missing Angel Juan* is an engaging mix of fantasy and reality, but enhanced this time by mystery and suspense. It is also magical, mystical, moving, mischievous, and—literally—marvelous. It establishes, once again, that Block is one of the most original authors of her generation—a brilliantly visionary writer with a talent strong enough to imagine worlds where paradise is a possibility; where every sight and sound of the natural world is a blessing; and where love, in its infinite variety, is both humankind's natural estate and heart-magic strong enough to redeem any loss. Reading this author's lyrical prose and engaging her refreshingly innocent and romantic sensibility is like being brushed by wings and kissed by angels.

At its best, as in the case of Brooks, Block, and Cormier, young adult literature offers the reader rewards as rich as adult literature can, and why not, since in these salutary cases, at least, it is a seamless part of the whole large world of literature. To deny this fact and to judge it by different critical standards is to ghettoize it and to diminish it, as too many reviewers do who seem to view any adult qualities as somehow detrimental, since, they sniff, adult novels "do not speak directly to the developmental needs of today's youth."[35]

Accordingly, adult qualities—if not criticized—are at least thought to be something to warn the reader about. A review of Chris Lynch's 1994 novel *Gypsy Davey* (Harper), for example, begins, "Lynch's *Shadow Boxer* [Harper, 1993], and *Iceman* [Harper, 1994], can easily be labeled as coming-of-age novels. Such categorizing isn't quite as accurate for his latest, which has the distinct feel of adult fiction."[36] Another review of this title betrayed both the still-prevalent lack of respect for the abilities of young adults as readers and the persistent view of literature as tool box: "The book would inspire serious discussions in English classes, and, particularly with the guidance of a good teacher, will give worthwhile insights into parenting and family issues."[37]

Young people—even the most tribalized—live in a world larger than adolescence and have needs that transcend the purely developmental. By focusing only on this aspect, YA literature has too often diminished the lives of its readers, just as the typical reviews have too often diminished the literature by focusing, in turn, only on the latest title and ignoring the body of an author's work or its place in the larger body of literature.

This deficiency is longstanding. As early as 1984 Norma Klein complained of the brevity of YA book reviews, which deny the opportunity "to cover the writer's development from the perspective of earlier books. . . . Thus, we have no sense of building a growing reputation in which each new book will be a part of a totality—a 'body of work.' "[38]

While reviews—because of their brevity, contemporaneity, and the deadline pressure under which they are written—seldom examine a work in a larger context, criticism—which is by nature retrospective—must do this and requires, therefore, the widest possible range of reading. As Paul Heins has reminded us, "Criticism deals with literature in perspective."[39]

In perspective, yes, in the sense that a novel is not an isolated phenomenon but exists, and must be evaluated, in the context of a writer's other work and in the context of similar work by other writers. But this raises a new question: from which perspective? There are, after all, a bewildering variety of types and schools of criticism and critical techniques. Which best serves young adult literature and the needs of its readers, and which, by calling out and praising excellence, best serves to enrich the literature?

There is no absolute answer to these questions. I suspect the most viable critical method will be the most—well, *magpie*, borrowing what is necessary from a variety of schools, disciplines, and individual critics.

John Gardner, for example, invited us to consider that style is the servant of substance, not vice versa, and that "technique for its own sake or for the sake of the artist's personal amusement and self-expression" is "empty nattering." [40]

From the New Critics we can learn reverence for the text, and through the application of literary/critical techniques to its analysis, we can find illumination. From the psychological critics we can learn the importance of character and how to judge and evaluate the integrity of their presentation. (Of less value in adding to our understanding of the work, I think, are biographical details of the authors' lives. It is interesting, for example, to know that Francesca Lia Block's father was an artist who specialized in still life, since this helps explain her fascination with *objets* and their omnipresence in the settings of her characters' lives, but I think this information does nothing to assist us in our evaluation of their contribution to the techniques she employs in establishing setting.)

Those of us who feel that relevance can lead to revelation will be grateful to Marxist criticism and—even more acutely—to the New Historicism (i.e., the study of literature in its historical and political context).

Whatever school or style is employed, the end of criticism is the same: enlightenment and enrichment of both the reader and of the literature itself. Criticism needs to be constructive, to build up rather than to tear down. It builds our skills as readers, too, making us more discerning and more ambitious even as it is building up the literature and making *it* more ambitious, more able to offer us readers understanding, even that wisdom that T. S. Eliot noted.

This kind of reading is not easy. It requires close attention and is not a passive but an active experience, an implied dialogue between the author and the reader. How to undertake it has been suggested by Mortimer Adler in his *How to Read a Book*: "You [the reader] know the book has more to say than you understand and hence it contains something that can increase your understanding. . . . What do you do then? Without external help of any sort, you go to work on the book. With nothing but the power of your own mind you operate on the symbols before you in such a way that you gradually lift yourself from a state of understanding less to one of understanding more."[41]

To my mind the best kind of book to offer this experience is the novel. Why? Because, I submit, of its unique capacity to educate not only the mind—by enabling us to intellectually comprehend the lives of others—but to educate the heart and the spirit, as well. The late Italo Calvino put it this way, in his *Six Memos for the Next Millennium*: "My confidence in the future of literature consists in the knowledge that there are things only literature can give us by means specific to it."[42]

Richard Peck had those specific means in mind, I think, when he wrote, "A novel isn't real life with the names changed."[43]

And Robert Lipsyte agrees. Of course fiction is different from real life (and from the bare factual bones of nonfiction), he told me in a 1993 interview; fiction has to make sense!

Yes, novels have to make sense, and when they do, they make it possible for us readers to make sense, as well, of the horrors and terrors, the imponderables and uncertainties of everyday life through the order and structure that art imposes on the life it observes. Lipsyte says it's like scaffolding that is built to give us readers the proper vantage, the proper distance from which to observe another life and, with a shock of recognition, to see ourselves in it.

Fiction gives us not only an external view of another life, however, but an internal one as well, through its empathic immediacy, the emotional rapport that it offers the reader; it enables us, in short, to eavesdrop on someone else's heart.

Yes, we can get a statistical profile of the adolescent problem drinker from a report in *Time* magazine, but to emotionally comprehend the problem, to understand how it *feels* to be trapped in that skin, we turn to Robert Cormier and his *novel, We All Fall Down.* To completely comprehend the experience of being a homeless kid, we turn to Paula Fox's *Monkey Island* or Theresa Nelson's *The Beggar's Ride* (both Orchard, 1991 and 1992, respectively). And to understand the emotional plight of impoverished, single-parent families, we look to Virginia Euwer Wolff's *Make Lemonade* (Henry Holt, 1993).

"There are limits to the amount of reality the novel form can encompass," Peck cautions. "Young adult novels test the boundaries."[44]

There are some who argue that it is not testing them strenuously enough.

Young adult author Chris Lynch is among these. In the *School Library Journal* piece referred to earlier, he has stated, "Among the writers I know, there is a distinct feeling of, well, less than awe at work produced for young adults. YA is looked at as the B-team of literature. . . . When writers hear the term 'Young Adult,' they get the feeling 'The gloves are on.' " [45]

They've had that feeling for decades, though. In 1975 Norma Klein acknowledged at least tacitly that it was the prevailing climate of opinion even then when she wrote, "I think we're condescending to adolescents when we imply that they aren't mature enough to face the, at times, jagged edges of reality today. They are as aware of the complexities as we are and will be turned off by books which attempt to simplify their experience." [46]

It is surely time to risk taking the gloves off and even throwing them away, to test those boundaries and to risk pushing them even farther back, if young adult literature is to be relevant and wisdom-offering to the most at-risk generation of young adults in our history. This means it must be unsparingly honest, even brutally candid, if necessary, both in the choice of subjects it risks addressing and in the openness with which it treats the material.

We need to encourage a new generation of young adult writers to follow the risk-taking and transformative example of Robert Cormier, who single-handedly changed young adult literature forever when he "set free the subject of despair."

I'm not sure that "despair" is quite the right word, though. What Cormier really set free was the acknowledgement of the very real presence of evil in young lives. As William Golding had done for an adult audience in his *Lord of the Flies*, so Cormier took his younger readers into the heart of darkness and turned the lights on there—showing them, and us, a place that, until he tested the boundaries, had been securely off-limits. A place, in fact, like the South Side of Chicago, where, as Stephen Braun recently wrote, "neighborhoods have repeatedly become the scenes of childhood savagery that dwarf even the fictionalized terrors of 'The Lord of the Flies.' "[47]

One of the scenes Braun describes is the horrifying one in which two ten- and eleven-year-old boys dropped a third boy—just five years old—to his death from a fourteenth-floor window because he would not steal candy for them.

Braun might also have been referring, though, to the case of two twelve-year-olds across the country from Chicago, in Wenatchee, Washington, who cold-bloodedly shot a transient to death, or the fourteen-year-old boy in Bath, New York, who murdered a preschooler by bludgeoning and strangling him, or the eleven-year-old in Chicago who cut the throat of an 83-year-old neighbor woman.

In a recent letter to *The Horn Book* magazine, a librarian questioned the praise that columnist Patty Campbell had given to several books that unsparingly addressed such heart-of-darkness events: "I wonder what kind of world we are presenting to our young people," Janet Fisher wrote, "when books like this are held up to them. Fiction should be a mirror of our world—is this how our world is? Yes, divorce is a fact of life, so is death, but do they have to be depicted as the norm in every book? Could we not present the other side of the coin a little more often? A happily balanced family life with young people who aspire to more than quick sex, for example?" [48]

Well, unfortunately the conventional model of American family life—a married couple with kids and a stable home—is on the verge of becoming the exception rather than the rule, the U.S. Census reports.

According to 1991 census data, only 50.8 percent of America's children now live in traditional "nuclear" families. [49]

Even when there are two parents, "many [teenagers] appear to live in virtually separate worlds from adults. Four in ten say their parents sometimes or often do not make time to help them."

"Even when my parents are here," one boy told a reporter, "it's like they're not, because they don't have any time." [50]

This is supported by the November 1994 "Harper's Index," which reported that the chances that a U.S. teenager has not spoken to either parent for more than ten minutes during the last month is one in five. [51]

This is more than a pity; it's a tragedy, since as Dr. Barbara Staggers, a physician who won the 1993 Lewis Hine Award for her work with young adults, says, "With all the kids I know who make it, there's one thing in common: an individual contact with an adult who cared and who kept hanging in with the teen through his hardest moments" [52]—exactly the kind of circumstance, for example, so eloquently described by Robert Lipsyte in his 1991 novel *The Brave* (Harper), in which the now-adult Albert Brooks hangs in with the troubled teenager Sonny Bear and saves him from self-destruction.

Unfortunately this *is* the exception in young adult novels, one traditional characteristic of which has been to avoid the inclusion of any significant adult presence, at all costs.

In real life the result of this absence of adults and family involvement is described by Luis J. Rodriguez: "For many members, the gang serves as family, as the only place where they can find fellowship, respect, a place to belong. You often hear the word *love* among gang members. Sometimes the gang is the only place where they can find it." [53]

Shades of *The Outsiders?* Well, yes—even, as Rodriguez presents it, to the dangerously romantic sentimentality.

The true reality of gang life is something different, as America discovered when a shocked nation read the particulars in the case of eleven-year-old Robert "Yummy" Sandifer, a Chicago gang member with twenty-eight charges on his rap sheet, twenty-three of them felonies.

Nevertheless, "He was adorable," an attorney told a *Newsweek* reporter. "I thought, no way this little pumpkin could be in a gang." [54]

But he was, and it was the death of him. Yummy shot to death a fourteen-year-old boy in a gang-motivated slaying and then was, himself, murdered by two other members of his own gang (themselves only fourteen and sixteen) to silence him before the police could arrest him.

Cases like Yummy's are hardly confined to Chicago. In 1992 there were 800 gang-related deaths in Los Angeles county: more than two a day, and nearly three times the 1985 total of 271. And experts fear that "with gang imagery increasingly reflected in fashion, music, song, movies, and television, violence is becoming the basis of a new antisocial subculture."[55]

Indeed, "Youth gangs have become almost as ubiquitous as violence itself in schools," Elizabeth Shogren reports. In 700 medium and large cities surveyed by the National League of Cities, gangs were blamed for having a "serious influence on violence in classrooms, playgrounds, and hallways. But the impact of gangs was not restricted to large urban centers. Forty percent of the suburban communities and non-metropolitan towns and cities surveyed said gangs were a factor in violence in their schools as well."[56]

"It's all based on anger and hatred, of self and others," Steve Valdivia, executive director of Community Youth Gang Services in Los Angeles, explains.[57]

This hatred is increasingly manifested not only in traditional gang warfare based on rivalry and considerations of turf and territory, but also in warfare inspired by racial differences and cultural stereotyping. In 1994, gang warfare between blacks and Latinos left seventeen dead and fifty wounded in Los Angeles's Venice area.[58]

Less than two months later, in the wealthy suburb of San Marino, a war between a Chinese gang and gangs of mixed Asian heritage left two dead and seven wounded.[59]

The reality of violence is everywhere, unfortunately—even in white, middle-class suburbs, those formerly peaceful places that provided the settings for all those forties and fifties teen romances. On November 19, 1994, *The New York Times* reported the clubbing to death with baseball bats of a sixteen-year-old boy in Fox Chase, Pennsylvania. No organized gangs were involved, but the death grew out of "a longstanding feud and rivalry between two middle-class communities."[60]

It appears increasingly obvious that the answer to Janet Fisher's troubled question is *Yes*, this *is* how the world is. And I'm afraid we do young adults no favors by pretending otherwise. As Richard Peck says, "Life keeps giving us new reasons to write about death."[61]

The late Norma Klein, never one to fear the hard-edged truth, said this: "If we admit that being a teenager at any time of history is, by some definition, terrible, then let us have books that acknowledge this, books that deal with some of these terrible problems without sugar coating and lies and evasion. Young people will be grateful for these books. They need them."[62]

Remember what Matt Fuller, that HIV-positive volunteer with the People with AIDS Coalition, said? "The time for denial is past."[63]

Robb Foreman Dew said it even better: "Whenever it's necessary to engage in deception in order to keep a secret, it's a good bet that you are indulging in a bit of concealment that is damaging to the soul."[64]

If young adult literature is to have any kind of validity in today's world, it can no longer afford to practice any kind of deception—no matter how benign.

Time to dignify the literature and its readers by trusting them with the truth.

The truth is that in 1993 "children suffered more physical and sexual abuse, severe neglect, exploitation, emotional abuse and lack of adequate food, shelter, and clothing than ever before." [65]

Time to give faces to all of these abused and exploited young people: people like Alex, a homeless, gay, HIV-positive fifteen-year-old living in Hollywood whose story was reported not by a young adult book but by a daily newspaper, *The Los Angeles Times*. Sexually active since he was thirteen, Alex says, "I never practiced safe sex. I just thought, 'I'm so cute, nothing will happen to me.' That's the way a fifteen-year-old thinks," he continues, "they can't deal with a reality like AIDS. Death and dying is something that seems so far away, they can't connect it to themselves." [66]

Literature can help make that connection, I think; and by so doing, it can help kids deal with a reality like AIDS, and maybe, just maybe, save lives in the process.

Ms. Minifred, the librarian in Patricia MacLachlan's luminous novel *Baby* (Delacorte, 1993), says, "In these books there is the power of a hundred hurricanes" (p. 43).

I treasure those words and find comfort in the sentiment they express, but I realize they may be a little too . . . *neat*, a little too *literary* to translate directly into reality. I was taken aback when I interviewed Latin American author Isabel Allende several years ago and, being familiar with her personal exposure to political upheaval, dictatorship, and exile, asked her about the power of books, naively presuming that she, too, would praise their hurricane power. Instead, her reply was a simple but passionate "No! Books have no power to change the world."

Well, not the world, perhaps, but I still stubbornly hope that books can change individual lives. As Norma Klein has written, "I may be asking a lot of books, but I'd like as many of them as possible to somehow make life easier for adolescents."[67]

I would too. But books won't change anything if they're a formulaic, problem-driven fiction inhabited by cardboard characters who only skate across the surface of reality. Instead, young adult books must constitute a grittily realistic literature inhabited by complex characters whose lives—both exterior and interior—invite us not only to empathize but to think. John Gardner said that "really good fiction has a staying power that comes from its ability to jar, turn on, move the whole intellectual and emotional history of the reader."[68]

This fiction must give faces to all young adults—straight and gay, black and white and brown, native born and newly immigrant. Homeless, impoverished, endangered, abused, afraid. And its writers must risk taking the gloves off to tackle dangerous subjects and to deal with them unflinchingly and honestly. Not to shock and scandalize and sensationalize but to tell the simple, plain, and unvarnished truth. For how can we change the world if we cannot first see it plain and then see ourselves, whole—warts and all— in it?

That is how literature might be able to change lives and, in the process, save them. That is what the very best books for young adults have always striven to do and what they must do even more vigorously in the future if the literature is to survive.

I am no great fan of rap music, but I serendipitously came across a lyric the other day from a group called the Disposable Heroes of Hiphoprisy. Let me share one verse, because it is so relevant to what *I've* been struggling to say:

> But death is the SILENCE
> In this language of violence.
> Death is the SILENCE
> But death is the silence
> In this cycle of violence
> Death is the SILENCE. [69]

We cannot permit young adult literature to be silenced. Everyone who cares about literature and about young people has a dead-serious responsibility to focus attention on, support, and defend the very best, most courageously outspoken, and bluntly honest of young adult books. By so doing, we strengthen *its* voice; we amplify it so that it can be heard by those who most need to hear it: the most-at-risk-ever young adults themselves.

NOTES

1. Babbitt, Natalie, "Between Innocence and Maturity," p. 143.
2. Canby, Vincent, "Youth Has Its Day as Movies Face Reality," *The New York Times*, October 24, 1982, 2:13.
3. Babbitt, Natalie, "The Purpose of Literature," p. 150–1.
4. Rochman, Hazel, "Young Adult Books: Childhood Terror," *The Horn Book*, LXI:598 (September/October 1985).
5. Townsend, "Standards," p. 33.
6. Chambers, Aidan, "Alive and Flourishing," in *Booktalk*. New York: Harper, 1985, p. 87.
7. Edwards, *Fair Garden*, p. 122.
8. Campbell, Patty, "Only Puddings Like the Kiss of Death: Reviewing the YA Book," *Top of the News*, 35:161 (Winter 1979).
9. Dunning, Stephen, "Criticism and the 'Young Adult Novel'" in Meade, p. 149.
10. Chambers, "Alive," p. 86.
11. Babbitt, "Between," p. 143.
12. Brooks, Bruce, "Imagination, the Source of Reading," *The New Advocate*, 5:81–2 (Spring 1992).
13. Lynch, "Today's YA Writers," p. 37.
14. Rose, Jacqueline, Review of *What Hearts* in *School Library Journal*, 38:116 (November 1992).
15. Lacher, Irene, "Coming of Age in the Printed Page," *The Los Angeles Times*, January 25, 1994, p. E2.
16. Grumbach, Doris, "A Life among the Pointed Firs," *The New York Times Book Review*, May 23, 1993, p. 19.
17. Chambers, "Alive," p. 87.
18. Edwards, "Rise," p. 95.
19. Rochman, "Young Adult Books," p. 598.
20. Chambers, "Alive," p. 88.
21. Egoff, "Beyond," p. 192.
22. Baskin, Barbara, et al., "The Search for Values: Young Adults and the Literary Experience," *Library Trends*, 37:70 (Summer 1988).
23. Edwards, *Fair Garden*, p. 76.
24. Gallo, Don, "What Should Teachers Know About YA Lit for 2004?" *English Journal*, 73:33 (November 1984).
25. Babbitt, "Purpose," p. 152.
26. Eliot, T. S., *Notes Towards the Definition of Culture.* Quoted in Paul

Heins, "Out on a Limb with the Critics," in Paul Heins, editor, *Cross-currents of Criticism Horn Book Essays 1968–1977*. Boston: The Horn Book, 1977, p. 80.

27. Townsend, "Standards," p. 26.

28. Edwards, *Fair Garden*, p. 123.

29. Pollitt, Katha, "Canon to the Right of Me . . ." *The Nation*, 253:330 (September 23, 1991).

30. Townsend, John Rowe, "The Reviewing of Children's Books," in Betsy Hearne and Marilyn Kaye, editors, *Celebrating Children's Books*. New York: Lothrop, 1981, p. 181.

31. McDonnell, Christine, "New Voices, New Visions: Bruce Brooks," The Horn Book, LXIII:188–91 (March/April 1987).

32. Gallo, ed., *Speaking*, p. 34.

33. Ingall, Marjorie, "Letter," *Publishers Weekly*, 24:10 (October 17, 1994).

34. Block, Francesca Lia, "Punk Pixies in the Canyon," *The Los Angeles Times Book Review*, July 26, 1992, p. 11.

35. Mertz and England, "Legitimacy," p. 120.

36. Zvirin, Stephanie, review of *Gypsy Davy* in *Booklist*, 91:318 (October 1, 1994).

37. Rausch, Tim, review of *Gypsy Davy* in *School Library Journal*, 40:145 (October 1994).

38. Klein, Norma, "My Say," *Publishers Weekly*, 225:106 (March 9, 1984).

39. Heins, "Out on a Limb," p. 404.

40. Yardley, Jonathan, "The Moral of the Story," *The Washington Post Book World*, April 17, 1994, p. 3.

41. Adler, Mortimer, *How to Read a Book*, revised and updated edition. New York: Simon & Schuster, 1972, pp. 7–8.

42. Calvino, Italo, *Six Memos for the Next Millennium* translated by Patrick Creagh. Cambridge, MA: Harvard University Press, 1988, p. 1.

43. Peck, *Mall*, p. 157.

44. *Ibid.*, p. 159.

45. Lynch, "Today's YA Writers," p. 37.

46. Klein, "Thoughts," p. 24.

47. Braun, Stephen, "Childhood Savagery Revisits Chicago's Tough South Side," *The Los Angeles Times*, October 15, 1994, p. A18.

48. Fisher, Janet, "Letter," *The Horn Book*, LXX:644 (November/December 1994).

49. Shogren, Elizabeth, "Traditional Family Nearly the Exception, Census Finds," *The Los Angeles Times*, August 30, 1994, p. A1.

50. Chira, Susan, "Worry and Distrust of Adults Beset Teen-Agers, Poll Says," *The New York Times*, July 10, 1994, p. 1.
51. "Harper's Index," *Harper's Magazine*, 289:11 (November 1994).
52. Foster, Douglas, "The Disease Is Adolescence," *The Utne Reader*, 64:53.
53. Rodriguez, Luis, "Rekindling," p. 58.
54. McCormick, John, "Death of a Child Criminal," *Newsweek*, CXXIV:45 (September 12, 1994).
55. Katz, Jesse, "County's Yearly Gang Death Toll Reaches 800," *The Los Angeles Times*, January 19, 1993, p. A1.
56. Shogren, Elizabeth, "Violence in Schools on Rise Across U.S.," *The Los Angeles Times*, November 2, 1994, p. A13.
57. Katz, "Country's," p. A23.
58. Crogan, Jim, "Trapped by the Terror of a Venice Street War," *The Los Angeles Times*, June 18, 1994, p. B1.
59. Torres, Vicki, "Officials Link Gang Rivalry to Party Slayings," *The Los Angeles Times*, August 19, 1994, p. B1.
60. Jones, Charisse, "Act of Youthful Savagery Stuns a Suburb," *The New York Times*, November 19, 1994, p. 1.
61. Peck, *Mall*, p. 107.
62. Klein, "Books," p. 236.
63. Fuller, Matt, "Marked Man," *The Advocate*, 669.6 (November 29, 1994).
64. Dew, Robb Foreman, *The Family Heart*. Reading, MA: Addison-Wesley, 1994, p. 207.
65. Rivera, Carla, "Child Abuse, Suicides Rising in L.A. County," *The Los Angeles Times*, November 9, 1994, p. A1.
66. Jones, Robert A., "Dangerous Liasons," "*The Los Angeles Times*, July 25, 1993, p. 13.
67. Klein, "Thoughts," p. 26.
68. Yardley, "Moral," p. 3.
69. Disposable Heroes of Hiphoprisy, "Language of Violence," in Bennett L. Singer, ed., *Growing up Gay/Growing up Lesbian*. New York: New Press, 1994, p. 248.

SELECTED BIBLIOGRAPHY

PRIMARY SOURCES

Alcott, Louisa May. *Little Women*. Boston: Roberts Brothers, 1868–69.

Anaya, Rudolfo. *Bless Me, Ultima*. TQS Publications, 1972.

Angelou, Maya. *I Know Why the Caged Bird Sings*. New York: Random House, 1969.

Annixter, Paul. *Swiftwater*. New York: A. A. Wyn, 1950.

Anonymous. *Go Ask Alice*. Englewood Cliffs, NJ: Prentice Hall, 1971.

Atkin, S. Beth. *Voices from the Fields*. Boston: Joy Street/Little, Brown, 1993.

Baldwin, James. *If Beale Street Could Talk*. New York: Dial, 1974.

Bauer, Marion Dane. *Am I Blue?* New York: Harper, 1994.

Beard, Henry and Christopher Cerf. *The Official Politically Correct Dictionary and Handbook*. New York: Villard, 1992.

Benary-Isbert, Margot. *The Ark*. New York: Harcourt, 1953.

Bennett, Jack. *The Hawk Alone*. Boston: Little, Brown, 1965.

———. *Jamie*. Boston: Little, Brown, 1963.

———. *Mister Fisherman*. Boston: Little, Brown, 1965.

Berck, Judith. *No Place to Be: Voices of Homeless Children*. Boston: Houghton Mifflin, 1992.

Bess, Clayton. *The Mayday Rampage*. Sacramento, CA: Lookout Press, 1993.

Block, Francesca Lia. *Cherokee Bat and the Goat Guys*. New York: Charlotte Zolotow/Harper, 1992.

———. *Ecstasia*. New York: ROC (NAL), 1993.

———. *The Hanged Man*. New York: Harper, 1994.

———. *Missing Angel Juan*. New York: Harper, 1993.

———. *Primavera*. New York: ROC (NAL), 1994.

———. *Weetzie Bat*. New York: Charlotte Zolotow/Harper, 1989.

Blume, Judy. *Forever*. New York: Bradbury, 1975.

Bonham, Frank. *Durango Street*. New York: Dutton, 1965.

Boylston, Helen. *Sue Barton, Student Nurse*. Boston: Little, Brown, 1936.

Brooks, Bruce. *Boys Will Be*. New York: Henry Holt, 1993.

———. *Everywhere*. New York: Harper, 1990.

———. *Midnight Hour Encores*. New York: Harper, 1986.

———. *The Moves Make the Man*. New York: Harper, 1984.

———. *No Kidding*. Harper, 1989.

———. *What Hearts*. New York: Laura Geringer/Harper, 1992.

Bunn, Scott. *Just Hold On*. New York: Delacorte, 1982.

Carlson, Lori M., editor. *Cool Salsa: Bilingual Poems on Growing Up Latino in the United States*. New York: Henry Holt, 1994.

———, and Cynthia L. Ventura, editors. *Where Angels Glide at Dawn*. New York: Harper, 1990.

Carter, Angela. *The Bloody Chamber and Other Adult Tales*. New York: Harper, 1979.

Cavanna, Betty. *Going on Sixteen*. Philadelphia: Westminster, 1946.

Childress, Alice. *A Hero Ain't Nothin' But a Sandwich*. New York: Coward McCann, 1973.

Cisneros, Sandra. *The House on Mango Street*. Houston, TX: Arté Público, 1983.

———. *My Wicked, Wicked Ways*. Bloomington, IN: Third Women Press, 1987.

———. *Woman Hollering Creek and Other Stories*. New York: Random House, 1991.

Cormier, Robert. *The Chocolate War*. New York: Pantheon, 1974.

———. *We All Fall Down*. New York: Delacorte, 1991.

Crew, Linda. *Children of the River*. New York: Delacorte, 1989.

Daly, Maureen. *Seventeenth Summer*. New York: Dodd, Mead, 1942.

Davis, Deborah. *My Brother Has AIDS*. New York: Atheneum, 1994.

Donovan, John. *Family: A Novel*. New York: Harper, 1976.

———. *I'll Get There: It Better Be Worth the Trip*. New York: Harper, 1969.

———. *Remove Protective Coating a Little at a Time*. New York: Harper, 1973.

———. *Wild in the World*. New York: Harper, 1971.

Donovan, Stacey. *Dive*. New York: Dutton, 1994.

du Jardin, Rosamond. *Practically Seventeen*. Philadelphia: Lippincott, 1949.

Duncan, Lois. *I Know What You Did Last Summer*. Boston: Little Brown, 1973.

———. *Killing Mrs. Griffin*. Boston: Little Brown, 1978.

Durant, Penny Raife. *When Heroes Die*. New York: Atheneum, 1992.

Emery, Anne. *Sorority Girl*. Philadelphia: Westminster, 1952.

Eyerly, Jeannette. *Bonnie Jo, Go Home*. Philadelphia: Lippincott, 1972.

———. *Drop-Out*. Philadelphia: Lippincott, 1963.

———. *Escape from Nowhere*. Philadelphia: Lippincott, 1969.

———. *The Girl Inside*. Philadelphia: Lippincott, 1966.

———. *A Girl Like Me*. Philadelphia: Lippincott, 1966.

———. *Radigan Cares*. Philadelphia: Lippincott, 1970.

———. *See Dave Run*. Philadelphia: Lippincott, 1978.

———. *The World of Ellen March*. Philadelphia: Lippincott, 1964.

Farley, Walter. *The Black Stallion*. New York: Random House, 1941.

Felsen, Henry Gregor. *Crash Club*. New York: Random House, 1958.

———. *Hot Rod*. New York: Dutton, 1950.

———. *Street Rod*. New York: Random House, 1953.

———. *Two and the Town*. New York: Scribner's, 1952.

Forbes, Esther. *Johnny Tremaine*. Boston: Houghton Mifflin, 1944.

Ford, Michael Thomas. *100 Questions and Answers about AIDS*. New York: New Discovery, 1992.

Fox, Paula. *Monkey Island*. New York: Orchard, 1991.

———. *The Slave Dancer*. New York: Bradbury, 1973.

Gaines, Ernest J. *The Autobiography of Miss Jane Pittman*. New York: Dial, 1971.

Garden, Nancy. *Annie on My Mind*. New York: Farrar, Straus, 1982.

Garner, James F. *Politically Correct Bedtime Stories*. New York: Macmillan, 1994.

Gipson, Fred. *Old Yeller*. New York: Harper, 1956.

———. *Savage Sam*. New York: Harper, 1962.

Gleitzman, Morris. *Two Weeks with the Queen*. New York: Putnam, 1989.

Golding, William. *Lord of the Flies*. New York: Coward McCann, 1962.

Goodwillie, Susan. *Voices from the Future: Our Children Tell Us About Violence in America*. New York: Crown, 1993.

Greene, Bette. *The Drowning of Stephan Jones*. New York: Bantam, 1991.

Guest, Judith. *Ordinary People*. New York: Viking, 1976.

Guy, Rosa. *Edith Jackson*. New York: Viking, 1978.

———. *The Friends*. New York: Holt, 1973.

———. *Ruby.* New York: Viking, 1976.

Hall, G. Stanley. *Adolescence: Its Psychology.* New York: D. Appleton, 1904.

Hall, Lynn. *Sticks and Stones.* Chicago: Follett, 1972.

Head, Ann. *Mr. and Mrs. Bo Jo Jones.* New York: Putnam, 1967.

Heinlein, Robert. *Farmer in the Sky.* New York: Scribner's, 1950.

———. *Stranger in a Strange Land.* New York: Putnam, 1961.

Henry, Marguerite. *King of the Wind.* Chicago: Rand McNally, 1948.

———. *Misty of Chincoteague.* Chicago: Rand McNally, 1947.

Hentoff, Nat. *I'm Really Dragged But Nothing Gets Me Down.* New York: Simon & Schuster, 1968.

———. *Jazz Country.* New York: Harper, 1965.

Hermes, Patricia. *Be Still My Heart.* New York: Putnam, 1989.

Hinton, S. E. *The Outsiders.* New York: Viking, 1967.

———. *That Was Then, This Is Now.* New York: Viking, 1971.

Holland, Isabelle. *The Man Without a Face.* Philadelphia: Lippincott, 1972.

Holman, Felice. *Slake's Limbo.* New York: Scribner, 1974.

Holt, Victoria. *Mistress of Mellyn.* New York: Doubleday, 1960.

Homes, A. M. *Jack.* New York: Macmillan, 1989.

Jordan, June. *His Own Where.* New York: Crowell, 1971.

Jordan, Mary Kaye. *Losing Uncle Tim.* Chicago: A. Whitman, 1989.

Kaye, Marilyn. *Real Heroes.* San Diego, CA: Gulliver Books/Harcourt, 1993.

Kerr, M. E. *Deliver Us From Evie.* New York: Harper, 1994.

———. *Dinky Hocker Shoots Smack!* New York, Harper, 1972.

———. *Night Kites.* New York: Harper, 1986.

Klein, Norma. *Mom, the Wolfman and Me.* New York: Pantheon, 1972.

Knowles, John. *A Separate Peace.* New York: Macmillan, 1960.

Koertge, Ron. *The Arizona Kid.* New York: Joy Street/Little, Brown, 1988.

Kuklin, Susan. *Speaking Out: Teenagers Take on Race, Sex & Identity.* New York: Putnam, 1993.

Lane, Rose Wilder. *Let the Hurricane Roar.* New York: Longmans, Green, 1933.

Lee, Harper. *To Kill a Mockingbird.* Philadelphia: Lippincott, 1960.

Levy, Marilyn. *Rumors and Whispers.* New York: Fawcett, 1990.

Lewis, Elizabeth Foreman. *Young Fu of the Upper Yangtze.* Philadelphia: John C. Winston, 1932.

Lipsyte, Robert. *The Brave.* New York: Charlotte Zolotow/Harper, 1991.

———. *The Contender.* New York: Harper, 1967.

———. *Jock and Jill.* New York: Harper, 1982.

Lynch, Chris. *Gypsy Davey.* New York: Harper, 1994.

————. *Iceman*. New York: Harper, 1994.

————. *Shadow Boxer*. New York: Harper, 1993.

MacLachlan, Patricia. *Baby*. New York: Delacorte, 1993.

Mazer, Harry, and Norma Fox Mazer. *Guy Lenny*. New York: Delacorte, 1971.

————. *I, Trissy*. New York: Delacorte, 1971.

Mazer, Norma Fox. *Up in Seth's Room*. New York: Delacorte, 1979.

McKinley, Robin. *Beauty*. New York: Harper, 1978.

Meader, Stephen W. *Snow on Blueberry Mountain*. New York: Harcourt, 1961.

Means, Florence Cranell. *Great Day in the Morning*. Boston: Houghton Mifflin, 1946.

————. *The Moved-Outers*. Boston: Houghton Mifflin, 1945.

————. *Our Cup Is Broken*. Boston: Houghton Mifflin, 1969.

————. *Rafael and Consuelo*. New York: Friendship Press, 1929.

————. *Shuttered Windows*. Boston: Houghton Mifflin, 1938.

Meyer, Carolyn. *Elliott and Win*. New York: Margaret M. McElderry/ Macmillan 1986.

Miklowitz, Gloria. *Good-bye Tomorrow*. New York: Delacorte, 1987.

Mitchell, Margaret. *Gone with the Wind*. New York: Macmillan, 1936.

Mori, Kyoko. *The Dream of Water*. New York: Henry Holt, 1994.

————. *Shizuko's Daughter*. New York: Henry Holt, 1993.

Murrow, Liza Ketchum. *Twelve Days in August*. New York: Holiday, 1993.

Nelson, Theresa. *The Beggar's Ride*. New York: Richard Jackson/Orchard, 1992.

————. *Earthshine*. New York: Richard Jackson/Orchard, 1994.

Neufeld, John. *Lisa, Bright and Dark*. New York: Phillips, 1969.

Neville, Emily Cheney. *It's Like This, Cat*. New York: Harper, 1963.

Newman, Lesléa. *Heather Has Two Mommies*. Boston: Alyson, 1989.

Oneal, Zibby. *War Work*. New York: Viking, 1971.

Pease, Howard. *The Tattooed Man*. New York: Doubleday, 1926.

Peck, Richard. *Are You in the House Alone?* New York: Viking, 1976.

————. *Don't Look and It Won't Hurt*. New York: Holt, 1972.

————. *The Ghost Belonged to Me*. New York: Viking, 1975.

————. *Remembering the Good Times*. New York: Delacorte 1985.

————. *Secrets of the Shopping Mall*. New York: Delacorte, 1979.

Pike, Christopher. *The Cold One*. New York: Tor, 1994.

Pinkwater, Daniel. *Young Adult Novel*. New York: Crowell, 1982.

Plath, Sylvia. *The Bell Jar*. New York: Harper, 1971.

Porte, Barbara Ann. *Something Terrible Happened*. New York: Richard Jackson/Orchard, 1994.

Potok, Chaim. *The Chosen*. New York: Simon & Schuster, 1967.

Salinger, J. D. *The Catcher in the Rye.* Boston: Little, Brown, 1951.

Scoppettone, Sandra. *Trying Hard to Hear You.* New York: Harper, 1974.

Sebestyen, Ouida. *Words by Heart.* Boston: Little, Brown, 1979.

Sherburne, Zoa. *Too Bad about the Haines Girl.* New York: Morrow, 1967.

Sleator, William. *House of Stairs.* New York: Dutton, 1974.

Soto, Gary. *Baseball in April.* San Diego, CA: Harcourt, 1990.

———. *Jesse.* San Diego, CA: Harcourt, 1994.

———. *Local News.* San Diego, CA: Harcourt, 1993.

Stolz, Mary. *Cezanne Pinto.* New York: Knopf, 1994.

———. *The Sea Gulls Woke Me.* New York: Harper, 1951.

———. *To Tell Your Love.* New York: Harper, 1950.

Sutton, Roger. *Hearing Us Out: Voices from the Gay and Lesbian Community.* Boston: Little, Brown, 1994.

Swarthout, Glendon. *Bless the Beasts and Children.* New York: Doubleday, 1970.

Tunis, John R. *The Iron Duke.* New York: Harcourt, 1938.

Twain, Mark. *Adventures of Huckleberry Finn.* New York: Webster, 1885.

Voigt, Cynthia. *When She Hollers.* New York: Scholastic, 1994.

Walker, Paul Robert. *The Method.* San Diego: Gulliver Books/Harcourt, 1990.

Wells, Helen. *Cherry Ames, Student Nurse.* New York: Grosset, 1943.

Wersba, Barbara. *Run Softly, Go Fast.* New York: Atheneum, 1970.

White, Robb. *Deathwatch.* New York: Doubleday, 1972.

White, Ryan, as told to Ann M. Cunningham. *Ryan White: My Own Story.* New York: Dial, 1991.

Wiener, Lori S., editor. *Be a Friend.* Chicago: A. Whitman, 1994.

Wilhoite, Michael. *Daddy's Roommate.* Boston: Alyson, 1990.

Wojciechowska, Maia. *Shadow of a Bull.* New York: Atheneum, 1964.

Woodson, Jacqueline. *The Dear One.* New York: Delacorte, 1991.

———. *I Hadn't Meant to Tell You This.* New York: Delacorte, 1994.

Wolff, Virginia Euwer. *Make Lemonade.* New York: Henry Holt, 1993.

Yep, Laurence. *Dragonwings.* New York: Harper, 1975.

———. *Dragon's Gate.* New York: HarperCollins, 1993.

———. *Sweetwater.* New York: Harper, 1973.

———, editor. *American Dragons.* New York: HarperCollins, 1993.

Zindel, Paul. *My Darling, My Hamburger.* New York: Harper, 1969.

———. *The Pigman.* New York: Harper, 1968.

———. *The Pigman & Me.* New York: Harper, 1992.

SECONDARY SOURCES

Abcarian, Robin. "Incest: Sexual Politics or a Matter of Therapy and Recovery?" *The Los Angeles Times,* November 27, 1994, pp. E1, E6.

Abramson, Jane. "*Still Playing It Safe: Restricted Realism in Teen Novels.*" *School Library Journal,* 22:38–39 (May 1976).

"ACLU Sues for Return of Book Removed from School," *Frontiers,* April 8, 1994, p. 19.

Adler, Mortimer. *How to Read a Book.* Revised and Updated Edition. New York: Simon & Schuster, 1972.

Alexander, Sue. "Putting Changes in Context," *The Sampler,* Summer 1994, p. 3.

Alm, Richard S. "The Glitter and the Gold." In *Literature for Adolescents: Selection and Use,* edited by Richard A. Meade and Robert C. Small, Jr. Columbus, OH: Merrill, 1973.

American Heritage Dictionary of the English Language, The. Third Edition. Boston: Houghton Mifflin, 1992.

"Americans in 2020," *The New York Times,* April 22, 1994, p. A7.

Babbitt, Natalie. "Between Innocence and Maturity." In *Young Adult Literature in the Seventies,* edited by Jana Varlejs. Metuchen, NJ: Scarecrow, 1978.

———. "The Purpose of Literature: Who Cares?" *School Library Journal,* 36:150–52 (March 1990).

Bachelder, Linda, et al. "Looking Backward: Trying To find the Classic Young Adult Novel," *English Journal,* 69:86–89 (September 1980).

Baker, John F. "1994 National Book Awards." *Publishers Weekly,* 241:26 (November 21, 1994).

Baldwin, Neal. "Writing for Young Adults." *Publishers Weekly,* 226:16–20 (October 19, 1984).

Barr, Donald. "Should Holden Caulfield Read These Books?" *The New York Times Book Review.* May 4, 1986, pp. 1, 50–51.

Baskin, Barbara, et al. "The Search for Values: Young Adults and the Literary Experience," *Library Trends,* 37:63–79 (Summer 1988).

Batchelder, Mildred L. "Learning about Sharing." In *A Sea of Upturned Faces,* edited by Winifred Ragsdale. Metuchen, NJ: Scarecrow, 1989.

Berger, Laura Standley, editor. *Twentieth-Century Young Adult Writers.* Detroit: St. James, 1994.

Block, Francesca Lia. "Punk Pixies in the Canyon," *The Los Angeles Times Book Review*, July 26, 1992, pp. 1, 11.

Bloom, Harold. *The Western Canon*. New York: Harcourt, Brace, 1994.

Blume, Judy. *Are You There God? It's Me, Margaret*. New York: Bradbury, 1970.

Braun, Stephen. "Childhood Savagery Revisits Chicago's Tough South Side," *The Los Angeles Times*, October 15, 1994, pp. A1, A18.

Bridgers, Sue Ellen. *Home Before Dark*. New York: Knopf, 1976.

Brookhiser, Richard. "The Melting Pot Is Still Simmering," *Time*, 141:72 (March 1, 1993).

Brooks, Bruce. "Imagination, the Source of Reading." *The New Advocate*. 5:79–85 (Spring 1992).

Brownstein, Ronald. "'94 Candidates Agree on 1 Goal," *The Los Angeles Times*, October 10, 1994, p. A5.

———. "Wilson Proposes U.S. Version of Prop. 187," *The Los Angeles Times*, November 19, 1994, p. 1.

Burgess, Anthony. *The Novel Now*. New York: Norton, 1967.

Burton, Dwight L. "The Novel for the Adolescent." In *Literature for Adolescents: Selection and Use*, edited by Richard A. Meade and Robert C. Small, Jr. Columbus, OH: Merrill, 1973.

Calvino, Italo. *Six Memos for the Next Millennium*. Cambridge, MA: Harvard University Press, 1988.

Campbell, Patty. "Only Puddings Like the Kiss of Death: Reviewing the YA Book," *Top of the News*. 35:161–62 (Winter 1979).

———. "Perplexing Young Adult Books: A Retrospective." *Wilson Library Bulletin*, 62:20-26 (April 1988).

———. *Presenting Robert Cormier*. New York: Twayne, 1991.

Canby, Vincent. "Youth Has Its Day as Movies Face Reality." *The New York Times*, October 24, 1982, 2:1, 13.

Carlsen, G. Robert, "Bait: 'Pro.'" *English Journal*. 70:8, 10 (January 1981).

———. *Books and the Teen-Age Reader*. New York: Harper, 1967.

———. "For Everything There Is a Season." In *Literature for Adolescents: Selection and Use*, edited by Richard A. Meade and Robert C. Small, Jr. Columbus, OH: Merrill, 1973.

———. "Teaching Literature for the Adolescent: A Historical Perspective." *English Journal*. 73:28–30 (November 1984).

Carnegie Corporation on Adolescent Development. *A Matter of Time*. Abridged Version. New York: Carnegie Corporation, 1994.

Carter, Betty. *Best Books for Young Adults: The History, the Selections, the Romance*. Chicago: American Library Association, 1994.

Carter, Betty, and Richard F. Abrahamson. *Nonfiction for Young Adults: From Delight to Wisdom.* Phoenix, AZ: Oryx, 1990.

Chambers, Aidan. *Booktalk.* New York: Harper, 1985.

Chelton, Mary Kay. "The First National Survey of Services and Resources," *Journal of Youth Services in Libraries,* 2:224–31 (Spring 1989).

Chevalier, Tracy, editor. *20th Century Children's Writers.* Third Edition. Detroit: St. James Press, 1989.

Chira, Susan. "Worry and Distrust of Adults Beset Teen-Agers, Poll Says," *The New York Times,* July 10, 1994, pp. 1, 9.

Cimons, Marlene. "Aim AIDS Prevention at Youth," *The Los Angeles Times,* June 3, 1993, p. A9.

———. "Clinton Stresses Priority, Names AIDS Policy Chief," *The Los Angeles Times,* November 11, 1994, p. A32.

———, and Ronald J. Ostrow. "Illicit Drug Use by Youths Shows Marked Increase," *The Los Angeles Times,* February 1, 1994, pp. A1, A10.

"Coming Out in Comic Strip Stirs Controversy," *Frontiers,* April 23, 1993, p. 17.

"Conference on Books in Spanish for Young Readers," *USBBY Newsletter,* XIX:10 (Spring 1994).

Corsini, Raymond J., editor. *Encyclopedia of Psychology.* New York: Wiley, 1984.

Cowley, Geoffrey. "What If a Cure Is Far Off?" *Newsweek,* CXXI:70 (June 21, 1993).

Crogan, Jim. "Trapped by the Terror of a Venice Street War," *The Los Angeles Times,* June 18, 1994, pp. B1, B3, B8.

Crutcher, Chris. "Healing through Literature." In *Authors' Insights,* edited by Donald R. Gallo. Portsmouth, NH: Boynton/Cook Publishers, 1992.

Daly, Maureen. "Maureen Daly." In *More Junior Authors,* edited by Muriel Fuller. New York: H. W. Wilson, 1963.

Davis, Terry. *Vision Quest.* New York: Delacorte, 1979.

Dawidoff, Robert. "In Real Life, the Funnies Aren't," *The Los Angeles Times,* April 2, 1993, p. B7.

DeLuca, Geraldine, and Roni Natov. "An Interview with Robert Cormier." *The Lion and the Unicorn.* 2:109–35 (Fall 1978).

Dew, Robb Foreman. *The Family Heart.* Reading, MA: Addison-Wesley, 1994.

Disposable Heroes of Hiphoprisy. "Language of Violence" in *Growing up Gay/Growing up Lesbian,* edited by Bennett L. Singer. New York: New Press, 1994.

Donelson, Kenneth L. "YA Literature Comes of Age," *Wilson Library Bulletin.* 52:241–47 (November 1977).

Dunlap, David W. "Minister Stresses Anti-Gay Message," *The New York Times*, December 19, 1994, p. A8.

Dunn, Ashley. "In CA the Numbers Add up to Anxiety," *The New York Times*, October 30, 1994, p. E3.

Dunning, Stephen. "Criticism and the 'Young Adult Novel.'" In *Literature for Adolescents: Selection and Use*, edited by Richard A. Meade and Robert C. Small, Jr. Columbus, OH: Merrill, 1973.

Early, Margaret J. "Stages of Growth in Literary Appreciation," *The English Journal.* 49:161-67 (March 1960).

Edwards, Margaret A. *The Fair Garden and the Swarm of Beasts: The Library and the Young Adult.* New York: Hawthorn, 1969.

––––––. "The Rise of Teen-Age Reading." *The Saturday Review*, XXXVII:88–89, 95 (November 13, 1954).

Egoff, Sheila. "Beyond the Garden Wall." In *The Arbuthnot Lectures: 1970–1979*, compiled by Zena Sutherland. Chicago: American Library Association, 1980.

––––––. *Thursday's Child.* Chicago: American Library Association, 1981.

Ehrman, Mark. "Separating the *Trigo* from the Chaff," *The Los Angeles Times Magazine*, March 7, 1993, p. 10.

Eliot, T. S. *Notes Towards the Definition of Culture.* In *Crosscurrents of Criticism: Horn Book Essays 1968–1979*, edited by Paul Heins. Boston: The Horn Book, 1977.

Engdahl, Sylvia. "Do Teenage Novels Fill a Need?" In *Writers on Writing for Young Adults,* edited by Patricia E. Feehan and Pamela Petrick Barron. Detroit: Omnigraphics, 1991.

Epstein, Connie. "A Publisher's Perspective," *The Horn Book.* LXVI:237–41 (March/April 1990).

"Every School Day," *Time,* 141:23 (January 25, 1993).

Feehan, Patricia E., and Pamela Petrick Barron, editors. *Writers on Writing for Young Adults.* Detroit: Omnigraphics, 1991.

Fisher, Janet. "Letter," *The Horn Book,* LXX:644 (November/December 1994).

Fong, Doris. "From Sweet Valley They Say We Are Leaving," *School Library Journal,* 36:38–39 (January 1990).

Ford, Michael Thomas. "Gay Books for Young Readers: When Caution Calls the Shots," *Publishers Weekly,* 241:24–27 (February 21, 1994).

Forisha-Kovach, B. "Adolescent Development." In *Encyclopedia of Psychology,* edited by Raymond J. Corsini. New York: Wiley, 1984.

Forman, Jack. "Paul Zindel." In *Twentieth-Century Young Adult Writers,* edited by Laura Standley Berger. Detroit: St. James, 1994.

Fuller, Matt. "Marked Man," *The Advocate,* 669:6 (November 29, 1994).

Selected Bibliography

Gallo, Don. "What Should Teachers Know About YA Lit for 2004?" *English Journal*, 73:31–34 (November 1984).

Games, Stephen. "Superstores, Narrow Choices," *The Los Angeles Times*, October 16, 1994, p. M5.

Garden, Nancy. "Banned: Lesbian and Gay Kids' Books Under Fire," *Lambda Book Report*. 4:11–13 (November/December 1994).

Gelman, David. "The Young and the Reckless," *Newsweek*, CXXI:60–61 (January 11, 1993).

Gonzalez, David. "Catholic Bishops Grapple With a 'Culture of Violence.'" *The New York Times*, November 26, 1994, p. 9.

Gorman, Christine. "Higher Education: Crocked on Campus," *Time*, 144:66–67 (December 19, 1994).

Gottlieb, Annie. "A New Cycle in 'YA' Books." *The New York Times Book Review*, June 17, 1984, p. 24.

Graeber, Laurel. "Robert Cormier," *Publishers Weekly*, 224:98–99 (October 7, 1983).

Grant, Cynthia. *Uncle Vampire*. New York: Atheneum, 1993.

Gray, Paul. "Carnage: An Open Book," *Time*, 142:54 (August 2, 1993).

———. "Hurrah for Dead White Males!" *Time*, 144:62–63 (October 10, 1994).

———. "Teach Your Children Well," *Time*, 142:68–71 (Fall 1993: Special Issue).

Grumbach, Doris. "A Life among the Pointed Firs," *The New York Times Book Review*, May 23, 1993, p. 19.

Hall, Lynn. *The Shy Ones*. New York: Avon.

Hamilton, Virginia. *The Planet of Junior Brown*. New York: Macmillan, 1971.

———. *Zeely*. New York: Macmillan, 1967.

"Harper's Index," *Harper's Magazine*, 289:11 (November 1994).

Harrison, Eric. "AIDS Is No. 1 Killer of Young Americans," *The Los Angeles Times*, December 2, 1994, p. A8.

Havighurst, Robert G. *Developmental Tasks and Education*. Quoted in David A. Russell, "The Common Experience of Adolescence," *Journal of Youth Services in Libraries*, 2:61 (Fall 1988).

Heins, Paul. "Out on a Limb with the Critics." In *Crosscurrents of Criticism: Horn Book Essays 1968–1977*, edited by Paul Heins. Boston: The Horn Book, 1977.

Hentoff, Nat. "Fiction for Teen-Agers," *Wilson Library Bulletin*, 43:261–65 (November 1968).

———. "Tell It as It Is," *The New York Times Book Review*, May 7, 1967, p. 3.

Heron, Ann. *Two Teenagers in Twenty*. Boston: Alyson, 1994.

Hinton, S.E. "Teen-Agers Are for Real," *The New York Times Book Review,* August 27, 1967, pp. 26–29.

Hochschild, Adam. "War and Peace, Part II," *The Los Angeles Times Book Review,* August 7, 1994, pp. 1, 11.

Hoffman, Mary. "Growing up: A Survey," *Children's Literature in Education,* 15:171–85 (1984).

Holland, Isabelle. "What Is Adolescent Literature?" In *Writers on Writing for Young Adults,* edited by Patricia E. Feehan and Pamela Petrick Barron. Detroit: Omnigraphics, 1991.

Holmes, Steven A. "Survey Finds Minorities Resent One Another Almost as Much as They Do Whites," *The New York Times,* March 3, 1994, p. A9

Honan, William H. "Columbia to Celebrate 75 Years of Great Books," *The New York Times,* November 16, 1994, p. B9.

Hughes, Robert. *Culture of Complaint.* New York: Oxford University Press, 1993.

Hull, John D. "Running Scared," *Time,* 144:93–99 (November 21, 1994).

Huntwork, Mary M. "Why Girls Flock to Sweet Valley High," *School Library Journal,* 36:137–40 (March 1990).

Hutchinson, Margaret. "Fifty Years of Young Adult Reading: 1921–1971," *Top of the News,* 30:24–53 (November 1973).

Ingall, Marjorie. "Letter," *Publishers Weekly,* 241:10 (October 17, 1994).

Jefferson, Margo. "Sweet Dreams for Teen Queens," *The Nation,* 234:613–17 (May 22, 1982).

Jenkins, Christine. "Young Adult Novels with Gay/Lesbian Characters and Themes 1969–1992: A Historical Reading of Content, Gender and Narrative Distance," *Journal of Youth Services in Libraries,* 7:43–55 (Fall 1993).

Jennings, Frank G. "Literature for Adolescents—Pap or Protein?" *English Journal,* 45:226–231 (December 1956).

Jones, Charisse. "Act of Youthful Savagery Stuns a Suburb," *The New York Times,* November 19, 1994, p. 1, 6.

Jordan, June. "Young People: Victims of Realism in Books and Life," *Wilson Library Bulletin,* 48:140-45 (October 1973).

Kantrowitz, Barbara. "Wild in the Streets," *Newsweek,* 122:40–46 (August 2, 1993).

Katz, Jesse. "County's Yearly Gang Death Toll Reaches 800," *The Los Angeles Times,* January 19, 1993, p. A1, 23.

Kellogg, Mary Alice. "The Romance Book Boom," *Seventeen,* 42:158 (May 1983).

Kendall, Elaine. "One Girl's Inventing of an American Self," *The Los Angeles Times,* March 4, 1994, p. E4.

Kerr, M. E. "1993 Margaret A. Edwards Award Acceptance Speech," *Journal of Youth Services in Libraries*, 7:25-30 (Fall 1993).

"Kids Need Libraries," *Journal of Youth Services in Libraries*, 3:197–207 (Spring 1990).

Klein, Norma. "Books to Help Kids Deal with Difficult Times." In *Writers on Writing for Young Adults*, edited by Patricia E. Feehan and Pamela Petrick Barron. Detroit: Omnigraphics, 1991.

———. "My Say," *Publishers Weekly*, 225:106 (March 9, 1984).

———. "Thoughts on the Adolescent Novel." In *Writers on Writing for Young Adults*, edited by Patricia E. Feehan and Pamela Petrick Barron. Detroit: Omnigraphics, 1991.

Knudsen, R. R., and May Swenson, editors. *American Sports Poems*. New York: Orchard, 1988.

Kolbert, Elizabeth. "Television Gets Closer Look as a Factor in Real Violence," *The New York Times*, December 14, 1994, pp. A1, 13.

Kraus, W. Keith. "Cinderella in Trouble: Still Dreaming and Losing," *School Library Journal*, 21:18–22 (January 1975).

Kunz, Tom. "Word for Word/Teen Magazines," *The New York Times*, April 24, 1994, p. E7.

Lacher, Irene. "Coming of Age in the Printed Page," *The Los Angeles Times*, January 25, 1994, p. E1, 2.

Landsberg, Michele. *Reading for the Love of It.* New York: Prentice Hall, 1987.

Latrobe, Kathy Howard. "Report on the Young Adult Library Services Association's Membership Survey," *Journal of Youth Services in Libraries*, 7:237–53 (Spring 1994).

Lee, Felicia R. "AIDS Toll on Elderly: Dying Grandchildren," *The New York Times*, November 21, 1994, p. A11.

Louie, Ai-Ling. "Growing Up Asian American," *Journal of Youth Services in Libraries*, 6:115–27 (Winter 1993).

Lyall, Sarah. "Publishing Chief Is Out at Viacom," *The New York Times*, June 15, 1994, pp. C1, 14.

———. "Viacom Acts to Calm Fears over Dismissal of Snyder," *The New York Times*, June 16, 1994, p. C1, 17.

Lynch, Chris. "Today's YA Writers: Pulling No Punches," *School Library Journal* "Up for Discussion," 40:37–38 (January 1994).

Malone, Michael. "Tough Puppies," *The Nation*, 242:276–80 (March 8, 1986).

Maltin, Leonard. *Leonard Maltin's Movie and Video Guide 1992.* New York: Signet, 1991.

"Massachusetts Governor Signs Bill to Protect Rights of Gay Youth," *Frontiers,* December 31, 1993, p. 24–25.

Mathis, Sharon Bell. *"The Slave Dancer* Is an Insult To Black Children." In *Cultural Conformity in Books for Children,* edited by Donnarae MacCann and Gloria Woodard. Metuchen, NJ: Scarecrow, 1977.

McCormick, John. "Death of a Child Criminal," *Newsweek,* CXXIV:45 (September 12, 1994).

McDonnell, Christine. "New Voices, New Visions: Bruce Brooks," The Horn Book, LXIII:188–91 (March/April 1987).

McElderry, Margaret K. "Across the Years, Across the Seas: Notes from an Errant Editor," Journal of Youth Services in Libraries, 7:369–80 (Summer 1994).

McGuire, Stryker. "Immigrant Schools: The Wrong Lessons," Newsweek, CXXII:23 (August 9, 1993).

Merrett, James. "High School Confidential," *Frontiers,* May 20, 1994, p. 45.

Mertz, Maia Pank, and David A. England. "The Legitimacy of American Adolescent Fiction," *School Library Journal,* 30:119–23 (October 1983).

Miles, Jack. "The Epiphanies of Love and Loss," *The Los Angeles Times Book Review,* November 13, 1994, pp. A, G.

Mori, Kyoko. Quoted in *USBBY Newsletter,* XIX:9 (Spring 1994).

Mydans, Seth. "A New Tide of Immigration Brings Hostility to the Surface, Poll Finds," *The New York Times,* June 27, 1993, pp. 1, 14.

Myers, Walter Dean. *Fast Sam, Cool Clyde, and Stuff.* New York: Viking, 1975.

Nilsen, Alleen Pace. "That Was Then, This Is Now," *School Library Journal,* 40:30–33 (April 1994).

———, and Kenneth L. Donelson. *Literature for Today's Young Adults.* Second Edition. Glenview, IL: Scott, Foresman, 1985.

———. "Literature for Today's Young Adults," Fourth Edition. New York: Harper, 1994.

———. "The New Realism Comes of Age," *Journal of Youth Services in Libraries,* 1:275–82 (Spring 1988).

"Numbers Game, The," *Time,* 142:14–15 (Fall 1993: Special Issue).

O'Brien, Maureen. "Tartikoff Gets Warner Imprint," *Publishers Weekly,* 241:16 (October 3, 1994).

O'Connor, John J. "In TV Entertainment, a Heightened Gay Presence," *The New York Times,* November 23, 1994, p. B6.

———. "Is the BBC Too Adult for American Viewers?" *The New York Times,* December 29, 1994, p. B5.

Ostrow, Ronald J. "Nearly 50% of 12th Graders Linked to Drug Use," *The Los Angeles Times,* December 13, 1994, p. A34.

Peck, Richard. *Love and Death at the Mall.* New York: Delacorte, 1994.

———. "The Silver Anniversary of Young Adult Books," *Journal of Youth Services in Libraries*, 7:19–23 (Fall 1993).

Peyser, Marc. "Reading Frenzy," *Newsweek*, CXXIV:71–72 (November 14, 1994).

Pollack, Pamela D. "The Business of Popularity: The Surge of Teenage Paperbacks," *School Library Journal*, 28:25–28 (November 1981).

Pollitt, Katha. "Canon to the Right of Me . . ." *The Nation*, 253:328–32 (September 23, 1991).

Quezada, S. Shelley. "Bridging the Pacific Rim: Selecting and Reviewing Latin American Children's Books." In *A Sea of Upturned Faces*, edited by Winifred Ragsdale. Metuchen, NJ: Scarecrow, 1989.

Rafferty, Terrence. "Superhero," *The New Yorker*, LXX:93–95 (May 23, 1994).

Ragsdale, Winifred, editor. *A Sea of Upturned Faces.* Metuchen, NJ: Scarecrow, 1989.

Ramsdell, Kristin. *Happily Ever After.* Littleton, CO: Libraries Unlimited, 1987.

———. "Young Adult Publishing: A Blossoming Market," *Top of the News*, 39:173–181 (Winter 1983).

Rausch, Tim. Review of *Gypsy Davy* in *School Library Journal*, 40:145 (October 1994).

Reed, J. D. "Packaging the Facts of Life," *Time*, 120:65–66 (August 23, 1982).

"Report Cites Heavy Toll of Rapes on Young," *The New York Times*, June 23, 1994, p. A8.

Rimer, Sabra. "Rights for Gay Students in Public School," *The New York Times*, December 10, 1993, p. E2.

Rivera, Carla. "Child Abuse, Suicides Rising in L.A. County," *The Los Angeles Times*, November 9, 1994, p. A1.

———. "Next! When Abnormal Becomes Normal," *The Los Angeles Times*, September 6, 1994, pp. E1, 4.

Roane, Kit R. "Two White Sport Coats, Two Pink Carnations," *The New York Times*, May 22, 1994, p. Y12.

Roback, Diane. "Hollywood and Horror," *Publishers Weekly*, 241:S14 (March 7, 1994).

Rochman, Hazel. *Against Borders: Promoting Books for a Multicultural World.* Chicago: American Library Association, 1993.

———. "A Fine Romance," *Booklist*, 91:125 (September 15, 1994).

———. "Young Adult Books: Childhood Terror," *The Horn Book*, LXI:598–602 (September/October 1985).

Rodriguez, Luis J. "Rekindling the Warrior," *The Utne Reader*, 64:58–59 (July/August 1994).

Rodriguez, Roberto, and Patrisia Gonzalez. "Censorship by Omission: When the Mainstream Ignores You," *The Los Angeles Times*, December 30, 1994, p. B7.

Rose, Jacqueline. Review of *What Hearts* in *School Library Journal*, 38:116 (November 1992).

Russell, David A. "The Common Experience of Adolescence," *Journal of Youth Services in Libraries*, 2:58–63 (Fall 1988).

"Safe Sex School Play Canceled," Frontiers, February 25, 1994, p. 25.

Santrock, J. W. "Adolescence." In *Encyclopedia of Psychology*, edited by Raymond J. Corsini. New York: Wiley, 1984.

SCBWI Bulletin, April/May 1994, p. 1.

Schlesinger, Arthur M., Jr. *The Disuniting of America: Reflections on a Multiracial Society*. New York: Norton, 1992.

Scoppettone, Sandra, "Some Thoughts on Censorship: An Author Symposium." In *Writers on Writing for Young Adults*, edited by Patricia E. Feehan and Pamela Petrick Barron. Detroit: Omnigraphics, 1991.

Shaffer, Kenneth R. "What Makes Sammy Read?" *Top of the News*, XIX:9–12 (March 1963).

Shales, Tom. "Talk Shows Are Now a Peephole on Our Neighbors, Family and Friends," *The Los Angeles Times TV Times*, September 4, 1994, p. 10.

Shapiro, Susan. "Going for the Lion's Share: Judith Regan," *The New York Times Magazine*, July 17, 1994, pp. 22–25.

Shirley, Fehl. "The Influence of Reading on Adolescents," *Wilson Library Bulletin*, 43:256–260 (November 1968).

Shogren, Elizabeth. "Survey Shows 4 in 5 Suffer Sex Harassment at School," *The Los Angeles Times*, June 2, 1993, p. A10.

———. "Traditional Family Nearly the Exception, Census Finds," *The Los Angeles Times*, August 30, 1994, pp. A1, 18.

———. "Violence in Schools on Rise Across U.S.," *The Los Angeles Times*, November 2, 1994, p. A13.

Shulman, Ken. "Bloom and Doom," *Newsweek*, CXXIV:75 (October 10, 1994).

Sidorsky, Phyllis G. Review of *Everywhere* in *School Library Journal*, 36:224 (September 1990).

Smith, Karen Patricia. "The Multicultural Ethic and Connection to Literature for Children and Young Adults," *Library Trends*, 41:340–353 (Winter 1993).

Stavn, Diane Gersoni. "Watching Fiction for Today's Teens: Notes of a Critical Voyeur," *School Library Journal*, 16:139–140 (November 1969).

Stine, R. L. Fear Street Saga, No. 3: *The Burning*. New York: Archway, 1993.

Stolberg, Sheryl. "Girls Seen More at Risk as AIDS Hits Adolescents," *The Los Angeles Times*, June 6, 1993, p. A8.

Streitfeld, David. "Pop Culture," *The Washington Post Book World*, November 13, 1994, p. 15.

Sutton, Roger. "The Critical Myth: Realistic YA Novels," *School Library Journal*, 29:33–35 (November 1982).

———. "Kind of a Funny Dichotomy: A Conversation with Robert Cormier," *School Library Journal*, 37:28–33 (June 1991).

Toffler, Alvin. *Future Shock*. New York: Random House, 1970.

"Toll-Free Teen Line Launched for Gay and Lesbian Youth," *Frontiers*, August 12, 1994, p. 21.

Torres, Vicki. "Officials Link Gang Rivalry to Party Slayings," *The Los Angeles Times*, August 19, 1994, pp. B1, B3.

Townsend, John Rowe. "The Reviewing of Children's Books." In *Celebrating Children's Books*, edited by Betsy Hearne and Marilyn Kaye. New York: Lothrop, 1981.

———. "Standards of Criticism for Children's Literature." In *The Arbuthnot Lectures*, 1970–1979. Compiled by Zena Sutherland. Chicago: American Library Association, 1980.

———. *Written for Children*. Third revised edition. New York: Lippincott, 1987.

Tsang, Daniel C. "State of the Young Gay," *Frontiers*, May 20, 1994, p. 39.

Tucker, Ken. "Nameless Fear Stalks the Middle-Class Teen-Ager," *The New York Times Book Review*, November 14, 1993, p. 27.

Tunis, John R. "What Is a Juvenile Book?" In *Crosscurrents of Criticism: Horn Book Essays 1968–1977*, edited by Paul Heins. Boston: Horn Book, 1977.

"Upset by Explicit Literature, Cortines Moves AIDS Center," "Around New York," *The New York Times*, March 23, 1994, p. B12.

Van Gelder, Robert. "An Interview with Miss Maureen Daly," *The New York Times Book Review*, VI:2 (July 12, 1942).

Varlejs, Jana, editor. *Young Adult Literature in the Seventies: A Selection of Readings*. Metuchen, NJ: Scarecrow, 1978.

Vogel, Jennifer. "Throw Away the Key," *The Utne Reader*, 64:56–60 (July/August 1994).

Walton, Edith H. "'Seventeenth Summer' and Other Works of Fiction." *The New York Times Book Review*, May 3, 1942, p. 7.

Waters, Harry F. "Teenage Suicide: One Act Not to Follow," *Newsweek*, 123:49 (April 18, 1994).

White, Ruth. *Weeping Willow.* New York: Farrar, 1992.

Wojciechowska, Maia. "An End to Nostalgia," *School Library Journal,* 15:13–15 (December 1968).

Woods, George. "Screening Books for Review," *Wilson Library Bulletin,* 41:168–172 (October 1966).

Yardley, Jonathan. "The Moral of the Story," *Washington Post Book World,* April 17, 1994, p. 3.

Yolen, Jane. "An Empress of Thieves," *The Horn Book,* LXX:702–705 (November/December 1994).

"Youth Crime, Workplace Violence Rising, Studies Say," *The Los Angeles Times,* July 25, 1994, p. A15.

Zuckerman, Eileen Goudge. "Nancy Drew vs: Serious Fiction," *Publishers Weekly,* 229:74 (May 30, 1986).

Zvirin, Stephanie. Review of *Gypsy Davy* in *Booklist,* 91:318 (October 1, 1994).

INDEX

Index

Index

Index

Index